Politics and Truth

SUNY Series in Political Theory:
Contemporary Issues
Philip Green, Editor

Politics *and* Truth

POLITICAL THEORY AND
THE POSTMODERNIST CHALLENGE

Theresa Man Ling Lee

STATE UNIVERSITY OF NEW YORK PRESS

Published by
State University of New York Press

©1997 State University of New York

All rights reserved

Printed in the United States of America

No part of this book may be used or reproduced in any manner whatsoever without written permission. No part of this book may be stored in a retrieval system or transmitted in any form or by any means including electronic, magnetic tape, mechanical, photocopying, recording, or otherwise without the prior permission in writing of the publisher.

For information, address the State University of New York Press,
State University Plaza, Albany, NY 12246

Marketing by Nancy Farrell
Production by Bernadine Dawes

Library of Congress Cataloging-in-Publication Data

Lee, Theresa Man Ling.
    Politics and truth : political theory and the postmodernist challenge /
Theresa Man Ling Lee.
        p. cm. – (SUNY series in political theory. Contemporary issues)
    Includes bibliographical references and index.
    ISBN 0-7914-3503-2 (hardcover : alk. paper). – ISBN 0-7914-3504-0
(pbk. : alk. paper)
    1. Political science. 2. Truth. 3. Postmodernism. I. Title. II. Series.
JA71.L435 1997
320' .01–dc21
                                                              97-3267
                                                                CIP

1 2 3 4 5 6 7 8 9 10

To My Parents

Who have so much faith in an education that they never had

獻給我的父、母親

感謝他門對我的教育的信心

Contents

Acknowledgments /ix

1. Introduction /1

Part I
Historical Overview

2. Plato: Truth, Nontruth, and Legitimate Power /15
3. Hobbes: The Science of Politics /39

Part II
Contemporary Conundrum

Prologue /63
4. Weber: Rationalization and Politics /67
5. Foucault: Discursive Politics and the Modern State /91
6. Arendt: Totalitarianism and the Human Condition /115

Part III
Conclusion

7. The Politics of Truth in Context: The Case of China /141
8. Politics, Truth, and Democratic Practice /155

Endnotes /161
Bibliography /211
Index /235

Acknowledgments

This book began as a Ph.D. dissertation at Princeton University. I started out with Foucault as my thesis topic. I turned to the works of Plato and Hobbes for the purpose of establishing the bases for Foucault's critique of these thinkers. I soon discovered that I was in fact more interested in the relationship between politics and truth. Under Alan Ryan's encouragement and supervision, I decided to tackle the problematic rather than the works of one particular thinker. Since my defense, Alan has always been supportive of my endeavor. I appreciate both his intellectual rigor and his friendship throughout the years.

While at Princeton, I was fortunate to study with Sheldon Wolin, among others. His approach to political theory has influenced me in important ways. I owe much to Sheldon for encouraging me to "try out my wings."

A number of individuals have helped me as I wrote the book. First, I want to thank Philip Green, the series editor, for showing an interest in the manuscript. Richard Vernon and two other anonymous reviewers made constructive suggestions on how to revise the manuscript.

Barry Allen's treatment of the subject of truth in philosophy and his careful reading of the introductory chapter to this book helped me enormously to set up the conceptual framework. His comments on the earlier draft of the Foucault chapter were immensely useful in revising a difficult part of the manuscript.

Ronald Beiner shared his personal copies of Arendt's manuscripts and read the Arendt chapter more than once. He also prompted me to reconsider the nature of postmodernist politics. Peter Swan offered his expertise on Weber.

Friends in the Department of Philosophy at Guelph were highly supportive. Ken Dorter helped improve my case on Plato in significant ways. Jay Lampert read the chapter on Foucault. Michael Ruse is an all-purpose strategist. Karen Wendling, who provides me with-much needed feminist comradeship, commented on the section on Hobbes. I also tried out the Foucault chapter with Marta Rohatynskyj in the Department of Sociology and Anthropology. Thanks to Ken Woodside in my own department for encouraging me along the way.

Jennifer Foster and Lucinda Kennedy helped to prepare the manuscript for publication. Gary Toop was instrumental in the final compilation of the bibliography. Lorraine Black and John Spafford contributed their technical skills.

The Research Board and the Dean's Office of the College of Social Science at the University of Guelph provided financial support. The Centre Michel Foucault at the Bibliothèque du Saulchoir in Paris offered an excellent research environment. Librarians and the circulation staff of the Dana Porter Library at the University of Waterloo facilitated access to its collection on contemporary continental philosophy. Katie McDonough of the Manuscript Division at the Library of Congress responded efficiently to my request for materials from a distance.

Students in my courses on politics and sexuality, contemporary political theory, and modern China all contributed to my thoughts on a number of related issues. These include feminist politics and epistemology, postmodernism and democratic praxis, cultural identity and universalistic discourse. The Toronto chapter of the Conference for the Study of Political Thought provides a lively intellectual forum for theorists and philosophers of different persuasions. Among them is Alkis Kontos, with whom I took my first political theory course.

The companionship and unreserved support of my friend Peter Goddard are invaluable. Peter also read and commented on the manuscript in its entirety.

Finally, I must thank Paul Cameron for showing me how to persist in spite of it all.

While all these individuals have contributed to this work, I alone of course bear the responsibility for what it is.

The author is grateful to the following publishers for kindly granting permissions to reprint excerpts from their publications (in order of citations): Excerpts from *Philosophical Papers*, vol. 1: *Objectivity, Relativism, and Truth*, by Richard Rorty, copyright © 1991 by Cambridge University Press, are reprinted by permission of Cambridge University Press. Excerpts from *Dialogue and Dialectic: Eight Hermeneutical Studies on Plato*, by Hans-Georg Gadamer, translated by P. Christopher Smith, copyright © 1980 by Yale University, are reprinted by permission of Yale University Press. Excerpts from "On Truth and Lies in a Nonmoral Sense," in *Philosophy and Truth: Selections from Nietzsche's Notebooks of the Early 1870s*, by Frederick Nietzsche, translated and edited by Daniel Breazeale, copyright © 1979 by Daniel Breazeale, are reprinted by permission of Humanities Press International, Inc. Excerpts from *The Methodology of the Social Sciences*, by Max Weber, translated and edited by Edward A. Shils and Henry A. Finch, copyright © 1949 by The Free Press; copyright renewed 1977 by Edward A. Shils, are reprinted by permission of The Free Press, an imprint of Simon & Schuster Inc. Excerpts from *Economy and Society*, 2 vols, by Max Weber, translated and edited by Roth and Wittich, copyright © 1978 by The Regents of the University of California, are reprinted by permission of The University of California Press. Excerpts from "Power and Sex: An Interview with Michel Foucault," in *Telos*, vol. 32, copyright © 1977 by Telos Press, Ltd., are reprinted by permission of Telos Press, Ltd. Excerpts from "The Subject and Power," by Michel Foucault, in *Michel Foucault: Beyond Structuralism and Hermeneutics*, 2nd ed., copyright © 1982, 1983 by The University of Chicago, are reprinted by permission of The University of Chicago Press. Excerpts from "Kant on Enlightenment and Revolution," by Michel Foucault, in *Economy and Society*, vol. 15, copyright © 1986 by Routledge Ltd., are reprinted with permission from Routledge Ltd. Excerpts from "Omnes et Singulatim: Towards a Criticism of "Political Reason," in *The Tanner Lectures on Human Values*, edited by Sterling McMurrin, copyright © 1981 by The Tanner Lectures on Human Values, are reprinted by permission of The University of Utah Press. Excerpts from "Foucault at the Collège de France II: A Course Summary 1979," by Michel Foucault, in *Philosophy and Social Criticism*, vol. 8, copyright © 1981 by Sage Publications Ltd., are reprinted by permission of Sage Publications Ltd.

Excerpts from "Intellectuals and Power," by Michel Foucault, in *Language, Counter-Memory, Practice*, edited by Donald F. Bouchard, translated by Donald F. Bouchard and Sherry Simon, copyright © 1977 by Cornell University, are reprinted by permission of Cornell University Press. Excerpts from "Truth and Politics," in *Between Past and Future*, by Hannah Arendt, copyright © 1954, 1956, 1957, 1958, 1960, 1961 by Hannah Arendt, are reprinted by permission of Viking Penguin, a division of Penguin Books USA Inc. Excerpts from "Philosophy and Politics: The Problems of Action After the French Revolution," by Hannah Arendt, copyright © 1990 by the Hannah Arendt Literary Trust, reprinted by permission of Harcourt Brace & Company. Excerpts from "The Archimedean Point," by Hannah Arendt, in *Ingenor* (Spring 1969), copyright © 1969 by the University of Michigan, College of Engineering, are reprinted by permission of the University of Michigan, College of Engineering. Excerpts from "On Hannah Arendt," by Hannah Arendt, in *Hannah Arendt: The Recovery of the Public World*, edited by Melvyn A. Hill, copyright © 1979 by Melvyn A. Hill, are reprinted by permission of St. Martin's Press, Inc.

CHAPTER ONE

Introduction

Twentieth-century politics is distinctive by way of how political ideas dominate the conduct of politics. This observation is the starting point of the book. The most obvious place to begin is the Cold War phenomenon, which divided the world after the Second World War into two opposing ideological camps—liberal democracy versus Leninist-Stalinist socialism. The very concept of a "cold war" is significant. Such a war is not simply an armed confrontation, "an act of force," as Clausewitz puts it. Ideas, as much as weapons, become an integral component of the arsenal. The propaganda and rhetoric of both sides of the ideological divide showed clearly that political ideas were not simply a rationale for war. If anything, conventional wars became a means to validate political ideas as truth. Indeed, much of the fanaticism characteristic of the Cold War era was sustained by the conviction that one was fighting for truth. Hans Morgenthau, in the classic *Politics Among Nations*, likens the Cold War to the religious wars of earlier times:

> As the religious wars of the sixteenth and seventeenth centuries were followed by the dynastic wars of the latter seventeenth and eighteenth centuries, as the latter yielded to the national wars of the nineteenth and the early twentieth centuries, so war in our time tends to revert to the religious type by becoming ideological in character. The citizen of a modern warring nation, in contrast to his ancestors of the eighteenth and nineteenth centuries, does not fight for the glory of his prince or the unity and greatness of his nation, but *he "crusades" for an "ideal," a set of "principles," a*

"way of life," for which he claims a monopoly of truth and virtue.[1]

In short, the Cold War was literally a contest of truth—a truth that is distinctly secular, invoking political ideas rather than religious principles.

An obvious question at this point is whether characterizing politics as a contest of truth remains relevant to our current condition. We are, after all, living in the post-Cold War era which, among other things, means that we are no longer living in a world polarized by warring ideological camps. Yet the demise of the Cold War does not make truth any less central to politics. First of all, we need to look at a set of contrasting phenomena in the decade leading to the end of the Cold War—the increasing politicization of knowledge in the then liberal democratic camp on the one hand, and the depoliticization of knowledge in the Leninist socialist camp on the other. This set of contrasting events importantly raised the issue of the role of political power in the certification of knowledge as truth.

The politicization of knowledge in the West is closely tied to the intellectual movement called postmodernism. Defined by Lyotard as "incredulity toward metanarratives," postmodernism began as a critical challenge to the ideals of modernity embodied in the Enlightenment—transcendent reason, objective knowledge, autonomous self, progressive history.[2] Inspired by Nietzsche, postmodernism represents no less than a wholesale attack on the pursuit of "Truth" in the entire Western philosophical tradition as a disguised form of the "will to power." The overall impact of questioning the Enlightenment ideals is to show that the certification of knowledge is as much a political as an epistemological issue. Postmodernism as such is fundamental to gearing the restructuring of university curricula in the last decade toward a self-consciously political direction. To some, the otherwise banal institutional process is transformed into one in which knowledge becomes quite literally, to borrow Clausewitz's words again, "a true political instrument, a continuation of political intercourse, carried on with other means."[3]

As the postmodernist effort to politicize knowledge gathered steam in the Western world in the 1980s, there was another movement to disentangle knowledge from politics on behalf of objectivity. These were the heady days in the former Soviet Union and the Eastern Bloc, as well as China, when state control over the circulation of information and knowledge was finally easing to facilitate domestic reforms. Taking advantage of this unprecedented political opportunity, intellectuals pushed hard to sever the link between knowledge and politics by insisting that the search for knowledge is no more than an intellectual activity.[4] For until then, not only did these socialist states fail to guarantee any freedom of expression, the ruling elites were in fact thoroughly cynical about the objectivity of knowledge. To them, there is simply no knowledge that is politically neutral. It was no accident that intellectuals had such a hard time in these socialist countries and that these regimes generally displayed an anti-intellectual stance. It is therefore important to remember that the final collapse of the socialist camp was preceded and accompanied by the depoliticization of knowledge.

These two contrasting episodes illustrated in concrete terms that the relationship between truth and politics is by no means clearcut. It is obvious that each of these movements in its own way helped to undermine the moral authority of its respective regime by redefining the boundary between truth and power. The message from those dissidents who challenged the former socialist states was that the pursuit of truth must be separated from the exercise of power precisely because the former is an intellectual activity in search of knowledge, not a political activity in search of power. Yet the message from their counterparts in liberal democratic states appears to be the reverse: the pursuit of truth cannot and should not be separated from politics because truth necessarily entails power.

How are we to judge between these two arguments? Is truth political or apolitical? Is there a theory of truth that is both intellectually viable and can account for these divergent claims? Let us be clear on what is at stake. It is simply intellectually and politically unsustainable to say that truth is political when those who hold political power in our society are not identical to those who certify knowledge while truth is apolitical when the two are identical. If truth necessarily entails power, one will simply be hard pressed to condemn the very attempt to monopolize truth as a means to consolidate power. It is thus significant that Václav Havel, in his famous essay "The Power of the Powerless," confronts the then Leninist-Stalinist regime as one in which "the centre of power is identical with the centre of truth."[5] He argues that the revolt available to ordinary men and women is the revolt to *"live within the truth,"* which is an attempt to reclaim the "'pre-political.'"[6]

The problem of ascertaining a sustainable relationship between truth and politics is especially pressing when one considers how the post-Cold War political discourse is evolving. What I have in mind is the process of global democratization, which has become the latest obsession of our times. That this is among the "hottest" current issues is in part due to the perception that the end of the Cold War has more to do with the collapse of the socialist camp than it does with disarray within the liberal democratic states.[7] There is a widespread sense that socialism is passé and that our future lies in some kind of "open" society. The obvious question that emerges is whether or not the liberal democratic states of the West constitute a viable and desirable model for the rest of the world. More often, however, the issue is put euphemistically as the prospect of global democratization.[8]

While the question of liberal democracy in the West as the model for the rest of the world is not new, the important twist in these post-Cold War days is that there is no longer a clear political alternative that the West as such can conveniently contrast itself against and claim superiority over. Taken positively, this may very well be a rare historical moment when citizens of the once "Free World" can reconsider the fundamental principles of liberal democracy without any palpable political threat.[9]

Typically (as during the Cold War days), one can expect the academic left to take on the role of the critic during such soul-searching moments. But this is no typical moment. There is a sense that a different radical alternative is needed. Postmodernism poses itself as such an alternative when its intellectual agenda is seized upon by some as the new basis for construing the voice of the marginalized and the oppressed. The difference is that now the critical role of the intellectuals is conducted with the blessing of Nietzsche rather than that of Marx.

It is against this background that I want to consider postmodernism as a political alternative, which claims to transcend the classical positions of both liberalism and Marxism. Like all political movements, however, postmodernism consists of a spectrum of positions. I shall take the movement as it has evolved in the United

States as my case in point. I identify Richard Rorty as occupying the conservative end and William Connolly the radical end. For all their difference, both of these extremes, and all the positions between them, turn out to share the age-old tradition that begins with Plato and that is the attempt to define the relationship between politics and philosophy. In short, the postmodernist attack on Truth is not only a critical posture vis-à-vis the philosophical foundation of liberalism. It also opens the way for a new kind of politics that makes truth with a small "t" vital to its rationale.

Postmodernism and Politics

Rorty's seminal work, *Philosophy and the Mirror of Nature*, is a thorough reflection on what he considers to be the "central concern" of philosophy, which is to formulate a "general theory of representation." For "to know is to represent accurately what is outside the mind" and philosophy has always seen itself as the ultimate adjudicator of "claims to knowledge."[10] In this provocative work, Rorty concludes that all philosophical attempts at a theory of representation are inadequate. Instead, he counsels us to take *"conversation* as the ultimate context within which knowledge is to be understood."[11] Philosophers should take the "ubiquity of language" seriously, in which case they will understand that philosophy can be no more than "a study of the comparative advantages and disadvantages of the various ways of talking which our race has invented."[12]

In the decade following the publication of *Philosophy and the Mirror of Nature*, Rorty emerged as a strong new voice in defense of liberal democracy. In *Consequences of Pragmatism*, Rorty says that in the "post-Philosophical" culture (that is, when pragmatism is *the* philosophy), "neither the priests nor the physicists nor the poets nor the Party were thought of as more 'rational,' or more 'scientific' or 'deeper' than one another."[13] By 1991, Rorty is prepared to say that following Dewey, he takes pragmatism not "as grounding, but as clearing the ground for, democratic politics."[14] In short, pragmatism facilitates our handling of political questions for what they are, in which solidarity by way of "intersubjective agreement," not "objectivity," is what really matters.[15]

Thus, philosophy, in the hands of pragmatists, is once again defining its relation with politics. This time there is, however, a profound difference in that philosophy is no longer the arbiter of politics. Rather, Rorty wants to "dephilosophize politics."[16] While philosophy as conversation can no longer justify politics, philosophy as conversation is not without its political preference. In this regard, Rorty quite comfortably settles for the "rich North Atlantic democracies." These democracies are informed by what Rorty labels as "postmodernist bourgeois liberalism." This brand of liberalism distinguishes itself from "philosophical liberalism," which is a "collection of Kantian principles" that make "transcultural and ahistorical" claims.[17] Rorty's declaration of his political affiliation has not gained him any sympathy, be it on the left or the right.[18] And if one wants to raise the issue of ethnocentric bias in Rorty's political preference, he is ready with the following defense:

> I use the notion of ethnocentrism as a link between antirepresentationalism and political liberalism. I argue that an antirepresentationalist view of inquiry leaves one without a skyhook with which to escape from the ethnocentrism produced by acculturation, but that the liberal culture of recent times has found a strategy for avoiding the disadvantage of ethnocentrism. This is to be open to encounters with other actual and possible cultures, and to make this openness central to its self-image. This culture is an *ethnos* which prides itself on its suspicion of ethnocentrism—on its ability to increase the freedom and openness of encounters, rather than on its possession of truth.[19]

Not surprisingly, in spite of the radical challenge posed by Rorty's pragmatism to the entire Western philosophical tradition, Rorty places himself more in the category of "reformist" rather than "revolutionary" politics.[20] This is why I put Rorty on the conservative end of the postmodernist political spectrum.

In contrast, the radical position is ready to take its revolt against the philosophical foundation of liberalism to the point of discrediting liberalism as political practice. Since this radical position actually has an alternative political platform, I shall call it postmodernist politics proper. Postmodernist politics advocates a new form of democracy, one predicated on an antifoundationalist notion of truth and a nonessentialist notion of the self. An antifoundationalist notion of truth is meant to dislocate closure and accentuate contestability in political discourse.[21] A nonessentialist notion of the self questions the desirability of any kind of emancipatory politics as it inevitably prescribes some form of universal identity for all individuals in the name of liberation. More generally, proponents of postmodernist politics argue that democratic politics cannot be conducted under the rubric of liberalism and Marxism as both are creatures of the Enlightenment project.

Of the radical postmodernist writings on democracy in the United States, the work of William Connolly, and increasingly that of Bonnie Honig, are among the most well-known. Inspired by a "post-Nietzschean sensibility," Connolly's goal is to establish a democratic practice that is appropriate for an increasingly global world. Connolly calls this "agonistic democracy," which he explicates as follows:

> A *democracy* infused with a spirit of agonism is one in which divergent orientations to the mysteries of existence find overt expression in public life. Spaces for difference to be are established through the play of political contestation. Distance becomes politicized in a world where other, topographical sources of distance have closed up. The terms of contestation enlarge opportunities for participants to engage the relational and contingent character of the identities that constitute them, and this effect in turn establishes one of the preconditions for respectful strife between parties who reciprocally acknowledge the contestable character of the faiths that orient them and give them definition in relation to one another.[22]

Presumably "agonistic democracy" recognizes "the indispensability of identity to life" without stifling differences.[23]

The flourishing of such practice requires rethinking the "modern" assumption of the state as the key repository of collective identity.[24] Most importantly, Connolly claims that there is a certain disjunction between temporality and spatiality in our times.[25] By this Connolly means a misfit between the sociopolitical reality of the late twentieth century and our historical state structure. "Agonistic democracy" would be an issue-driven politics that transcends the limit of territorial politics necessarily entailed by the modern nation-state. In Connolly's words:

> Democratic politics must either extend into global issues or deteriorate into institutionalized nostalgia for a past when people believed that the most fundamental issues of life were resolvable within the confines of the territorial state. The contemporary need, perhaps, is to supplement and challenge *structures of territorial democracy* with a politics of *nonterritorial democratization of global issues*.[26]

Thus, postmodernist politics as Connolly envisions it is a politics uniquely tailored to a global rather than bipolar world. By presenting itself as a challenge to liberal democracy, Connolly's case for postmodernist politics is a perfect illustration of what its advocates see as wrong with state-centered politics. The postmodernist critique of such politics can be summarized as follows. First, behind all theories of state sovereignty is a political vision driven by the "impulse towards the total ordering of political phenomena."[27] Second, such a vision is nothing short of a "metanarrative" of order, which is a narration "with a legitimating function" and thereby forecloses contestation.[28] Third, state-centered politics is thus by definition antidemocratic. In short, what informs Connolly's stance against state-centered politics is an antifoundationalist philosophical orientation.

Placing Truth in Politics

This book is written against the political and intellectual backdrop outlined above. More specifically, we want to find out the basis for postmodernist political critique within the Western philosophical tradition. Implicit in the critique are a series of related questions. Why does it matter politically how truth is validated? Does the claim to having truth necessarily imply a certain claim to authority by those who possess truth? If so, how does truth translate into political power? Is a foundationalist notion of truth antidemocratic by implication? Is a contextualist notion necessarily democratic, as the postmodernists tend to suggest?

Part I, where I examine the works of Plato and Hobbes, is a selected historical survey of how these issues have been tackled. While both thinkers are known to be unreservingly averse to the practice of democracy, their views on truth and its relation to politics are importantly different. The question we ask is if it is indeed the conception of truth that sets Plato's politics apart from Hobbes's.

But first let me outline the analytical framework that informs my choice of Plato and Hobbes as representative of the Western philosophical tradition. In *Truth in Philosophy*, Barry Allen makes a useful distinction between two distinct conceptions of truth in the history of Western philosophy—classical and modern. The common assumption of both is that "the truth depends on something whose existence and identity is determined quite apart from conventional practice." This something is "what *has to exist*" if there is truth at all. Allen calls this existential presupposition of truth "truth's *ontological a priori*."[29] It is in terms of this "*ontological a priori*" that Allen draws the following distinction:

> The chief difference between classical and modern philosophies of truth concerns truth's ontological a priori: a difference in the entity posited as determining, ontologically, the possible existence and content of truth. In modern philosophy, it is not nature or substance but the self-evident sameness of what is and what is affirmed when a subject is reflectively aware of itself as presently feeling, thinking, or apparently perceiving one thing and not another which demonstrates, against all skeptical doubt, the possibility of a true-making sameness between thought and being.[30]

Accordingly, Plato is a philosopher who espouses the classical notion of truth and Hobbes the modern conception. This fundamental contrast between the classical and the modern notions of truth will inform my treatment of Plato and Hobbes as political thinkers.

Chapter 2 addresses Plato's view on the relationship between philosophy and politics. Plato maintains that "what *has to exist*"—"truth's *ontological a priori*"—is in fact the essence of things, which can only be apprehended by reason. Plato also makes a necessary connection between this highly abstract and essentialist notion of truth and the good.[31] I will demonstrate how this connection is crucial to Plato's politics. However, I will also argue that while Plato's politics has to be understood in light of his notion of truth, politics as such has nothing to do with the validation of philosophical truth.

Chapter 3 treats Hobbes as a political thinker who embraces the modern conception of truth. Central to this analysis is Hobbes's view on science, which is predicated on the claim that unless we create our own object of knowledge, we can never be sure of what we know. In other words, Hobbes's epistemology is one that shifts the emphasis from what there is to be known to what it is about the knower that makes knowledge possible. This modern conception of truth is at the heart of Hobbes's nominalism, which maintains that truth is an attribute of language rather than of things. I argue that the Leviathan is created to ensure that truth as an artificial construct remains stable over time as it is instrumental to political order.

The historical survey in Part I appears to confirm the postmodernist critique of the Western philosophical tradition as one that supports a totalistic political vision and antidemocratic practice. But what is already beginning to emerge, as we shall see, is that while Hobbes may not be a consistent nominalist, his notion of truth is suspiciously postmodernist in important ways. With this contrast in place, Part II deals specifically with three twentieth-century thinkers—Weber, Foucault, and Arendt (in the order in which they will be discussed). For students of politics, all three are well known for their highly critical views of contemporary Western society, which may be summarized by a one-word description. For Weber, it is rationalization. For Foucault, it is normalization. And finally, for Arendt, it is totalitarianism. But there are two things that all three have in common which make them uniquely suited to my project. First, none of the three can be easily tagged with a political label. This means that all three will be particularly pertinent to those interested in nonliberal, non-Marxist political alternatives. Second, as thinkers who lived in a post-Nietzschean world, all three are highly critical of the philosophical tradition that started with Plato. As we shall see, the shared anti-Platonic stance among Weber, Foucault, and Arendt is crucial to how each considers the role of knowledge in politics, although their views differ in important ways. The works of Weber, Foucault, and Arendt can therefore be usefully juxtaposed for the purpose of understanding the relationship between politics and truth in the context of twentieth-century politics.

Part II begins with Weber. In Chapter 4, I interpret Weber's conception of social science as a unique blend of Kantian epistemology and Nietzschean antimetaphysics. Placed in this context, rationalization as an analytical category represents Weber's ambitious attempt to capture the ontological tension between the abstractness of thinking and the concreteness of living. Politics, like all other life activities, is inevitably shaped by this tension. The predicament of late modernity is that the balance is tilted increasingly toward the side of abstractness. Accordingly, Weber advocates a political posture through his concept of vocation as a means to tilt the imbalance. My claim is that Weber's politics ought to be read as a profound indictment of a world dominated by abstract thinking. At the same time, Weber's highly personal form of politics is a statement on the limit of the state as the venue for meaningful political action. In this sense, Weber anticipates postmodernist politics. Yet it will be mistaken to label Weber a postmodernist in the way the term is defined in the book. For what Weber wants to restore through politics is not the contingent self, but rather a world mediated by the thinking as well as the spirited self.

Chapter 5 considers Foucault, perhaps the most celebrated thinker of our times, and one who is often regarded as having laid the philosophical groundwork for postmodernist politics. Foucault's "genealogy" of modernity tells the story of a normalizing society sustained by a complex network of power relations disguised in the name of Truth. It is against this background that Foucault points to the need to redirect political analysis away from the state in order to focus on the matrix of disciplinary power. I shall argue that contrary to his postmodernist rhetoric, the state plays a crucial role in Foucault's study of power. Foucault's work ought to be read as part of the "liberal" project, which is, as Foucault defines it, informed by the principle that "there is always too much government." I suggest that this is the proper context to place the political significance of Foucault's intellectual engagement. I note, however, that Foucault's philosophical reconsideration of the notion of truth as a historical construct poses a real political quandary. This is when the state and the sovereign definer of truth are one.

The obvious choice of a thinker whose work can help us to tackle the problem is Arendt. Chapter 6 examines Arendt as a political observer who has given us one of the most powerful contemporary indictments of totalitarianism. In her study of totalitarianism, Arendt's originality lies in the juxtaposition between a philosophical notion of truth that begins with Plato and the unique sociopolitical reality of late modernity which renders this notion viable in practice. The outcome of Arendt's analysis is an insight into the profound antipolitical nature of philosophical truth. This view is clearly tied to Arendt's theory of political action, one that is premised on the human condition of plurality. The point about politics is to celebrate human plurality through the formation of opinions. This is not to deny a place for truth in politics, as opinion needs to be guided by what Arendt refers to as "factual truth." But truth, be it in a philosophical or factual form, cannot take the place of constant engagement in thinking and judging which Arendt asks of everyone.

Part III deals with the link between democratic practice and a contextualist notion of truth. Chapter 7 focuses on post-Mao China as a case study. It is significant that one of the first signs of change in post-Mao China was an epistemological debate on the nature of truth conducted with official sanction. This episode was a perfect example of how truth is central to a discourse of legitimation. What came out of an intense debate was a contextualist notion of truth to signal the beginning of a China that was supposed to be more tolerant of political differences. But I argue that the liberating power of a contextualist notion of truth is illusory because it can be just as easily monopolized by the state. Truth with a small"t" is no better guarantor of democracy than Truth with a big"T".

Chapter 8 reexamines the relationship of truth and politics in the context of contemporary politics in the Western world. I assess the promise of postmodernist politics by focusing on identity politics. I argue that all the thinkers considered in this study will have reservations about the nature of identity politics. The different grounds of their objections serve as an appropriate way to end a book that addresses the theme of truth and politics.

Part I

HISTORICAL OVERVIEW

CHAPTER TWO

Plato: Truth, Nontruth, and Legitimate Power

IN ONE OF THE MOST WIDELY READ and debated texts in the tradition of political theory, Plato's *Republic*, we see a paradigmatic attempt to establish the claim of truth to sovereignty. Central to the whole argument of the *Republic* is the role of knowledge in politics. Now, for Plato, true knowledge is philosophy, and the state is just only when it is under the rule of one who knows the truth—the philosopher king. In the words of Socrates,

> Cities will have no respite from evil, my dear Glaucon, nor will the human race . . . unless philosophers rule as kings in the cities, or those whom we now call kings and rulers genuinely and adequately study philosophy, until, that is, political power and philosophy coalesce, and the various natures of those who now pursue the one to the exclusion of the other are forcibly debarred from doing so.[1]

The ideal state is meant to embody justice for all. However, realizing this ideal will also require the total control and manipulation over those subject to the rule of the just. Karl Popper, in his influential book *The Open Society and Its Enemies*, notes that in practising justice, the philosopher king in effect brings about injustice to individuals as justice demands "some kind of equality in the treatment of individuals."[2] Accordingly, Plato's notion of justice is considered by Popper as a form of perverted justice—"totalitarian justice"—whereby the interest of the state takes precedence over that of the individual.[3]

In thus characterizing the *polis*, Popper establishes himself as one of the most vocal critics of Plato. This reading claims that

Plato's politics is informed by a philosophy characterized by "methodological essentialism." It is this essentialism that supports the postulation of "one absolute and unchanging ideal," which in turn justifies Plato's sweeping "Utopian engineering."[4]

But what if the *Republic* is never meant to be a blueprint for political action? This is indeed the view most commonly associated with Leo Strauss. Strauss claims that the nature of Plato's *polis* is, in effect, a nonissue in that the so-called ideal state, when actualized, is no more than an absurdity.[5] The absurdity of the situation demonstrates that the just city is not meant to be realized. "It is impossible because it is against nature" for evil to disappear from the city.[6] This is the limit of the city which is not for philosophy to remedy. On this reading, Socrates' ideal *polis* is thus a mere mockery of the impossible.

Most students in political thought are familiar with these two diametrically different interpretations of Plato's *Republic*. What I would like to highlight here is rather the all-too-easily overlooked commonality between Popper and Strauss. By this I mean the view that the *polis* is highly unpalatable and that this is a direct consequence of Plato's philosophy, which is the ultimate repository of transcendent truth. For Popper, the undesirability is due to Plato's conviction that politics can be modelled after philosophy.[7] For Strauss, the undesirability is due precisely to Plato's view that politics and philosophy are inherently incongruent.

Both of these positions have been much debated.[8] Instead of treading the familiar grounds of why Plato's politics as laid out in the *Republic* is problematic according to these two positions, I suggest that we turn to a radically different interpretation of Plato's politics. I have in mind Gadamer's reading, which maintains that neither Plato's philosophy nor his politics is absolute in character. The choice of Gadamer is not random in that philosophical hermeneutics is very much a part of the postmodernist intellectual project as defined in the introductory chapter. In the words of Gadamer, "the hermeneutic consciousness . . . recognises that in the age of science the claim of superiority made by philosophic thought has something vague and unreal about it."[9] It is thus significant that we examine what Gadamer has to say about the relationship between knowledge claims and political power in Plato.[10]

Section I of the chapter is devoted to this purpose. We shall see that central to Gadamer's position is the argument that dialectic is the link between Plato's theory of knowledge and theory of rule. This argument constitutes the ground for Gadamer's further claim that there is a necessary connection between philosophy and politics in Plato's thought where there is room for both philosophical truth and open politics. In sections II and III, I turn to the *Republic* and the *Laws* respectively in an effort to assess Gadamer's reading. I demonstrate that at the heart of Plato's politics is a paradox—philosophy is the only legitimate guide to politics and yet the political can never approximate the philosophical. In light of this argument, section IV accounts for why the kind of connection between the openness of dialectic and the persuasive governmental technique as set forth by Gadamer becomes questionable.

I

Dialectic and Hermeneutics

Generally, Gadamer supports a reading of Plato as a philosopher who does not regard philosophy to be a fixed set of doctrines that can be inculcated. This is why Plato rejects treatises and lectures as appropriate media for conveying to the "general public" what philosophy is.[11] Indeed, Gadamer claims that the central theme of the "Seventh Letter" (which Gadamer considers authentic) is none other than Plato's theory of teaching and learning, which is the art of dialectic—the "untiring movement back and forth"—conducted by way of talking.[12] If we take into account that dialogue is the preferred way for Plato to state his thoughts as well as the ambivalent and inconclusive way in which his dialogues often end, it does appear that Plato has no set doctrine to teach.

It is this openness of the Platonic dialogue that Gadamer's hermeneutics takes seriously. On this reading, the Platonic dialogue, which typically proceeds through a series of questions and answers, is dialectic sine qua non. Gadamer regards dialectic as the paradigm for the most basic human quest for meaning. As noted in *Truth and Method*, the "art of questioning" is raised to a "conscious art" in the Socratic-Platonic dialectic. This art is not to be confused with *techne*. For dialectic is not a form of "craft that can be taught" in order to "master the knowledge of truth."[13] Rather, as

Gadamer sees it, dialectic, being the "art of asking questions," brings the object questioned into a "state of indeterminancy." Gadamer suggests that "questioning is not the positing, but the testing of possibilities."[14] It is in this sense that a true question achieves "openness." The openness provided by questioning is the way to advance what one knows. For to ask, one must know that "one does not know."[15] Hence, dialectic represents the true "art of thinking," which progresses through persistence in asking. This is to suggest that the person seeking for knowledge must "preserve his orientation towards openness."[16]

Dialectic therefore has a clear moral precept. One has to be tolerant of differences to remain open. This tolerance constitutes the basis for genuine communication in the form of "conversation." In the words of Gadamer:

> It [conversation] requires that one does not try to out-argue the other person, but that one really considers the weight of the other's opinion. Hence it is an art of testing. But the art of testing is the art of questioning. . . . To question means to lay open, to place in the open. As against the solidity of opinions, questioning makes the object and all its possibilities fluid.[17]

Dialectic, by engaging language through the "process of question and answer, giving and taking, talking at cross purposes and seeing each other's point," is able to facilitate genuine "communication of meaning." This is what hermeneutics attempts to achieve "with respect to the written tradition." Hence, to describe the "work of hermeneutics as a conversation with the text" is more than just a metaphor. In conducting a dialogue with the text, hermeneutical reading avoids the pitfall of any "dogmatic abuse" of words.[18] This is the ground for Gadamer to maintain that there is an intimate connection between dialectic and hermeneutics.[19]

Dialectic and Politics

While Gadamer does not specify the sociopolitical conditions conducive to hermeneutics,[20] Gadamer's overall emphasis on the "openness" of dialectic must entail a certain political commitment to the centrality of dialogue in politics.[21] This position is most clearly borne out in Gadamer's reading of Plato's politics. Indeed, for Gadamer, if the Platonic dialogue has the important role of protecting words from "dogmatic abuse," the Platonic political program demonstrates the viability of politics conducted through persuasion rather than the inculcation of dogma. It is in this sense that Gadamer's interpretation of Plato's political philosophy suggests a distinct parallel in the relationship between the structure of knowledge and the conduct of politics.

In *The Idea of the Good in Platonic-Aristotelian Philosophy*, Gadamer notes that "the clumsy and circuitous demonstration" of the possibility of the ideal state in the *Republic* demonstrates precisely its "*im*possibility".[22] Yet in distinguishing his interpretation from Strauss's,[23] Gadamer is careful to point out that Plato seeks more than just showing the irresolvability of the "conflict between theōria and politics" through the absurdity of such a conflict.[24] Rather, Gadamer suggests that

> Reading dialectically means relating these utopian demands in each instance to their opposite, in order to find, somewhere in between, what is really meant—that is, in order to recognize what the circumstances are, and how they could be made better. Per se, the institutions of this model city are not meant to embody ideas for reform. Rather, they make truly bad conditions and the dangers for the continued existence of a city visible e contrario.[25]

Accordingly, Gadamer maintains that there is a positive message to the paradox of the philosopher king:

> The point "in between" to which Plato directs us here is a state so arranged that the exercise of the power of government will be carried out as a public office and not exploited as a chance to advance one's own interests.[26]

The observation that there is a constructive didactic purpose to the *Republic* enables Gadamer to call Plato's *polis* an "educational state" appropriately.[27] The *Republic* as a whole is taken to be an exercise in "looking about for a cure for ailing states." The positive goal of "constituting an ideal state in words" is to *cultivate* "the just political attitude of its citizens," which Gadamer maintains is the very thing that makes a just state possible.

Thus, Gadamer's position is that not only is there no conflict between philosophy and politics in Plato's "educational state," philosophy in fact renders politics more effective. Accordingly, the "ideal state" in Plato's *Republic* is about how philosophy and politics can and should coalesce:

> This constitution is not meant, as a better-designed institution, to reform an existing state but to found a new state—which, however, means to form human beings who can construct a genuine state. Plato's *Republic*, as an educational state, is a design for man, and the founder of the republic is someone who forms men. And if Plato hoped throughout his life for political efficacy and tried his hand at it, it was always through philosophy. Politics, in particular, set him the task of leading people to philosophy, because it is only people who have been led to philosophy who in turn can order others—and that means a whole state—in a way that relates to what true understanding aims at: the idea of the good.[28]

By suggesting that the main purpose of the *Republic* is educational, Gadamer maintains that the appropriate means of bringing about a just state is through education. More specifically, it is a form of education that is dialectical in method and ontological in aim. Just as the Platonic dialectic aims to impart knowledge through the fluidity of illuminating conversation rather than the rigidity dictated by written statements, Plato's politics facilitates change by persuasion rather than imposition. Such is the hallmark of a just state, where there is a parallel between the openness and tolerance characteristic of the Platonic dialogue and a political program that is nonauthoritarian in advocating its cause.

II

Rule of the Wise

How sustainable is Gadamer's interpretation of the connection between Plato's theory of knowledge and his theory of rule? To answer this question, I suggest that we turn to the *Republic* as a text that not only deals with the constitution of a perfect state, but also the desirability and possibility of translating true knowledge into the practice of statecraft. We must note that crucial to Gadamer's interpretation is that the process of dialectic suggests openness. However, as I shall argue, this reading fails to address Plato's insistence that dialectic is the only way to truth and that there is Truth to be attained by one who is engaged in dialectic. It is thus imperative that we ask whether these two points compromise the openness implied by dialectic in any important ways.

In the quote cited at the beginning of the chapter, Plato states that a city will have "no respite from evil" until philosophers rule as kings. Philosophers are defined as "those who love the spectacle of truth."[29] Hence, to decipher what this way of life entails and why it can combat evil, we need to investigate into the ability to pursue truth and the nature of the truth itself.

The first question that is in order is whether the ability to pursue truth is unique to the philosophers. We begin with Plato's view on education as explicated in the parable of the cave. Here Plato notes that life without education is like the life led by the prisoners of an underground cave, who live in the world of shadows. Education is likened to the process whereby a prisoner is released from bondage and is forced to travel upward until one is able to reach the light. Education as such is a process of self-discovery and liberation from a form of "shadowy" existence by removing the external impediments.[30] In Socrates' words,

> Education then is the art of doing this very thing, this turning around, the knowledge of how the soul can most easily and most effectively be turned around; it is not the art of putting the capacity of sight into the soul; *the soul possesses that already but it is not turned the right way or*

looking where it should. This is what education has to deal with.[31]

That education is a process of recovering what is inherent in us is a view that Plato holds consistently. This theme is discussed in other works of his, most famously in *Meno*. Here Socrates attempts to demonstrate that "seeking and learning are in fact nothing but recollection." To prove this, Socrates makes one of Meno's slaves, who has never received any formal education, reason out the fundamental geometrical principles that define all squares. Although the exchange between Socrates and the slave is laden with Socrates' suggestive questions, the fact remains that Socrates is "simply interrogating him [the slave] on his own opinions" regarding the square under examination, without giving the slave "any instruction or explanation." Having thus proven successfully that even an uneducated slave can become knowledgeable without being taught, Socrates proceeds to make the claim that the human soul is "forever in a state of knowledge."[32] Hence,

> If the truth about reality is always in our soul, the soul must be immortal, and one must take courage and try to discover—that is, to recollect—what one doesn't happen to know, or, more correctly, remember, at the moment.[33]

Moreover, not only is learning the recovery of what is inherent in us, the ability to do so is in fact a universal quality that we all have in our possession. The philosopher, in pursuing truth, is doing no more than what everyone else is in principle capable of doing. As we shall see, this capacity to realize what Socrates takes to be the universal human quality turns out to be a crucial point in justifying the rule of the philosophers.

Let us now return to the philosophers' way of life by looking into the nature of the truth that is being pursued. In *Meno*, Socrates defines knowledge as "truth about reality," which is acquired when "true opinions" are "tied down" by reason. To achieve this, "true opinions" have to be repeatedly "aroused by questioning."[34] This, then, is the process of learning properly conducted, to which Meno's slave has a brief exposure. Learning will eventually take one to a completely different order of things, which represents the "reality." This is why to know is to have the "truth about reality."

With this, we come to one of the most studied aspects of Plato's theory of knowledge—the Forms.

Briefly stated, this theory postulates the following.[35] For each thing that exists, there is a Form that is its essence—that which is "more real" than the thing itself. As Gregory Vlastos suggests, the "real" is "that which is cognitively dependable, undeceiving."[36] A Form as such is stable and unchanging, unattached to any particular object. It is the Forms that constitute the realm of "the intelligible." They are the "objects of thought," as opposed to the "objects of sight" that constitute the realm of "the visible." Moreover, the senses may corrupt the intellect:

> I was afraid that by observing objects with my eyes and trying to comprehend them with each of my other senses I might blind my soul altogether. So I decided that I must have recourse to theories, and use them in trying to discover the truth about things.[37]

It is in the realm of "the intelligible" that we "recover" truth. Truth thus acquired transcends particularity and specificity. Truth is not fact, for there is "nothing stable or dependable" in facts. Facts belong to the realm of "the visible," which means that they "fluctuate just like the water in a tidal channel, and never stay at any point for any time," as with everything else in this realm.[38] Thus, when we tally up all these conditions that make truth possible, it becomes clear that for Plato, "truth-claims owe nothing to sensory observation and everything to logical inference and analysis."[39] Senses can never tell us what an object "really" is, only reason can perform this task. Truth is reason *par excellence*. What "can be thought" is what "can be."[40]

Now that we know what the nature of truth is, we can appreciate more fully the reason for Plato's assertion that the capacity to learn is inherent in all of us. The assertion in effect upholds the capacity to learn as a universal quality that defines being, regardless of who we are as distinct individuals. In other words, the philosopher, by contemplating the realm of "the intelligible," realizes being. This is how the philosopher lives the authentic life, that is, the life most truthful to who we "really" are.

However, while we may all potentially become philosophers, Plato does not appear to count on this potential in his ideal *polis*.

Indeed, in several places in the *Republic*, Plato indicates that only a handful of citizens will become philosophers in reality. The myth that we are all "earth-born brothers," in Book III, is construed on the ground that there is a political need to keep everyone content since only those with the mixture of gold, as opposed to a mixture of silver or bronze and iron, can become rulers.[41] Again, in Book V, Socrates states plainly that "some people have a natural aptitude for philosophy and for leading the state, while others have not that aptitude and must follow the leader."[42] It turns out that the majority of people will not have the aptitude and will have no choice but to "follow the leader." Accordingly, the ruling class will be elitist in the *polis*:

> Then a whole city which is established according to nature would be wise because of the smallest group or part of itself, the commanding or ruling group. This group seems to be the smallest by nature and to it belongs a share in that knowledge which, alone of them all, must be called wisdom.[43]

The same conclusion is repeated in the *Statesman*.[44] There, the stranger tells young Socrates that it is "only in the hands of the select few or of the enlightened individual" that we find the "right exercise of political power which is itself the one true constitution."[45]

We now have in our hands one of those many much-contested absurdities that are present in the *Republic*, namely, how should we reconcile Plato's claim that the ability to acquire knowledge is universal with his elitist theory of rule? Rather than giving Plato a way out in the Straussian fashion (that is, Plato does not mean what he says), I suggest that this pair of seemingly contradictory claims can be resolved by examining Plato's tripartite schema of the soul. As is well known, Plato divides the soul into three different components—reason, spirit, and appetite. All three are present at all times in every individual. To become a philosopher means that reason is able to precede over spirit and appetite, as reason is the only component of the soul that can relate to truth. While we all have the potential to let reason take charge, the predominance of reason over the other two components is by no means something that we can simply take for granted. Hence, in Plato's classification of the community, the philosophers constitute a special breed that requires years of rigorous training before reaching the end of the upward journey to truth.[46] This is why, in any given political community, what we find in reality is that only a selected few possess the art of statesmanship. As young Socrates points out in the *Statesman*, it is simply "quite out of question" for a considerable number of men to be capable of acquiring the art of statesmanship. If "statesmanship" were an art that could be acquired by many, it would be "the easiest of all arts," which clearly nullifies the prerogative that only philosophers are qualified to be kings.[47]

Justice and Power

Up to this point, we have dealt with the claim that the philosophers should rule because they are more knowledgeable and, hence, wiser than nonphilosophers. But Plato does not simply assert that the wise must rule. He wants to convince us that it is *just* for the wise to rule. As we shall see, it is this claim that makes Platonic politics a uniquely uncompromising form of politics.

We recall that in Plato's hierarchical view of knowledge, grasping the Forms is the highest type of mental activity that can be rightfully called the act of the intellect. No doubt in Plato's mind, this is reason working hard to exert its "tether" over opinion.[48] Yet in the upward journey from darkness to light, not all Forms are equal. The journey is literally a climb in which the end marks the highest point of the climb and gives one a panoramic view. It is therefore significant that Plato places none other than the Form of the Good in this privileged position. In Plato's words, "in the intelligible world the Form of the Good is the last to be seen, and with difficulty; when seen it must be reckoned to be for all the cause of all that is right and beautiful. . . . "[49] The Truth coincides with the Good.[50]

It seems clear enough why reaching the end of one's upward climb in the realm of the intelligible is to engage our rational capacity to its utmost and thereby give one the panoramic view, that is, the Truth. However, what exactly is the connection between the development of one mind's and the development of one's character? While only reason can take us through the climb, we must remember that in Plato's tripartite schema of the soul, the spirit and the appetite are simultaneously present in each of us and constitute a constant source of distraction within us. Thus, to finish the journey and to stay at the top is a real test of one's character. The feat indicates that not only has one engaged one's reason to its fullest potential, but that one is able to exercise self-control. For self-control is when reason is able to control the appetite and the spirit.[51] Only when reason is in control can the three parts of the soul be in harmony.[52] Justice is then achieved:

> Justice . . . does not lie in a man's external actions, but in the way he acts within himself, really concerned with himself and his inner parts. . . . be it about the acquisition of wealth, the care of his body, some public actions, or private contract. In all these fields he thinks the just and beautiful action . . . to be that which preserves this inner harmony and indeed helps to achieve it, wisdom to be the knowledge which oversees this action, an unjust action to be that which always destroys it, and ignorance the belief which oversees that.[53]

Likewise, justice in the city is achieved only when reason is in full control. And since governments are born "from the characters of the men who live in the cities,"[54] philosophers, being indisputably the most reasonable, should rule as kings. The rule of the philosopher king is "aristocracy." Accordingly, all other forms of governments are categorically corrupt, as they are controlled by nonphilosophers. The first corrupt form of government is when the philosophers king is still in charge, but only nominally. This is due to the inevitably of mistakes, even among the best philosopher kings. One critical area where mistakes will occur is in mating, so that the breed of the ruling class is no longer as pure as it should be and thereby resulting in an inferior type of philosopher king.[55] Accordingly, the second form of corruption emerges when the *polis* is dominated by those who love honor and victory more than wisdom. This constitutes "timarchy," which can easily deteriorate into "oligarchy." Oligarchy is defined as a form of government controlled by those who love wealth more than anything else. The next level of corruption takes place when "democracy" sets in. Correspondingly, this is when the "appetitive" begins to rule over the other parts of the soul, for the "democratic man" is one who thinks that "all pleasures are equal and must be equally prized."[56]

Justice and Action

It is important to note that justice, both at the individual and collective level, is defined by Plato as first and foremost a condition. Such a condition is one in which there is order to a hierarchical arrangement, that is, when each of its constituent components is in its proper place.[57] We recall that in the description of the just individual cited earlier, just action is no more than a manifestation of the inner state of the soul. Hence, for Plato, what truly defines justice is the state of one's soul. Action per se is secondary to the essence of justice.

Why is Plato so suspicious of action? The exchange between Socrates and Polemarchus in Book I is illuminating in this regard. Here, Socrates challenges the definition of justice as a craft of benefitting one's friends and harming one's enemies. Socrates points out that such a definition amounts to reducing justice into a craft with a specific function in specific circumstances, just like the crafts of medicine and cooking. More specifically, as Polemarchus suggests, such a definition of justice means that the just man is "most able to benefit his friends and harm his enemies" in fighting a war. When further pressed by Socrates that the definition implies that the just man is useless in peacetime, Polemarchus defends his view by pointing out that in times of peace, justice helps maintain contracts. This view is challenged by Socrates as unsustainable since it makes justice most useful only in safeguarding property, not when the property is actually in use. For example, when one needs to keep a lyre safe, justice is required. Yet when one wants to put the lyre in use, it is the musician's craft, not justice, that is most useful. In the words of Socrates, "so with all other things, justice is useless in their use, but useful when they are not in use." As Socrates rightly points out, if this were indeed the case, justice is hardly "a very important thing." More fundamentally, however, Socrates objects to the definition of justice as a craft of benefitting one's friends and harming one's enemies because this means that the just man, when practising justice, can in fact harm someone. And when men are harmed, "they deteriorate in their human excellence" and will only "become more unjust." In short, Socrates renders Polemarchus's definition logically incoherent by pointing out that the definition in effect states that it is in the very nature of justice to breed injustice.[58]

In this exchange with Polemarchus, Socrates establishes two very significant points. First, unlike any given craft, justice is not object and need oriented. Rather, the practice of justice has a general rather than a specific effect. Hence, justice, when engaged, is not a craft that aims only at benefitting a particular object at a particular moment. The second and more important point is that justice differs from all forms of crafts in that crafts are by definition knowledge of technical know-how. The effective performance of crafts such as medicine, cookery, and sailing requires practice and experience, which are characteristic of the world of action. The practical world of action that all craftsmen inhabit is thus separated most distinctly from the contemplative world of philosophers, who exemplify justice.

This latter point helps us to gauge Plato's definition of justice as a state of being at its most profound level. Indeed, given Plato's understanding of the real, there seems no other way but to relegate action to a secondary status. For as we act, we are reproducing what is contemplated in thought. Action as such is no more than an imitation of the Forms, that is, the real. Action, being an image, is by definition part of the realm of the visible.[59] Thus, thought is permanent and universal; action is transient and particular. A just person is always just even when the person is not acting. Yet every action the just person engages in is just.

To point out that action per se is secondary to Plato's theory of justice is crucial. It is in treating action as an imitation of the Form that explains Socrates' rather scornful response to the request of Glaucon and Adeimantus regarding the possibility of bringing the ideal *polis* into existence. As Socrates puts it,

> "Is it possible for anything to be realized in deed as it is spoken in word, or is it the nature of things that action should partake of exact truth less than speech, even if some deny it? Do you admit it or not?" "I do," he [Glaucon] said. "Then don't insist," said I, "that I must exhibit as realized in action precisely what we expounded in words."[60]

At the end of Book IX, an exchange between Socrates and Glaucon further confirms that to "act out" the just city is not Plato's primary concern. It goes,

> I understand, he [Glaucon] said, you mean in the city which we were founding and described, our city of words, for I do not believe it exists anywhere on earth.
> Perhaps, I [Socrates] said, it is a model laid up in heaven, for him who wishes to look upon, and as he looks, set up the government of his soul. It makes no difference whether it exists anywhere or will exist.[61]

These exchanges point out that for Plato, what counts is that the ideal *polis* is what is *true*, not what is realizable. This is a critical distinction that challenges the kind of interpretation set forth by Gadamer. More precisely, the point is not so much what Plato wants to see realized in the *polis*, but what he defends in principle. After all, what is defended in principle in this ideal *polis* is a regime sustained by systematic deception as well as complete manipulation and control of those under its rule. Hence, in the end, Gadamer, like Strauss, is too quick to dismiss the *polis*. However, unlike Strauss, Gadamer does it in the name of bringing politics closer to the demands of philosophy. For Gadamer's Plato, as we may recall, is one who wants to cure the "ailing states" by using the philosophical method of dialectic.

III

The Second Best

To recapitulate, I introduce Gadamer's reading of Plato as a contrast to the more commonly known interpretations offered by Popper and Strauss. More specifically, as noted in section I, Gadamer juxtaposes his own reading with that of Strauss. The question posed by Strauss can be stated as follows: should Plato's political project be taken seriously in light of his philosophy? Gadamer's answer to this is no if the project is taken literally, yes if it is appropriated dialectically. In section II, I have shown how Gadamer's reading does not satisfactorily explain why we should not take Plato's words in the *Republic* seriously when in fact for Plato, words are closer to Truth than action. But let us for the moment assume that Plato never really means to realize the ideal *polis* of the *Republic*, whether literally or dialectically, and consider the picture of Plato's "second best" *polis*—one ruled by laws.[62]

We begin by asking what it is that makes rule-by-law second to rule-by-philosopher king. In the *Statesman*, we are told that the latter is superior because it is more responsive to ever-changing circumstances.[63] This is quite in keeping with Plato's overall critique of how written words, when cast in rigid formal style, can easily become dogma.[64] However, I will contest that the more compelling explanation is associated with Plato's claim that just as action is secondary to the definition of justice, law is never the complete rendering of justice properly understood. That law, like action, is incomplete, is a direct consequence of the limit of language.

In the *Statesman*, Plato makes the claim that language has a more privileged status in representation than any other form of representation. There, the stranger said to Socrates that "a definition couched in words is a better description of a living creature than a drawing or any model of it can be. . . . "[65] This view of the representation power of language echoes what is expressed in one of Plato's earlier dialogues, *Cratylus*. Here, a name is defined as "an instrument of teaching and of distinguishing natures."[66] However, we must bear in mind that a name is no more than a tool of communication. After all, "the knowledge of things is not to be derived from names. . . . They must be studied and investigated in themselves."[67] In other words, even though language may be the best form of representation, it is nonetheless an "image" of truth.

That language is not itself truth does not make language arbitrary. Indeed, there is a "correctness" to names. In *Cratylus* the legislator is identified as the "maker of names" and thus laws stipulate names. However, in order to ensure that correctness be attained in naming, the "maker of names" is subject to a judge. The judge is none other than the "dialectician." In the end, the philosophers are "the first imposers of names."[68] Truth gets to judge language. This analysis of Plato's view on language accounts for why a regime under rule-by-law is the second best on a basis that is thoroughly consistent with Plato's theory of truth. Just as linguistic representation is second to truth, rule-by-law is second to rule-by-philosopher king.

Rule-by-Law and Absolute Power

In the *Laws*, about which Gadamer does not have much to say, we get a glimpse of the prototype of a regime under rule-by-law in the state of Magnesia. While those who occupy the high offices of the state are referred to as "rulers," the Athenian told us that it is in fact more appropriate to regard them as "servants of the laws." In his words:

> If I have called them "servants of the laws" it's not because I want to mint a new expression but because I believe that the success or failure of a state hinges on this point more than on anything else. Where the law is subject to some other authority and has none of its own, the collapse of the state, in my view, is not far off; but if law is the master of the government and the government is its slave, then the situation is full of promise and men enjoy all the blessings that the gods shower on a state.[69]

Plato thereby establishes rule-by-law as the supreme principle of this less than ideal polity, in which those in office should be subordinate to the law of the state.

Yet overseeing the law is the Nocturnal Council, which is an exclusive body made up of a selected few. The Council is meant to function as a "resistance" mechanism built into the laws to prevent them from being reversed.[70] The law of the state as such is subject to permanent review by the Council. In light of this critical constitutional provision, it is important that we consider who can become members of the Council. As discussed earlier, Plato's view in *Cratylus* is that the legislator, as the "maker of names," ought to be judged by the dialectician, that is, the philosopher. Indeed, the election mechanism to be in place suggests that the Nocturnal Council will be "in effect an intellectual and moral aristocracy."[71] In the end the Nocturnal Council is no more than "a device for the subordination of legislation and government to philosophy."[72] At the philosophical level, the stipulation for the Nocturnal Council is of course justified as Plato's way of safeguarding truth against the corruptive influence of the world of actions.

Plato insists that compliance to the laws, as to the philosopher king, is absolute. There is no justifiable cause for reform, let alone revolt, from below. In *Crito*, Socrates refused Crito's offer to facilitate an escape for him even though Socrates himself agreed that he was unjustly punished. His reason is that a city will surely be "turned upside down" if the "legal judgments which are pronounced in it have no force but are nullified and destroyed by private persons."[73] More importantly, legal judgments of the state are binding on all citizens residing in the state without the need for periodic express consent from the citizens. For by residing in a state, one is in effect giving what amounts to tacit consent to its legitimacy. And this is precisely what Socrates had done by staying in Athens all his life. In his words:

> It is a fact, then, they would say, that you are breaking covenants and undertakings made with us, although you made them under no compulsion or misunderstanding, and were not compelled to decide in a limited time. You had seventy years in which you could have left the country, if you were not satisfied with us or felt that the agreements were unfair.[74]

Presumably, the moral justification for stipulating that ordinary citizens be totally submissive to the authority of the state is that they will be subject to "reasonable" laws. The philosophers are, after all, the ultimate initiators of laws.

Rule-by-Law and Censorship

Do the constitutional features described above constitute sufficient basis for us to conclude that the state of Magnesia is as "hierarchical and authoritarian" as the ideal *polis*?[75] Critics like Trevor Saunders argue that the two states are in effect "the same Platonic state," that is, a state "governed by persons with metaphysical insights." The only difference is that in the *Republic*, "the hypothesis of Callipolis is that that kind of rule is achievable;" whereas, in the *Laws*, "the hypothesis of Magnesia is that it has not yet been achieved, and may indeed never be...."[76] One can challenge such an observation by pointing out that the provision for something like the Nocturnal Council resembles a rather standard practice of modern liberal democratic state. We have, after all, professional judges, who occupy positions not democratically elected, to oversee the legality of policies adopted by elected officials. Indeed, rule-by-law is now generally regarded as an important constitutional safeguard against the arbitrariness of individuals. Thus, this particular provision need not be taken as a conclusive sign of Plato's anachronistic "tribalism," which is a central theme in Popper's critique of Plato.[77]

Perhaps there is more sharing of power in Magnesia than in the ideal *polis*. But let us for the moment suspend our concern for the institutional setup of Magnesia and attempt to tackle the nature of the state from another perspective. One crucial issue that has not been addressed so far is the jurisdiction of the state. What we find is that in this land, the laws are all-encompassing. They prescribe "the duties we owe to children, relatives, friends and fellow-citizens, as well as the service heaven demands we render to foreigners; they will tell us the way we have to behave in the company of each of these categories of people...."[78] In fact, when we look at the list of legislation in the *Laws*, it is quite clear that the laws are to cover every single aspect of life—from marriage to procreation, from education in the womb to sport and military training of adults, from regulation of property, trade, and commerce to regulation of art and literature.

It is the last item—art and literature—that I want to pursue as it obviously touches on Gadamer's view that dialectic cannot be meaningfully engaged unless one is tolerant of differences. Earlier I noted that Gadamer fails to take into account the political implications of Plato's insistence that dialectic, in the form of "living speech," is the only appropriate mode of inquiry leading to truth.[79] Indeed, how far is Plato willing to go to ensure that the political climate be optimal to the engagement in dialectic? How tolerant is Plato to other modes of discourse that may not be compatible with his?

In the *Republic*, the question of censorship first appears in Book II when the concern for the kind of stories to be told to the "young and tender" is first raised.[80] The role of "story tellers" is thus brought under political scrutiny. As the dialogue unfolds, it becomes clear that these story tellers mean more specifically the poets. The critique of poetry is obviously a subject important enough to Plato that he returns to it in Book X. Here we learn that art is on the whole problematic because it is imitative. An artist makes a representation of an object perceived by the senses, which is itself already an image of the "real," that is, the "Form." Hence, the artist, as an imitator, is one "whose product is at three removes from nature."[81] Art in general, and poetry in particular, simply cannot generate true knowledge. But worse still, it is the moral consequence of imitation that Plato is concerned about. As pointed out by Gadamer,

> Thus this critique of mimetic poetry cuts much deeper than it had at first appeared. It not only criticizes the false and dangerous contents of mimetic art or the choice of an unseemly mode of representation. *It is at the same time a critique of the moral consequence of "aesthetic consciousness."* The very experience which is [*sic*] had in delusory imitation is in itself already the ruination of the soul. For the deeper analysis of the inner constitution of the soul has made evident that aesthetic self-forgetfulness opens the way for the sophists' game with the passions to infiltrate the human heart.[82]

Plato's case against poetry and the necessity to "banish poetry from the city" is therefore based on an ontological concern.[83] Poetry hinders the soul's journey to the Good by its appeal to passion rather than reason. "Aesthetic self-forgetfulness" is nothing less than forgetfulness of being.[84]

In the *Laws*, the message that poetry needs to be controlled is equally clear. A poet should not be allowed to compose anything "that conflicts with society's conventional notions of justice, goodness and beauty." Thus, it is stipulated that no work can be shown to any private person until it has first been submitted to the "appointed assessors and to the Guardians of the Laws."[85] In short, poets are totally stripped of their creative capacity and become a kind of "craftsmen" serving the law.[86]

It is in this context that the state of Egypt was hailed as the first state that recognized the importance of control over "artistic creativity." Apparently, according to the Athenian, paintings that were produced in Egypt ten thousand years ago were "no better and no worse than those of today" because any "modification and innovation" outside the prescribed forms stipulated by the state was prohibited. This stifling of creativity did not seem to bother the Athenian a bit. In fact, he said to Cleinias, the Cretan, that this was "simply a supreme achievement of legislators and statesmen."[87]

If artistic pursuit hinders the soul's journey to the Good, it is not surprising that the lack of control over "artistic creativity" can lead to political chaos. In discussing the decline of Athenian democracy, the Athenian relates political confusion to "confusion" in artistic forms in no uncertain terms:

> Gripped by a frenzied and excessive lust for pleasure, they [composers] jumbled together laments and hymns, mixed paeans and dithyrambs, and even imitated pipe tunes on the lyre. The result was *a total confusion of styles*. Unintentionally, in their idiotic way, they misrepresented their art, claiming that in music there are no standards of right and wrong at all, but that the most "correct" criterion is the pleasure of a man who enjoyed the performance, whether he is a good man or not. On these principles they based their composition, and they accompanied them with propaganda to the same effect. Consequently they gave the ordinary man not only a taste for breaking the laws of music but the arrogance to set himself up as a capable judge.[88]

Accordingly, in music, as in all other aspects of life, it is dangerous for the ordinary person to believe that one is a "capable" judge. Hence, if the legislator has even just a "rough idea of what constitutes 'correctness' in matters musical," then one ought not to have any "qualms about giving the whole subject systematic expression in form of a law." Likewise, one should do the same with all other art forms "equally without qualms."[89]

IV

Dialectical Openness and Political Closure

The preceding two sections examine the relationship between philosophy and politics in Plato by focusing primarily on the *Republic* and the *Laws*. I show that it is indeed the possession of truth by philosophers that justifies their claim to absolute power in Plato's *polis*. However, I do not think that this is due to Plato's belief that politics can be modelled after philosophy, as critics like Popper suggest.[90] Nor do I subscribe to Strauss's view that because the philosophical and the political cannot converge, Plato's political project is to be dismissed as a mere mockery of the impossible.

My position on the issue, that is, the relationship between philosophy and politics in Plato, can perhaps be best stated by way of why I find Gadamer's position to be unsustainable. We recall that central to his reading is the observation that since dialectic is an open-ended mode of inquiry, the kind of politics advocated by Plato must be conducive to and compatible with such a philosophical quest. In an attempt to explore Gadamer's Plato, I suggested earlier that we need to take into consideration Plato's insistence that dialectic is the only way to truth and that there is Truth to be ascertained. The concern that I have is that both of these claims can substantially compromise the openness of dialectic.

First of all, while the philosophical method needed for the pursuit is one that requires an inquisitive style of openness and flexibility, it is, after all, as Plato maintains, the only method of discovering truth for oneself. The method may be nondogmatic in style, but Plato is adamant that dialectic is the only way to truth.

More importantly, we need to ask why dialectic is the privileged mode of philosophical inquiry. In Plato's view, philosophical truth is beyond the grasp of language. Thus, truth cannot be fully conveyed through a "treatise" or a "lecture." While language is superior to all other forms of representation, it is nonetheless representation. That truth explored through the medium of language is inevitably incomplete is due to the basic inadequacy of language as such. Truth imparted through language is not and cannot be the whole of truth. This is why dialogue is the preferred form of communication for Plato. Dialogue, compared to written texts, is a more appropriate venue for indicating the incompleteness of any human attempt to capture all of truth. In short, if Plato appears to be nondogmatic when he is engaged in the process of recovering truth, he is so because the style of inquiry dictates this openness, not because he is receptive to other possible ways of ascertaining truth. Even Gadamer appears to qualify Plato's openness at one point when he says,

> Plato's critique of poetry, a critique which culminates in his rejection of aesthetic consciousness, is intended to support the claim which he makes for his own dialogues. . . .
>
> Thus the poetry of Plato's dialogues is certainly not the model for that poetry which would be allowed in the ideal state. But it is the real poetry which is able to say what is educational in actual political life.[91]

In discussing Plato's relation to despotism, Sheldon Wolin notes that "there is no homology existing between Plato's theory of knowledge and his theory of rule."[92] When this kind of interpretation is juxtaposed with Gadamer's, it clearly points to a rather different conception of how Plato's theory of knowledge is connected to his theory of rule. Wolin's interpretation allows one to draw a stark contrast between how political power is exercised through imposition and how philosophical truth is imparted through persuasion.

I agree with Wolin in that for Plato, there is no truth in politics. But this is so not because there is complete disjunction between Plato's theory of knowledge and his theory of rule. Rather, it is precisely because of Plato's view on how true knowledge is acquired that his theory of rule is formulated accordingly. To sum up, this theory of rule is one of absolute power which derives its legitimacy from a notion of truth that makes ultimate claim to justice. Yet the irony is that the act of ruling, even in the ideal *polis*, is at best an imitation of a rational order. The reason being that given Plato's view of truth, the antithesis between truth and politics is inherently irreconcilable nor should it be reconcilable. In the end, the real world of politics is the world of nontruth. For "everything that is born must perish. Not even a constitution such as this [the ideal *polis*] will last forever but it must face dissolution. . . ."[93]

In essence, truth, for Plato, signifies a state of mind that is distinct from the domain of action. It is knowing in the abstract, not experiencing in the concrete, that confirms the truth of being. Arendt makes an important observation when she points out that "Plato was the first to introduce the division between those who know and do not act and those who act and do not know" and that such a separation has remained "at the root of all theories of domination."[94] This theme on the conflict between philosophy and politics is one that I shall return to in the chapter on Arendt. The particular formula that Plato has provided for his version of complete domination by those who know over those who do not know is arrived at by equating truth with knowing and nontruth with action.

CHAPTER THREE

Hobbes: The Science of Politics

AMONG THE FIRST IMAGES THAT HOBBES'S political philosophy evokes is the stark reality of the state of nature, which is described as "solitary, poore, nasty, brutish, and short."[1] Equally known is Hobbes's solution to this unlivable state of nature—the figure Leviathan. For those familiar with the Book of Job, the figure is clearly a powerful one which can unequivocally invoke awe: "On earth it [Leviathan] has no equal, a creature without fear. It surveys everything that is lofty; it is king over all that are proud."[2]

Hobbes's depiction of the life of man without the intervention of politics as well as his solution are part of what Hobbes himself calls the "civil science." As Tom Sorell notes, for years the standard reading of Hobbes's civil science is that it owes its "scientific status" to its "links with the natural science."[3] Thus we find C. B. Macpherson, for example, claiming that Hobbes, like Galileo, reasons by way of the "resolutive-compositive" method. As described by Macpherson, "the resolutive part was the way to reach the required simple basic propositions; the compositive was the way to build the complex ones from those." The first thirteen chapters of *Leviathan* are thus crucial in that they provide the necessary building blocks for Hobbes's commonwealth. Accordingly, society is reduced to an aggregate of individual persons. These individuals are further broken down into a bundle of appetites and aversions which, when left unregulated, can only lead to a state of war. It is therefore imperative that we ensure the orderly operation of individual drives. This is what politics is all about and as such, the commonwealth is likened to a piece of well-designed machinery. On this reading, Hobbes's science of politics is mechanistic and deterministic.[4]

More recent works have, however, attempted an alternative interpretation of Hobbes's civil science.[5] Critics like Alan Ryan and Tom Sorell suggest that his civil philosophy is a self-contained science based more on the model of geometry rather than physics. The key difference between geometry and physics is that geometry entails knowledge that is thoroughly our own making whereas physics deals with an external world that is by no means a human artifact.[6] Hence, the first thirteen chapters in *Leviathan* are not necessarily an integral aspect of Hobbes's civil philosophy. For civil philosophy is simply not founded on a "scientific" psychology of human nature in the way that Macpherson has suggested.[7]

Given the contrasting views on the nature of Hobbes's science of politics, it is obvious that we need to begin by asking what science is to Hobbes before deciphering his civil philosophy. In chapter 1, I draw upon the distinction between the classical and modern notions of truth as the starting point for our investigation into the relationship between truth and politics. The modern notion is distinguished from the classical notion in that the emphasis is shifted from what there is to be known to what it is about the knower which validates knowledge. Hobbes's epistemological stance is generally taken to be nominalist. I shall explore Hobbes's nominalism as an instance of the modern notion of truth, which focuses the validation of knowledge on the knower. I argue that Hobbes's view on science cannot be properly understood unless we take into account this fundamental aspect of nominalism. Thus considered, the inquiry into the nature of science in Hobbes is as much an inquiry into the nature of human beings as knowers.

It is important to ascertain the scientific nature of Hobbes's politics. Science for Hobbes is knowledge *par excellence* and in his mind, the purpose of knowledge is to render action effective. As he puts it, "the end of knowledge is power" and "the scope of all speculation is the performing of some action, or thing to be done."[8] Thus, if the key to science lies indeed in the proper engagement of our capacity to know, then we need to ask whether the individual as knower enhances and empowers the individual as political actor. Yet Hobbes's social contract, which represents the epitome of scientific reasoning in politics, suggests that the most effective form of political action at the individual level is none other than to surrender the "Right of Governing" oneself to Leviathan.[9] This means that by the act of authorization, individuals have in effect given up their power to be political actors. Correspondingly, one needs to ask if by this same act of authorization, individuals have also ceased to be knowers of truth. I argue that the act of authorization does indeed encompass both. More precisely, Hobbes is making the case that truth must remain the monopoly of those who hold power if power were to be effective and truth were to be sustainable at all. The irony of this claim is of course that while it may be scientific reasoning that justifies the indispensability of Leviathan, in the end it is not science that binds individuals to the commonwealth.

I

Knowledge and Experiments

Let us turn to Hobbes's view on experiment as the starting point of our inquiry into what science is. Beginning from the 1650s on, Hobbes was involved in a debate with Robert Boyle over the postulation of vacuum. Underlying this specific controversy was a more fundamental issue, which is the role of experiments in the validation of knowledge. Boyle was a leading advocate of experimental practices as the cornerstone of the scientific study of natural phenomena; whereas Hobbes challenged Boyle's claim that experiments can yield the kind of certainty necessary to scientific knowledge.[10]

According to Boyle, the importance of experiment lies in its capacity to generate the "matter of fact" that serves as the foundation of knowledge. There are three technologies involved in establishing "matters of fact." They are material technology, literary technology, and social technology, which are all interrelated.

First and foremost in the experimental procedure is the use of material technology by way of a "purpose-built scientific machine" that mediates between the "perceptual competences of a human being and natural reality itself." It is the machine, an impersonal device, rather than the observer, that produces the result of the observation. Moreover, to secure the empirical basis of experimentally generated knowledge, the procedure has to be witnessed not just once but through the "multiplication of witnesses." The assumption is that something that is true can be witnessed over and over again. Each witness is also supposed to be a check on the other. To maximize the number of witnesses, "virtual witnessing" is accepted provided that a certain image of an experimental scene can be accurately reproduced in the reader's mind. In theory, the "multiplication of witnesses" is unlimited. The rules for writing an experimental report are therefore of paramount importance. The writer must convince the readers that he or she is no more than a disinterested observer reporting an observation that mirrors nature. This is how literary technology becomes relevant. Finally, by making collective witnessing a prerequisite for validating the results of experiments, Boyle has introduced a social component to the production of knowledge. An experiment must always take place in a public space so that it is accessible by either direct witnessing or "virtual" witnessing. An "experimental community" is thus created and certain forms and conventions are stipulated to ensure its solidarity.[11]

Together, these three technologies are meant to make nature, rather than man, the source of assent. That is to say, the experimental procedure assumes that there is an objective nature to be validated and that this act of validation can be done objectively by making it a collective act mediated by an impersonal device. However, the experimental procedure puts man in a passive role in the production of knowledge. Knowledge is an attempt by individuals to understand or, at best, to explain what is "out there." The idea of a human being actively creating one's own object of knowledge is alien to Boyle's experimental approach. Moreover, experimental practices limit science to producing descriptive and/or explanatory knowledge. Prescriptive knowledge will not be within the domain of this particular conception of science.

Knowledge and Language

How does Hobbes's view differ from Boyle's? In *Leviathan*, Hobbes states that there are two forms of knowledge. First, there is "Knowledge of Fact," which is "nothing else, but Sense and Memory." This form of knowledge is definitive in that a "fact" is something that we either see happening or remember having happened. "Knowledge of Fact" is the "Knowledge required in a Witnesse," which is the kind of knowledge that Boyle's experimental program is designed to recover.[12] Facts taken together may constitute "experience," which is "a Memory of successions of events in times past." We need "Prudence," not "Reasoning," to put these events together. Hence, knowledge based on experience cannot yield absolute certainty in that "the omission of every little circumstance" may alter the effect and can frustrate "the expectation of the most Prudent." More important for our purpose here is that human beings, as knowers, can only play a passive role in the generation of this form of knowledge. For knowledge of facts is based on the senses, which are no more than receptive organs vis-à-vis the external world. As such, knowledge of facts is by no means distinctive of human cognitive activity. Hobbes states bluntly that experience can be found in "Brute Beasts" as well as in man.[13]

The other form of knowledge is *"Knowledge of the Consequence of one Affirmation to another."* Hobbes considers this to be "scientific discourse," which begins with the "Definitions of Words, and proceeds by Connexion of the same into generall Affirmations" until the "Conclusion" is reached. Hence, science is "Knowledge of the consequence of words."[14] It is "conditionall" because each cognitive step is dependent on the previous one. Unlike knowledge of facts, scientific knowledge is acquired by "reason." According to Hobbes, reason is distinctive in the following way: "Reason is not as Sense, and Memory, borne with us; nor gotten by Experience onely; as Prudence is; but attayned by Industry."[15] For "Reasoning" is defined as the *"Reckoning* (that is, Adding and Subtracting) of the Consequences of generall names agreed upon, for the *marking* and *signifying* of our thoughts . . .[16]

This understanding of the nature of reasoning certainly does not put reasoning in a very creative role. It seems all that reasoning does is play with words. Indeed, Hobbes states that "the faculty of Reasoning" is "consequent to the use of Speech."[17] In other words, our capacity to employ language is a necessary condition for the engagement of reason. It is thus crucial that we examine Hobbes's view of language and its role in the creation and validation of knowledge.

Hobbes begins with the recognition that God is the "first author of Speech." Yet he also reminds us that with the tower of Babel, men were condemned to "the diversity of Tongues" and left to their own resources. "Speech" was invented in order to transfer our

"Mentall Discourse" into "Verbal" or "the Trayne of our Thoughts" into a "Trayne of Words."[18] This way two purposes are served:

> The first use of names, is to serve for *Markes*, or *Notes* of remembrance. Another is, when many use the same words, to signifie (by their connexion and order,) one to another, what they conceive, or think of each matter; and also what they desire, feare, or have any passion for. And for this use they are called *Signes*.[19]

That is to say, language helps to facilitate our sense of consistency within ourselves and with others. Language as such is distinctively anthropomorphic and it is that which sets us apart from animals.[20] In short, without language we can still experience and exercise prudence. But it is only with language that we can reason.

To state the significance of language differently, we can say that without language reason will not able to go beyond the empirically given. Hobbes claims that "there being nothing in the world Universall but Names; for the things named, are every one of them Individuall and Singular."[21] Moreover, "where Speech is not, there is neither Truth nor Falsehood." In other words, truth and falsehood are no more than "attributes of Speech." Truth therefore "consisteth in the right ordering of names in our affirmations." For someone in search of "precise truth," one "had need to remember what every name he uses stand for; and to place it accordingly."[22] This brings Hobbes to draw the following conclusion about the use and abuse of language:

> So that in the right Definition of Names, lyes the first use of Speech; which is the Acquisition of Science: And in wrong, or no Definition, lyes the first abuse; from which proceed all false and senseless Tenets.[23]

Science and Civil Philosophy

Geometry is thus rightly "the onely Science." For in geometry, "men begin at settling the significations of their words; which settling of significations, they call *Definitions*; and place them in the beginning of their reckoning."[24] Only then can science, as "the knowledge of Consequences," be produced.[25] An example of this "knowledge of Consequences" is that any straight line drawn through the center of a circle "shall divide it into two equall parts."[26] This knowledge, while "conditionall" in that it depends on the postulation of a circle and a straight line, is the only way to ascertain truth that is "generall, eternall, and immutable."[27] To conduct proper philosophy, one must therefore proceed the same way as one would proceed in geometry. Indeed, Hobbes's formal definition of philosophy is modelled after that of geometry:

> By Philosophy, is understood *the Knowledge acquired by Reasoning, from the Manner of the Generation of any thing, to the Properties; or from the Properties, to some possible Way of Generation of the same; to the end to bee able to produce, as far as matter, and humane force permit, such Effects, as humane life requireth.*[28]

This is why Hobbes thinks that Boyle's experimental scientist cannot claim to be a philosopher. An experimental scientist is unable to produce true science precisely because he proceeds from "Fact," which is nothing but "Sense" and "Memory," rather than "Reason."[29] Moreover, the experimental scientist does not create one's own object of study. In Hobbes's view, the concept of a scientific study of nature is a contradiction in terms because only when we create our own object of study can we claim to have perfect knowledge of the object. As Hobbes puts it:

> Of arts, some are demonstrable, others indemonstrable; and demonstrable are those the construction of the subject whereof is in the power of the artist himself, who, in his demonstration, does no more but deduce the consequences of his own operation. The reason whereof is this, that the science of every subject is derived from a precognition of the causes, generation, and construction of the same; and consequently where the causes are known, there is place for demonstration, but not where the causes are to seek for. Geometry therefore is demonstrable, for the lines and figures from which we reason are drawn and described by ourselves. . . . But because of natural bodies we know not

the construction, but seek it from the effects, there lies no demonstration of what the causes be we seek for, but only of what they may be.[30]

In contrast to geometry, the study of natural phenomena can never be demonstrated in any conclusive fashion because "there is no effect which the power of God cannot produce by many several ways." Hence, it is unlikely that the doctrine of natural cause will ever have any "infallible and evident principles."[31]

What we now have is a theory of knowledge that maintains that unless an object of knowledge is at the same time of our own making, we cannot verify that object of knowledge with reasoning. As Donald Hanson notes, "the idea of maker's knowledge is altogether fundamental to Hobbes's work, because it sets the boundaries at the level of principle of what can be known with perfect certainty and what can be known only hypothetically and conditionally."[32] But to the extent that reasoning is "consequent to the use of Speech," truth is no more than a language game. As we shall see in the next section, the political implication of this claim certainly puts Hobbes in tune with postmodernists like Lyotard, who maintains that "there is no need to resort to some fiction of social origins to establish that language games are the minumum relation for society to exist."[33]

The kind of knowledge that is required in civil philosophy is clearly knowledge based on the model of geometry. For one thing, as Hobbes states in *Leviathan*, " . . . the matters in question are not of *Fact*, but of *Right*, wherein there is no place for *Witnesses*."[34] More importantly, however, is the simple truth that "we make the commonwealth ourselves."[35] Hobbes starts with the observation that the political is not part of the natural world. God has created nature *ex nihilo* but it is man who creates the "commonwealth" or the state. In approximating this godlike act, man needs to give life to this human creation just as God gives life to the natural world as part of his divine creation. To give life to the commonwealth is to give power to one "Man" or an "Assembly of men" to act as our common superior.[36] Consequently, Leviathan is likened to an "Artificiall Man" possessing an "Artificiall *Soul*," which is the "*Soveraignty*." "*Sedition*" is the equivalent to "*Sicknesse*" and "*Civill war*" death.[37] Through this sequence of metaphors, Hobbes has made it clear that there is nothing more destructive to politics than civil war because this amounts to challenging the very thing that gives life to the commonwealth—sovereignty.

II

Truth and Political Order

But why is civil war so deadly? In *Behemoth*, which was Hobbes's analysis of the causes of the English Civil War, dissension in religion was singled out as the main culprit. At the beginning of "Dialogue I," Hobbes presents us with a list of those responsible for the war. First on the list were Presbyterian ministers, followed by Papists, then by various Protestant sects. Members of the House of Parliament, who were mostly educated individuals corrupted by the ideal of "popular government," ranked only fourth. Finally, there were the city of London and other towns of trade, opportunists, and those common people who were naive but arrogant.[38]

To appreciate Hobbes's view on the Civil War, we need to begin with Hobbes's conviction that we are responsible for what we have made just as God is ultimately responsible for his creation. It is therefore fundamental that we have a clear sense of the boundary between our domain and God's in order that we know where our responsibilities lie. Hobbes, citing the Bible as his authority, makes the following distinction:

> Our Saviour himself expressly saith, (John 18.36) *My Kingdome is not of this world.* Now seeing the Scripture maketh mention but of two worlds; this that is now, and shall remain to the day of Judgment . . . and that which shall bee after the day of Judgement, when there shall bee a new Heaven, and a new Earth; the Kingdome of Christ is not to begin till the generall Resurrection.[39]

This, on Hobbes's reading, is the correct interpretation of the Bible regarding the division of domain between God and man. The commonwealth is distinctly the kingdom of this world.

"The greatest, and main abuse of Scripture" is therefore the attempt to prove that "the Kingdome of God . . . is the present

Church."[40] All subsequent misreadings of the Bible follow from this erroneous premise. According to Hobbes, what was challenging the sovereign in his time was the Church attempting to establish itself as the master of "this world." To make the matter worse, the "Kingdome of God" in its earthly form had turned into what Hobbes referred to as the "Kingdome of Darknesse." For the Church was dominated by a "Confederacy of Deceivers" who attempted to "obtain dominion over men in this present world" by "dark, and erroneous Doctrines."[41]

It is significant that Hobbes should single out the Church spreading "erroneous Doctrines" about its role in worldly affairs as the main cause of civil unrest in his times. This diagnosis discloses Hobbes's conviction that political order must begin with and be sustained by a linguistic order. In Hobbes's words, without speech, "there had been amongst men, neither Common-wealth, nor Society, nor Contract, nor Peace."[42] Philosophically, Hobbes's nominalism would no doubt support the claim that not only is naming the beginning of reasoning, but the beginning of order as well. It is, after all, the "Law of Nature," which is "a Precept, or general Rule, found out by Reason," that orders man to "*seek Peace.*"[43] Clear and precise language is prerequisite to law and order. As Hobbes puts it:

> The Light of humane minds is Perspicuous Words . . . but by exact definitions first snuffed, and purged from ambiguity; *Reason* is the *pace*; Encrease of *Science*, the *way*; and the Benefit of man-kind, the *end*. And on the contrary, Metaphors, and senslesse and ambiguous words, are like *ignes fatui*; and reasoning upon them, is wandering amongst innumerable absurdities; and their end, contention, and sedition, or contempt.[44]

But there was also a historical basis for Hobbes's conviction. For this, I suggest that we turn to Thucydides who, by Hobbes's own acknowledgment, had influenced Hobbes in significant ways.[45] In assessing Thucydides' contribution as a historian, Hobbes notes the following:

> For the principal and proper work of history being to instruct and enable men, by knowledge of actions past, to

bear themselves prudently in the present and providently towards the future: there is not extant any other (merely human) that doth more naturally and fully perform it, than this of my author.[46]

Among other things, Thucydides, in his account of the Peloponnesian War, reminds us of the vulnerability of *logos*, understood as the human capacity for rational discourse, in the midst of war. The submergence of *logos* can be seen in the manipulation of language. As Robert Connor notes in his book *Thucydides*, the historian belonged to a school of Greek thought that maintained that language is conventional and the association between name and things is a result of "human use and habit" rather than "nature or divine dispensation."[47]

If language is conventional, then we simply cannot count on language to provide us with any independent criteria for judgment. Accordingly, the occurrence of civil war, in which a society's convention is usually challenged, is when language is most vulnerable to manipulation. The abuse of language that goes hand in hand with the calamities of war becomes most apparent in Thucydides' analysis of the civil war in Corcyra.[48] The war first broke out in 427 B.C. between the pro-Athenian, democratic faction and the pro-Spartan, oligarchic faction, which then spread to the rest of the Greek world. There was a general breakdown of law and order, resulting in extreme violence and death. Language underwent changes that were reflective of the events of the time. Hobbes translates Thucydides' description of the situation as follows:

> The received value of names imposed for signification of things, was changed into arbitrary. For inconsiderate boldness, was counted true-hearted manliness: provident deliberation, a handsome fear: modesty, the cloak of cowardice: to be wise in every thing, to be lazy in every thing. . . . He that had been so provident as not to need to do the one or the other, was said to be a dissolver of society, and one that stood in fear of his adversary. In brief, he that could outstrip another in the doing of an evil act, or that could persuade another thereto that never meant it, was commended.[49]

It is, however, not so much the arbitrariness of the meanings of words per se that concern Thucydides. Rather, the collapse of linguistic conventions signifies for him something more fundamental—the collapse of *logos*, which is the human capacity for rational discourse. This capacity operates by way of making distinctions with the important requirement that distinctions are meaningful only if the standards for differentiation can be sustained over time. Given Thucydides' assumption that there is no inherent meaning to words, the stability of language becomes paramount as it provides the medium with which we make distinctions and, hence, judgments.

It would be unlikely for this kind of analysis presented by Hobbes's most respected historian to have escaped his attention. Connor aptly juxtaposes Thucydides and Hobbes in the following way:

> Corcyra's political anarchy readily symbolizes a moral anarchy. Now all the conventions of Greek life—promises, oaths, supplication, obligations to kin and benefactor and even that ultimate convention, language itself—give way. It is Hobbes's *bellum omnium contra omnes*.[50]

This juxtaposition allows us to reconsider Hobbes's state of nature from a different perspective. The state of nature is importantly about the equality of condition in that each man is subject equally to the threat of violent death. But more fundamentally, it is about the collapse of distinction. In Hobbes's words, there is "no *Mine* and *Thine* distinct."[51] If we cannot even make such a fundamental distinction, then all else must be rendered meaningless. This is why Hobbes maintains that in the state of nature, we will not be able to distinguish the right from the wrong, the just from the unjust. Hobbes's own words in describing this state of moral anarchy are significant: "The *notions* of Right and Wrong, Justice and Injustice have no place."[52] I emphasize the word "notions" because I think Hobbes literally regards the collapse of language as a more fundamental threat than the "unjust" action itself. For Hobbes, moral reasoning will be "consequent to the use of Speech."

Hobbes must therefore see the importance of a central authority to enforce the rules of discourse. That is to say, while Hobbes does not turn to a transcendental concept of truth to establish the indisputable nature of truth, he does turn to unquestionable authority to make sure that whatever the "truth" is, it is not to be disputed. Sheldon Wolin aptly calls the Leviathan the "sovereign definer."[53] In other words, Hobbes is arguing for an arbiter of this political and linguistic community which is over and above the community itself. In understanding the role of Leviathan in this way, we also come to a different appreciation of the nature of the social contract.

Formally, the social contract is a contract made between men to give up their natural right to do anything deemed necessary for self-preservation. For the "Law of Nature" has instructed men that the state of nature is unsustainable and ultimately self-destructive.[54] As such, the social contract is an institutional agreement on the limits of one's rights. But to the extent that the "Law of Nature" is no more than "a Precept, or generall Rule, found out by Reason" and that "Reason," as noted earlier, is "nothing but *Reckoning* . . . of the Consequences of generall names agreed upon," the social contract is also a "linguistic contract."[55] As in verifying a proposition such as "*two and three makes five*," Hobbes points out that this requires a process of "calling to minde the order of those numerall words, that it is so appointed by the *common consent* of them who are of the same language with us, (as it were by a certaine contract necessary for humane society). . . ." Hobbes further states that "this assent shall be called knowledge, and to know this truth is nothing else, but to acknowledge that it is made by our selves."[56] In the end, the creation of a political domain is a distinctively human act precisely because it is language that provides the binding thread.

Politics and Being

Hobbes must recognize that although his nominalism may convince us of the necessity for an arbiter of truth, nominalism can equally render the job of the arbiter of truth rather ineffective and frustrating. Hence Hobbes says, "That a Common-wealth, without Sovereign Power, is but a word, *without substance*, and cannot stand."[57] Here, I want to emphasize in particular Hobbes's use of the word "substance." In this regard Hobbes's claim concerning the relationship between assertion and substance in *Elements in Philosophy* is illuminating:

> Now these words *true, truth,* and *true proposition,* are equivalent to one another; for truth consists in speech, and not in the things spoken of; and though *true* be sometimes opposed to *apparent* or *feigned,* yet it is always to be referred to the truth of proposition; for the image of a man in a glass, or a ghost, is therefore denied to be a very man, because this proposition, *a ghost is a man,* is not true. . . . And therefore truth or verity is not any affection of the thing, but of the proposition concerning it.[58]

Heidegger notes perceptively that Hobbes's nominalism is an instance of "extreme nominalism," in which the question of "whatness" is centered entirely on the copula "is." In Heidegger's words:

> *What is* the thing? From the nominalist viewpoint this means: What is the reason for the assignment of two different names to the same thing? To utter the "is" in the proposition, to think the copula, means to think the ground of the possible and necessary identical relatedness of subject and predicate to the same thing. What is thought in the "is," the ground or cause, is whatness (realitas). Accordingly, the "is" announces the essentia or the quidditas of the res which is asserted about in the assertion.[59]

Hobbes is thus caught in a fundamental contradiction, whereby there appears to be a connection "between the *actuality* of a being and the *truth of the assertion* about this actual being."[60] Heideigger continues to say:

> Despite his whole nominalistic attack on the problem, the "is" means, for Hobbes, too, more than a mere phenomenon of sound or script which is somehow inserted between others. The copula as a coupling of words is the index of the thought of the cause for the identical referability of two names to the same thing. The "is" means the whatness of the thing about which the assertion is made. Thus beyond the pure verbal sequence there emerges a manifold which belongs to assertion in general: identifying reference of names to a thing, apprehension of the whatness of the thing

in this identifying reference, the thought of the cause for the identifying referability. Subjected to the constraint of the phenomena involved in the interpretation of the assertion as a sequence of words, Hobbes more and more surrenders his own initial approach.[61]

In short, Heiddeger is pointing out that Hobbes is not a consistent nominalist. For Hobbes in the end believes that there is one correct way of naming. This occurs when the copula "is" corresponds to "whatness." In this sense, naming is by no means a totally arbitrary act. Naming can only be true if it indicates what is being named is *what is*.

Given the high stake involved in naming, it is only logical for Hobbes to insist that Leviathan should have the "Soveraign Power, to be Judge, or constitute all Judges of Opinions and Doctrines, as a thing necessary to Peace, thereby to prevent Discord and Civill Warre."[62] However, such a power is not only instrumental to the maintenance of peace and order in the commonwealth as is generally assumed. Heidegger's critique enables us to appreciate at the most profound level what is at stake for Hobbes in declaring Leviathan to be the only sovereign definer. What I am suggesting here is that for Hobbes to claim that the case for Leviathan is a true proposition, by his own reasoning this instance of truth must also correspond to being. This means that Hobbes is in effect making an ontological case for why the state of nature, which is necessarily a state of war, is *not* an alternative to the commonwealth. Since we are constantly living under the "continuall feare, and danger of violent death" in the state of nature, the state of nature is quite literally the negation of being. If the frontispiece of the *Leviathan* shows that the body of the sovereign is made up of numerous individual bodies, it is because the body of Leviathan sets the perimeter for the very condition of life by reaffirming life itself. One finds an interesting parallel account of the relationship between truth and existence more than two hundred years later, when Nietzsche said the following:

> From boredom and necessity, man wishes to exist socially and with the herd; therefore, he needs to make peace and strives accordingly to banish from his world at least the most flagrant *bellum omni contra omnes*. This peace treaty

brings in its wake something which appears to be the first step toward acquiring that puzzling truth drive: to wit, *that which shall count as "truth" from now on is established*.[63]

Moreover, what needs to be considered in this ontological account of Hobbes's case for Leviathan is that being for Hobbes is more than physical survival. While one's life is under constant threat in the state of nature, the state of nature is importantly also a condition deprived of commodious living and culture. It is no accident that Hobbes defines safety as not simply "bare Preservation, but also all other Contentments of life."[64] Thus, according to Hobbes, it is the duty of those who govern "to furnish their subjects abundantly, not only with the good things belonging to life, but also with those which advance to delectation" in order that the subjects "may grow strong and lusty."[65] This explains, for example, why Hobbes stipulates for the legislation of "publique charity." The law of the commonwealth should provide for those who fail to maintain themselves "by accident unevitable." In Hobbes's view, it is simply uncharitable to leave these people at the mercy of "uncertain Charity" of "private persons."[66] As the feminist critic Kathleen Jones notes, "Hobbes's delineation of sovereign authority" is a "paradoxical wedding." It is the coupling of the "external features of paternal, disciplinary rule—the body of the father—with maternal, preservative interests—the caretaking of the mother."[67]

III

Political Order and Indoctrination

Leviathan's sweeping mandate undoubtedly points to the political significance of how Hobbes propounds to legitimate the mandate on a continuing basis. Hobbes's social contract recognizes the right of each individual to authorize Leviathan into existence. This points to the centrality of human agency in accepting submission to authority. Yet the exercise of human agency is only meaningful if we have real alternatives to choose from. Hobbes's prima facie case is that all reasonable beings will accept his solution. But

Hobbes is not taking any chances either. As he puts it: "Its therefore the duty of those who have the chief Authority; to root those [perverse doctrines] out of the mindes of men, not by commanding, but by teaching; not by the terrour of penalties, but by the perspicuity of reasons."[68] This assertion is likely based on Hobbes's conviction that that even "the power of the mighty hath no foundation but in the opinion and belief of the people."[69] Elsewhere, Hobbes talks about the difference between overcoming and conquering an enemy. One overcomes by brute force, but one can never conquer by brute force. Conquering requires the cooperation of those who are overcome—a promise to obey.[70] Hence, there is good reason to think that Hobbes is aware that power needs to be *recognized*.

It is against this background that we consider Hobbes's view on indoctrination. As Hobbes notes, "*Man is made fit for Society not by Nature, but by Education. . . .*"[71] He also claims that the "Common-peoples minds . . . are like clean paper, fit to receive whatsoever by Publique Authority shall be imprinted in them."[72] These observations are certainly suggestive of a program of indoctrination. Accordingly, there are "Publique Ministers" whose duty is "to teach, or to enable others to teach the people their duty to the Soveraign Power."[73] However, Hobbes recognizes that the state alone cannot do the job of teaching people the proper doctrine. This is why reforming university is crucial to the viability of Hobbes's commonwealth.

The reality in Hobbes's time was that most common people received their "civill" and "morall" doctrines from the Preachers and the Gentry, who in turn received theirs at the university. Unfortunately, in Hobbes's view, "the *Universities* have been to this nation, as the wooden horse was to the Trojans."[74] In fact, Hobbes even claims that "the core of rebellion . . . are the Universities."[75] Since we cannot do away with the university, the only solution left is to discipline it. In Hobbes's words,

> There [the Academies], the true, and truly demonstrated foundations of civill Doctrine are to be laid, wherewith young men being once endued, they may afterward both in private and publique instruct the vulgar. . . . I therefore conceive it to be the duty of Supreme Officers to cause the true elements of civill Doctrine to be written, and to

command them to be taught in all the Colledges of their severall Dominions.[76]

The key issue here is to ensure that young people attending the university be taught to obey the king as the only head of this worldly kingdom and that the king owes his crown to "no man, ecclesiastic or other."[77]

Those who attend universities may indeed have the benefit of reasoning out Hobbes's civil science as the political solution to civil unrest. For these people, they are the likely beneficiaries of the kind of "moral and epistemological individualism" that Alan Ryan notes in Hobbes—a form of individualism that is free from the authority of the Church and in which "each man must make up his mind for himself."[78] However, it is unclear whether the "vulgar" will ever be able to exercise such autonomy. After all, the subjects are told that every doctrine that the sovereign preaches is in accordance to the "Commandments."[79]

Judged against the objective of securing a universal recognition of the sovereign, *Leviathan* is thus more a work of persuasion rather than a scientific treatise based on irrefutable facts. This is the line of interpretation that I see as originating in Sheldon Wolin's *Hobbes and the Epic Tradition of Political Theory* and elaborated by David Johnston in *The Rhetoric of Leviathan*.[80] This approach emphasizes the need for creating an appropriate political culture that will be conducive to the establishment of Hobbes's version of the commonwealth. As Tom Sorell notes, Hobbes's civil science in fact contains "more advocacy than explanation."[81] More recently, Ryan's challenge to reading Hobbes's state of nature as a version of prisoner's dilemma further adds to the significance of this approach. As Ryan puts it, the Hobbesian man is not "a utility maximizer, but a disaster-avoider." In fact, for the Hobbesian man, "fear of the return to the state of nature" is the operative motive and Hobbes "spent much of *Leviathan* trying to persuade them [the subjects] to keep their eyes on the object of that fear."[82]

One remaining issue is the related question of censorship. Here Hobbes maintains that censorship should be applied only to that which challenges the power of Leviathan and consequently, threatens peace. Or to put this more positively, Leviathan should not attempt to have control over activities that are not disruptive of public order. For this is to put unnecessary burden on Leviathan's shoulder. On this basis, there appears to be ground to conclude that a reasonable portion of our private life will be exempted from state control in Hobbes's commonwealth. Yet, as pointed out by Ryan, "toleration" will only be defended on utilitarian ground in Hobbes's Leviathan.[83] Hence, if freedom of speech is not ruled out a priori by Hobbes, it is also not defended in principle. As Hobbes puts it:

> In cases where the Soveraign has prescribed no rule, there the Subject hath the liberty to do, or forbeare, according to his own discretion. And therefore such Liberty is in some places more, and in some lesse; and in some times more, in other times lesse, according as they that have the Soveraignty shall think most convenient. [84]

IV

The Philosopher King vs. Leviathan

In this concluding section, I shall compare Hobbes with Plato in order to draw together the various issues discussed in this chapter and the previous one. An obvious observation about Plato and Hobbes is that they both maintain that politics and truth overlap—the legitimate sovereign is also one who holds the truth. Moreover, in both cases, the sovereign power is absolute and fundamentally antidemocratic. Thus both Plato and Hobbes subscribe to a view of authority that sustains "a mode of discourse that gives expression to rank, order, definition, and distinction."[85] Not surprisingly, at the end of Part 2 of *Leviathan* we find Hobbes comparing his work with Plato's. Hobbes commends on Plato's distinctive contribution by his advocacy of the rule of "Philosophers" as the only effective means to end "the disorders of State" and "Civill Warre."[86] The similiarities between the two thinkers, however, end here.

As discussed in the previous chapter, for Plato, "Truth" exists and it can be recovered through dialect. It is the acquisition of truth that entitles one to sovereign authority. Moreover, because truth, by definition, puts an end to speculation and argumentation, the claim of truth to sovereignty is absolute. For Hobbes, although there is no inherent truth, truth has to be sustained or else chaos will set in. The point is to make "truth" stable and consistent within a political community. This is where Leviathan comes in. Hence, while the sovereign holds the truth, the sovereign does not have the "truth" in hand before acquiring power.

Another important difference between Plato and Hobbes is that there is a face to Plato's philosopher king. One must remember that the *Republic* is importantly about the education of one's soul. The philosopher king is the most knowledgeable and virtuous person. Although the famous frontispiece of *Leviathan* has a face, Hobbes says, "I speak not of men, but (in the Abstract) of the Seat of Power. . . . "[87] Leviathan is, in the end, an office—a position in the hierarchy of power. Hobbes makes a case for Leviathan based on an indispensable *function* that only Leviathan, metaphorically speaking, can perform and that is to put an end to an absolutely intolerable state of chaos. Hobbes's theoretical innovation lies in emptying Leviathan of any personal traits, thus making Leviathan effectively the institutional safeguard against the unpredictability of individual political actors. Hobbes has thereby depersonalized political power, which is an important contribution to the development of modern liberalism. Moreover, Hobbes's Leviathan is no philosopher king. Its claim to power is not on moral grounds nor does it exist to promote a moral order.

One case in point is the question of censorship. In the previous chapter, the nature of censorship in Plato's *polis* is discussed. There, I pointed out that according to Plato, any form of discourse that hinders the soul's journey to the Good ought to be censored. In particular, poetry as an art form is categorically banned as it threatens the quest for truth and authenticity.

In contrast, there is no categorical censorship of poetry in Hobbes's commonwealth. In fact, as David Johnston notes, Hobbes regards poetry as a valid form of discourse, along with philosophy, history, and rhetoric. Hobbes even deals with the "forms of elocution or style appropriate to each of these arts."[88] Johnston argues that while Hobbes maintains that philosophy is the only way to arrive at the truths of the "Science necessary for Soveraigns,"[89] he also realizes that philosophical writing may not be the most effective means of *communicating* precepts to a large audience.[90] After all, *Leviathan* is meant to teach "both how to govern, and how to obey."[91] Hence, Johnston makes the following observation:

> From a literary point of view, then, *Leviathan* can be seen as the closing point of a circle that begins with a contrast between the power of the visual image and the powerlessness of the moves through the "dry discourse" of strict philosophical demonstration, and returns once again to the "speaking picture" of poetry—now, to be sure, in the service of science.[92]

In Hobbes's own words,

> But where these precepts [of true Philosophy] fayle, as they have hetherto fayled in the doctrine of Morall vertue, there the Architect (*Fancy*) must take the Philosophers part upon herselfe. He therefore that undertakes an Heroique Poeme . . . must not onely be the Poet, to place and connect, but also the Philosopher, to furnish and square his matter, that is, to make both body and soule, coulor and shaddow of his Poeme out of his owne store. . . . [93]

From this passage, we can see that Hobbes really does not object to poetry as a form of discourse unless, of course, it is a "subversive" poem. But then we must note that in such a case, it is the content of the poem that will be censored, not the form per se. In contrast with Plato, Hobbes has no epistemological or moral case against poetry as a mode of communication.

As I have argued, the justification for Leviathan is ultimately what Hobbes sees as a distinctively human effort to preserve what is equally human—politics and language. As Amos Funkenstein notes, "no other thinker [Hobbes] of the seventeenth century argued as consistently as he did for the constructive character of all human manifestations—language, science, political order."[94] Language underlies the employment of reason, while the whole point of politics is to establish the rule of reason rather than that of passion. Yet the problem for Hobbes is that there is no inherent guarantee to our capacity for rationality.[95] Thus, Hobbes turns to truth by inventing a "sovereign definer" to ensure that neither politics nor language is to be destroyed at the whim of individuals. But what is dangerous about this doctrine is the proposition that the *idea* of an absolute power can save us. It does not give one much room to fight against what may follow should this power be abused. For by removing truth from politics, Hobbes has left us completely at the mercy of one who defines the truth for us.

Given Hobbes's nominalist view of truth and the claim that such a notion of truth is what justifies absolute power precisely because there is no "Truth," Hobbes is uniquely situated to understand the politics of this century. Plato's essentialist notion of truth needs no justification from power. Truth is "self-sufficient" for Plato; politics is at best an imitation. However, for Hobbes, truth is a nonissue unless it is coextensive with power. Ironically, as pointed out earlier, this nominalist view of truth actually grounds power on a more abstract plane than Plato's essentialist view. After all, Hobbes thinks that it is more important to promote the very notion of truth itself rather than its content. If we think hard about the various wars fought in this century in the name of truth, we have to start wondering, like Hobbes, whether there can be truth without power.

Part II

CONTEMPORARY CONUNDRUM

Prologue

ONE WAY OF RESTATING THE DIFFERENCE between the classical and the modern notion of truth as explicated by Allen is to say that there is a shift from what there is to be known as truth to who the knower is that validates knowledge as truth. This means that with the modern conception of truth, the focus is on the knower. But the change in focus does not necessarily mean that the knower is thereby actively determining what there is to know. Historically, the modern notion of truth entailed within its perimeter the Enlightenment. Indeed, the earlier period of the Enlightenment was dominated by empiricism, which tends to assign a rather passive role to the mind. Thus, we find Locke characterizing the mind as "white Paper, void of all Characters, without any *Ideas.*"[1]

As Norman Hampson notes, Kant, along with Rousseau, were the two thinkers who brought forth a major breakthrough in the second half of the eighteenth century. Together they repositioned the centrality of humanity in the larger order of the universe by rediscovering the "inner voice," which had hitherto been drowned by the scientific and philosophical speculation of the earlier Enlightenment.[2] The "heart" was accepted as the "legitimate consort of the head." The recovery of emotion does not, however, mean that "the artist usurped the position formerly occupied by the scholar." Rather,

> Both turned to the emotions for guidance they had previously expected of their reason. Sentiment came to be accepted as the source of a kind of knowledge to which intelligence could not aspire, and as the arbiter of action. But if feeling became pilot, reason remained in command.

... The definition of their respective roles could never be established with finality but there was no question of the elimination of reason.[3]

Yet posterity considers Kant, more so than Rousseau, "as the philosopher who summed up the achievement of the Enlightenment."[4] This is significant as it was indeed Kant who set the boundary of human knowledge in its distinctly modern framework. From Kant on, reality is always mediated reality. The "I think," as the formal proposition of apperception, is what makes knowing possible. In Kant's words,

> It must be possible for the "I think" to accompany all my representations; for otherwise something would be represented in me which could not be thought at all, and that is equivalent to saying that the representation would be impossible, or at least would be nothing to me.[5]

As the "form of apperception," the "I think" is "not itself an experience." Rather, the "I think" "belongs to and precedes every experience" and as such, it is "a *merely subjective condition*" of knowledge.[6]

Thus, the empiricism of the earlier Enlightenment with its implied materialist determinism is superceded by a rational being with full agency in the pursuit of knowledge. In Kant's transcendental schema, the knower is no longer the passive processor of raw data. Richard Schacht sums up Kant's achievement as follows:

> Before Kant . . . it had been thought that the mind took its cue from an independently existing nature. Kant's "revolution" consisted in his reversal of this picture: nature as we know it is now understood, not as existing independently of the mind, but rather as having no existence independent of it and as taking its cues (forms, structures, qualities) from the latter. The mind, therefore, far from being merely a sort of passive mirror, is seen as playing a very active role indeed in the generation of experience.[7]

In short, with Kant, there is no turning back to the classical notion of truth. The modern notion of truth situates squarely the question of "subjectivity" at the very center of philosophical inquiry, as it is the "domain where thought and existence are unified; where what is judged and said cannot fail to coincide with what is."[8]

A plausible reading of the history of philosophy after Kant is to see Nietzsche's questioning of truth itself as the most thoroughgoing effort to tease out the implication of Kant's epistemology. As Alexander Nehamas suggests, Nietzsche's perspectivism can be seen as "an effort to move away from the idea that the world possesses any features that are in principle prior to and independent of interpretation."[9] To me, Nehamas's definition of perspectivism is the most lucid way of expliciting what is at issue for Nietzsche when he claims that "facts are precisely what there is not, only interpretations."[10] Such a reading places Nietzsche's perspectivism on a logical continuum generated by a conception of truth that is centered on subjectivity.

In art we see an interesting parallel development. The Spanish philosopher José Ortega y Gasset summarizes the history of Western arts as follows: "First things are painted; then, sensations; finally, ideas."[11] To Ortega y Gasset this development is indicative of a series of fundamental changes in the relation between the artist and the object of painting, in which the artist's attention was first "fixed on external reality; then, on the subjective; finally, on the intrasubjective."[12] The prototype of the third phase is cubism, which marks the beginning of twentieth-century art as a distinctive era. Picasso, who along with Braque founded cubism, was known to have said the following: "I paint objects as *I think them*, not as I see them."[13] Nehamas notes,

> Picasso created something in the very act of depicting it—not simply a new way of looking at the world but, equivalently, *a new aspect of the world to look at*. The equivocal manner in which this and other similar achievements have to be described matches perfectly the ambiguities in Nietzsche's own attitude toward truth and reality.[14]

As Carl Schorske describes in his classic *Fin-de-Siècle Vienna: Politics and Culture*, post-Nietzschean European culture was a world of its own that defied the analytical categories hitherto available to intellectual historians of his generation, amongst whom progress was assumed.[15] Schorske's own study of *fin-de-siècle* Vienna, a time of tremendous political and social disintegration, leads him to conclude that all over Europe the "rational man" of "traditional liberal culture" was no longer deemed viable. Rather, "rational man has had to give place to that richer but more dangerous and mercurial creature, psychological man. This new man is not merely a rational animal, but a creature of feeling and instinct."[16] The twentieth century is therefore appropriately the "age of subjectivist culture," which is characterized by "a sense that unified experience lies beyond the grasp of the modern self and that malaise and self-conscious guilt have become inextricably intertwined with 'culture.'" There emerges a "special sensitivity to human feelings, psychological truths, the authenticity of emotion"; in short, a "preoccupation with the 'inner self.'"[17] Thus considered, cubism is perhaps the quintessential twentieth-century expression of subjectivist culture, where thought and existence are unified through intrasubjective aesthetic.

One way then to appropriate Nietzsche's impact on the twentieth century is to say that with Nietzsche, the question of truth becomes a question of history. More precisely stated, history, understood as an account of human experience, takes on new analytical significance when philosophy's claim to the throne is in question. Truth is, in Nietzsche's words, "a movable host of metaphors, metonymies, and anthropomorphisms; in short, *a sum of human relations*. . . . "[18] Nehamas aptly describes Nietzsche's perspectivism as "not so much a traditional theory of knowledge but as the view that all efforts to know are also efforts of particualr people to live particular kinds of lives for particular reasons."[19]

What happens to politics in this "age of subjectivist culture"? It is to this question that we turn in the second part of the book.

CHAPTER FOUR

Weber: Rationalization and Politics

STRADDLING THE NINETEENTH AND TWENTIETH CENTURIES, Weber rightly serves as our point of departure. Wilheim Hennis interprets Weber's "central question" as the specificity of modernity placed in the broader context of Weber's "'qualitative' interest in the history of Humanity (*Menschentum*)." The "conduct of life (*Lebensführung*)" therefore became the logical "object of *investigestion*." More specifically, Weber was interested in the "'rationalization of *Lebensführung*.'"[1] This means that the much-studied Weberian concept of rationalization is first and foremost an anthropological question. That is to say, while rationalization is often taken to be Weber's way of capturing the social forces and institutional arrangements that come to define modern societies of the West, in the end it is the impact of these changes on the "nature of human experience" that Weber was most concerned about.[2]

Against this interpretation, how then does Weber's anthropological project tie in to the problematic of the relationship between truth and politics? First of all, it appears that truth is the less controversial of the two concepts, as most critics seem to agree that Weber's philosophy of social science is essentially antifoundationalist. However, Weber's politics has been the subject of much debate. This in part is due to the fact that Weber himself did not have a clearly defined political position. One can discern simultaneously liberal and illiberal, pluralist and elitist, democratic and antidemocratic elements in Weber's political writings.

In light of these contradictory positions, one approach accounts for Weber's apparent lack of principled stance by way of his antifoundationalism. Leo Strauss, for example, states that by denying us the "true value system," Weber's social science "necessarily leads to nihilism or to the view that every preference, however evil, base, or insane, has to be judged before the tribunal of reason to be as legitimate as any other preference."[3] Wolfgang Mommsen, having noted the various "antinomical structures" in Weber's political thought, comes to similar conclusion. On this reading, since Weber accepts the Nietzschean premise that science cannot "formulate definitive truths," "everything would again come down to the autonomy of the individual person who, though having a moral obligation to rationality, was basically free to choose."[4]

Both of these interpretations in fact resemble a very common criticism levelled against postmodernism these days. The argument put forth is that an antifoundationalist notion of truth is politically ineffectual if not outright dangerous. In this sense Weber is a precursor of postmodernism and all its negative political impact.

In this chapter, I shall examine the relationship between Weber's social science and his politics. As we shall see, Weber's methodology, his diagnosis of the predicament of modernity, and his prescription for resistance are all interrelated. Ironically, this interrelation is an indication of the insidiousness of rationalization. For the process of rationalization is essentially about our appropriation of the external world as a set of abstract rules. Weber's analysis points to the single-mindedness and the pervasiveness of this pursuit. Hence, if Weber's diagnosis is to be taken seriously, one has to conclude that the prescription he advocates is disturbingly a sign of our time. For the solution is no more concrete than the abstract rules that the solution is supposed to deal with. By this, I mean to suggest that Weber's prescription does not address the possibility for "real changes" in the world. This inability to act, as I will point out, is consequent upon Weber's intellectual standpoint, which is indeed antifoundationalist in its thrust. However, I will also argue that while Weber may not have an effective course of political action to offer, Weber does have a principled political stance. For him, the "political" is to counter the rationalization of the conduct of life. It is political not because it is a contest of grounding politics on antifoundationalism instead of foundationalism. Rather, the struggle is a struggle between reason and passion.

I

Weber's Methodology

Our starting point is Weber's methodology of social science. As Christian Lenhardt notes, Weber's epistemology cannot be properly understood without situating it in the tradition of German idealism. More specifically, Lenhardt maintains that Weber had appropriated one strand of Kantian idealism, which is "critical idealism," as opposed to "absolute idealism." Critical idealism as such is not a "philosophy of the absolute." Rather, critical idealism believes that it has "strengthened reason by cutting away what is considered to be false claims on absolute ground."[5] Central to Weber's methodology is the concept of objectivity. As we shall see, the concept is indeed Weber's way of nullifying "false claims on absolute ground," without, however, foregoing the possibility of knowledge.

In the essay "'Objectivity' in Social Science and Social Policy," Weber notes that "modern epistemology...ultimately derives from Kant."[6] Like Kant, Weber begins with the presupposition that "'scientific truth exists and it is valid,'" recognizing, however, that there is a limit to this scientific truth. For it is only under "certain presuppositions of thought" that truth is "possible and meaningful."[7] We must note here that Weber's main concern is what is *meaningful* for the investigator of social phenomena, not just what is meaningful for the actors involved. It is in this context that Weber accepts the Kantian postulation of the insurmountable disjunction between the "infinite reality" and the "finite human mind." Any analysis of such an "infinite reality" by our "finite" mind will have to rest on the assumption that scientific investigation can only focus on a "finite portion" of such a reality and that the portion is selected on the ground that it is "worthy of being known."[8]

Weber maintains that how one selects a finite portion is a question that cannot be answered scientifically. Rather, the question is a "cultural" one. Weber defines culture as a "finite segment of the meaningless infinity of the world process, a segment on which *human beings* confer meaning and significance." As "cultural beings," we are thus "endowed with the capacity and the will to take a deliberate attitude towards the world and to lend it *significance*." The distinctiveness of our existence lies precisely in the fact that we are constantly engaged in carving out a segment that is meaningful and significant.[9]

Weber calls those disciplines that deal with human events in accordance with their cultural significance "cultural sciences." Social science is a bona fide cultural science, as it is fundamentally concerned with a science of interpretation that attempts to understand "the characteristic uniqueness of the reality in which we move." Since the object of investigation and the investigator are both "cultural beings," Weber recognizes that there is simply "no absolutely 'objective' scientific analysis of culture." In the end, no analysis can be independent of "special and 'one-sided' viewpoints."[10] More precisely, "understanding" [*Verstehen*] is achieved with the help of the "ideal-type," which is not to be confused with a "hypothesis" or a straightforward "description of reality." Rather, according to Weber, an ideal-type is a "unified analytic construct" formed by "the one-sided *accentuation* of one or more points of view." An ideal-type is thus defined as follows:

> It is a conceptual construct [*Gedankenbild*] which is neither historical reality nor the "true" reality. It is even less fitted to serve as a schema under which a real situation or action is to be subsumed as one *instance*. It has the significance of a purely ideal *limiting* concept with which the real situation or action is *compared* and surveyed for the explication of certain of its significant components. Such concepts are constructs in terms of which we formulate relationships by the application of the category of objective possibility. By means of this category, the adequacy of our imagination, oriented and disciplined by reality, is judged.[11]

Yet it must be noted that this is purely a logical judgment. Weber is very emphatic that it should not be confused with "value-judgments," which are based on "ideals" (that is, moral judgments).[12] With the construction of an ideal-type, Weber claims that the distinctiveness of our viewpoints will come out most clearly as a result of the contrast between empirical reality per se and the ideal-type. An ideal-type then, being a theoretical construct of "one-sided *accentuation* of one or more points of view," exposes the social scientist to face the intellectual consequence of what one has chosen to be the "finite portion" from the "infinite reality."[13] The "objectivity" of the social sciences is therefore dependent on "the fact that the empirical data are always related to those *evaluative ideas* which alone make them *worth knowing*" and that the "significance" attributed to the data can only be "derived from these evaluative ideas."[14] Accordingly, Weber defines the relationship between the objective and the subjective as follows:

> The *objective* validity of all empirical knowledge rests exclusively upon the ordering of the given reality according to categories which are *subjective* in a specific sense, namely, in that they present the *presuppositions* of our knowledge and are based on the presupposition of the *value* of those *truths* which empirical knowledge alone is able to give us.[15]

With this theory of objectivity, Weber's social science is meant to transcend the limits of both positivism and intuitionism. Weber's objection to the positivists is that in their quest for "general" laws of the social realm, they purge meaning from the object of investigation as well as from the investigator. Weber criticizes the intuitionists in their effort to "empathize" by way of "'reproduction in immediate experience.'" He points out that what the empathizing historian can reproduce is essentially the "*first-person* value feelings." Hence, "'intuition,'" being essentially constituted by the "emotional contents of the observer," cannot form the basis for "empirical, historical knowledge of real relations."[16]

Two themes emerge from this analysis of Weber's methodology. First, it is impossible for a "social scientist" to claim to have attained absolute and exhaustive knowledge of the object of investigation. Here, the impact of Nietzsche's perspectivism on what emerged as a form of *fin-de-siècle* Kantian epistemology seems clear. I shall not venture into the details of the connection between Nietzsche and Weber.[17] Suffice to say that Weber himself acknowledged Nietzsche's profound influence,[18] which entailed Nietzsche's "destruction of all metaphysical concepts" and his "diagnosis of the time: God is dead."[19] Second, because the knower is first and foremost a "cultural being," what one chooses to study—that is, where one "cuts" into the "infinite reality"—necessarily reflects the value system of the investigator. This suggests that what one knows is what one *chooses* to know. There is no such thing as passive knowledge. The Weberian social scientist is a living cognitive being with full agency. The significance of this claim will be explored later.

II

The Enchanted World and Its Transformation

The question of where Weber himself chooses to cut into "reality" now appears to take on new significance. As noted earlier, Weber's central concern is with the "rationalization of *Lebensführung*" of modernity. What then is at stake for Weber to pose the question of modernity in such terms? As we shall see, this question is importantly an ontological question in that at issue is none other than the possibility of authentic being. The Nietzschean twist to this ontological quest is that it is investigated as a historical rather than a metaphysical problematic.

If there is one line that sums up Weber's concept of rationalization, it is that rationalization is the story of the mind's triumph over nature, culminating in the world of disenchantment that modernity finds itself in. A rationalized world is a world in which "principally there are no mysterious incalculable forces that come into play."[20] But rationalization is by no means inevitable. For while we are cultural beings who attempt to make sense of the world around us by conferring meaning and significance to an otherwise "meaningless infinity," the very act of conferring meaning does not necessarily exhaust the world of "mysterious incalculable forces."

In fact, according to Weber, the enchanted world of the primitive is precisely one where meaning and "mysterious incalculable forces" coexist. The primitive were bound to nature in such a way that they were totally dependent upon its elemental forces. These primitive people believed that there were gods and spirits that ruled over and through these forces although these forces remained a mystery to the primitive.[21] Yet this mystery did not lead to passivity on their part. The primitive tried to cajole nature through magic directed toward the gods and spirits.[22] Magic thus became a mediating agency between the gods and the primitive. Rituals and sacrifices were the means by which the primitive coped with the external world. There were specific means to deal with specific gods, and thereby the plurality of spirits was maintained.[23]

The plurality of spirits is critical because it constitutes precisely the ground for meaningful existence. The plurality of gods means that there is more than one god who makes competing claims on the loyalty of man. As Fredric Jameson has suggested, "pluralism for Weber means *pantheism*, not peaceful coexistence but a Homeric battlefield, in which 'different gods struggle with one another, now and for all times to come. . . . '"[24] Since it is impossible to please all gods simultaneously, it becomes necessary to choose one god instead of another at any given point in time. One god will be pleased but the others will be offended. The stakes are high. Thus, one chooses with conviction and passion rather than indifference. This very act of choosing authenticates human beings as cultural beings. In Weber's words, "The 'culture' of the individual certainly does not consist of the *quantity* of 'cultural values' which he amasses; it consists of an articulated *selection* of culture [*sic*] values."[25]

Polytheism and the tension of choosing in the midst of plurality are therefore the characteristics of an enchanted world. The mirror image of the enchanted world is the world of disenchantment—"a world robbed of gods."[26] The transformation of a world filled with gods to a world robbed of gods is the process of rationalization. Rationalization as such is characterized by the attitude of the mind toward the world that informs the process. As Weber points out, this attitude is the "belief that if one but wished one *could* learn it [the world] at any time."[27] Thus, nothing appears to be mysterious anymore. Weber insists that this apparent transparency can only be an act of the mind operating in abstractness. For "if one proceeds from pure experience," one can only arrive at "polytheism."[28] Pervasive "intellectualization" thus constitutes in Weber's view a crisis of meaning in modernity as intellectualization attempts to replace the existential space of the "Homeric battlefield" with unity of thought.

As a historical process, rationalization is the convergence of several "cultural" configurations in the capitalist society of the

West. These configurations include the rise of Protestant ethics in religion, the claim of science as the paradigm of knowledge, and the emergence of bureaucracy as the form of organization. These phenomena are "cultural" in that they all began as human efforts to make sense of an otherwise senseless world. I shall focus particularly on the rise of Protestant ethics, as it is the prototype of the rationalization of the conduct of life.[29]

Religion

The replacement of polytheism by monotheism is no doubt critical to the evolution of religious beliefs as it signifies that man is no longer simply proceeding from "pure experience."[30] But from the Weberian perspective of understanding history as a history of rationalization, the emergence of Calvin's doctrine of predestination in Christianity signifies an even more significant break-off point. Weber maintains that religion originated in man's attempt to make sense of human suffering. Religion is, in brief, the answer to the question "why is there suffering?". This same question is asked by the fortunate and the unfortunate alike. Accordingly, there emerged a "theodicy of good fortune" and a "theodicy of suffering" to legitimize the good life enjoyed by the fortunate and to account for the suffering of the unfortunate. With Calvin's doctrine of predestination, however, the "theodicy" of good fortune and of bad fortune becomes beyond the reach of one's daily experiences. More precisely, as we shall see, the doctrine of predestination robs believers of the means to cajole God.[31]

The relationship between Calvin's doctrine of predestination and the rise of capitalism is the subject of the Weberian classic, *The Protestant Ethic and The Spirit of Capitalism*.[32] There, Weber argues that it is Calvinism that provides the sanction for "a systemic rational ordering of the moral life as a whole"—the most important contribution of ascetic Protestantism to the development of capitalism in the West.[33]

The development of this "systemic rational ordering of the moral life as a whole" actually arises from an irrational situation brought about by the *radicalization* of the "fear of damnation" in Calvin's doctrine of predestination. This doctrine is predicated first of all on the postulation of an insurmountable distance between God and his people in which "god does not exist for men, but men for the sake of God." Calvinists are constantly haunted by the belief that God chooses only a small number of followers to receive his "eternal grace" and that there is no recourse of telling who the chosen few are. To think that one's good deed can make a difference to one's destiny after death is inappropriate since this is based on the assumption that God's will can be persuaded by human effort. Thus, unlike Catholicism, Calvinism does not advocate the accumulation of single cases of good works as a means to "purchase" salvation. Moreover, the elimination of priests means "the elimination of magic as a means to salvation," as "the priest was a magician who performed the miracle of transubstantiation." Finally, to make the matter worse from the point of view of the believers, the doctrine maintains that it is impossible to tell the difference between the elect and the non-elect by external behavior.[34]

In his study of the history of Calvinism, Weber argues that this harsh doctrine of predestination had an immense psychological impact on early generations of believers. The individual suffered from an "unprecedented inner loneliness" and immense sense of helplessness. There was no fellow man, "no priest," "no Sacraments," "no Church," "no God" to whom one could turn. The fear of damnation, because of this doctrine, became in effect unbearable for the individual.[35]

It is clear that the radicalization of the fear of damnation is correlated with the Calvinist postulation that God's will is not subject to human calculability. This is achieved by making God less anthropomorphic and more abstract. Unlike polytheism, Calvin's God is not the god of thunder and lightning, nor is he the god of rain. In short, Calvin's God does not resemble any image conjured up by humanity based on the concrete experiences of everyday living.

The extreme harshness of the situation demands a "thorough" solution. The followers were told to lead "a life of good works combined into a *unified system*" by engaging themselves in "intense worldly activities."[36] Yet all these "good works" are now ironically used to constitute "the technical means, *not of purchasing salvation, but of getting rid of the fear of damnation.*"[37] In other words, when looked at more cynically, good works display at any rate possible election. Thus, followers are tempted to be good in the hope of showing, if not achieving, election for the otherworldly existence.

This is how ascetic monasticism, which was originally practised in the medieval monasteries, became the ideal model of everyday conduct.[38] Asceticism becomes a calling not just to a handful of saintly characters, but to all believers. What it involves is "a systematic method of rational conduct" with the purposes of freeing man from "irrational impulses" and "subjecting man to the supremacy of a purposeful will." Calvinism therefore brings with it a doctrine of an "innerworldly asceticism," the significance of which lies in the "religionization of means."[39] What this entails is the integration of the rational organization of daily life within a religious framework, whereby such rational organization of life is seen as a religiously sanctified means of life. But we must bear in mind that the Calvinist doctrine of predestination still condemns its believers in the permanent state of uncertainty. It is only when Protestantism converged with capitalism that the pathos of a religious way of life was thoroughly lost to rationalization.

The relationship between the development of Protestant asceticism and that of the ethos of capitalism is portrayed in Weber's own words as follows:

> Christian asceticism, at first fleeing from the world into solitude, had already ruled the world which it had renounced from the monastery and through the Church. But it had, on the whole, left the naturally spontaneous character of daily life of the world untouched. Now it strode into the market-place of life, slammed the door of the monastery behind it, and undertook to penetrate just that daily routine of life with its methodicalness, to fashion it into a life in the world, neither of nor for this world.[40]

Stated in less metaphorical language, those values sanctioned by Protestant asceticism in practical life, like industry and frugality, are precisely those that lend support to the kind of capitalism characteristic of the Occident. The Puritan outlook, which grew out of Calvinism, "stood at the cradle of the modern economic man." But as capitalism developed, the religious rationale gave way to the "secularizing influence of wealth." The care for external goods, instead of being like a "light cloak" that can be "thrown aside at any moment," has become "an iron cage." Encased in the "tremendous cosmos of the modern economic order," modern men, unlike the prototypical Puritans, are "forced" to work in a calling. For modern men, as the acquisitive economic men, have lost sight of the religious end that originally inspired the calling and made it meaningful.[41]

Science

If a disenchanted world is a world emptied of gods, then it is science that gives men the means to rob the world of gods. For science is the most concrete embodiment of the very attitude that informs rationalization, which is that in principle, one "could" know everything. A rationalized world is a world in which everything is thought to be calculable by the scientific mind. By insisting that everything can "be reduced to rational explanation," science questions all "religious, moral, and metaphysical beliefs."[42]

What the scientific mind strives for is knowledge that is objective, dispassionate, and methodical. Yet while science makes universal propositions, the specific content of scientific knowledge is constantly changing. In fact, it is in the very nature of scientific work to be "'surpassed'" and "outdated."[43] Thus, scientific knowledge feeds into the modern world where the chain of *"ad infinitum"* progress is thought to be both possible and desirable. Ironically, unlike "some peasant of the past," the modern man, being caught up in the very "progressiveness" of civilized life, can no longer die "satiated with life."[44]

However, the scientific mind has also come to disown the common sense of the individuals in its claim that knowledge is inexhaustible. The knowledge of specialists becomes the order of the day. In the introduction to *The Protestant Ethic and the Spirit of Capitalism*, Weber notes that "expert studies," in which "only the specialist is entitled to a final judgment," is a "condition of any valuable work in the modern world."[45] Thus, the claim that "one can, in principle, master all things by calculation" is somewhat evasive. As Weber puts it, we have conquered the barrier of distance but unless one is a physicist, one does not really know how the streetcar gets into motion.[46]

In any case, the scientific mind promises a certitude that is attainable only when the mind is completely divorced from one's existential experience. The important point is that the advent of science has fostered an attitude of the mind that has exhausted the world of mystery. Yet "increasing intellectualization and rationalization do *not*, therefore, indicate an increased and general knowledge of the conditions under which one lives."[47]

Bureaucratization

If science has delivered us knowledge that promises to be objective, dispassionate, and methodical, then bureaucracy is the organizational counterpart of such an epistemological paradigm. For the hallmark of bureaucracy is to translate living beings into files and numbers, rendering them readily accountable and accessible. This is how bureaucracy promises "precision, speed, unambiguity, knowledge of the files, continuity, discretion, unity, strict subordination, reduction of friction and of material and personal costs."[48]

The efficient operation of bureaucracy is guided by two principles: "'without regard for persons'" and "calculable rules."[49] These two principles clearly complements one another and are particularly suited to facilitate the modern capitalist order. The more pervasive bureaucracy becomes, the more it is able to "dehumanize" and eliminate "from official business love, hatred, and all purely personal, irrational, and emotional elements which escape calculation." In short, the "special virtue" that bureaucracy can offer to capitalism is to subject individuals to the rule of calculability by disregarding them as living beings.[50]

III

Reenchantment and Modernity

I have hitherto highlighted aspects of Weber's analysis of rationalization as historical process. To recapitulate, we examine how the Protestant ethic contributes to the capitalist ethos; how science has equipped us with the mental attitude required to exhaust the world of mystery and how bureaucracy meets the needs of capitalist development. On Weber's reading, all these developments have contributed to the predicament of modernity, which is a world meant to be without uncertainty and, hence, a world devoid of meaningfulness. In particular, Weber's interpretation of the connection between Protestantism and capitalism indicates that rationalization means first and foremost the rationalization of the conduct of life, whereby the primordial human act of balancing among different gods and spirits is lost to a methodical and dispassionate way of life.

As discussed earlier, the methodology of Weber's social science postulates that where a social scientist "cuts" into the "infinite reality" is indicative of one's value system. By applying Weber's claim to his own choice of subject for investigation, it becomes clear that what Weber values is the existential context for meaningful action. As noted earlier, the pathos of modern man according to Weber is that he can no longer die "'satiated with life.'" And when "death is meaningless, civilized life as such is meaningless."[51]

Is there any way out of this rational world? Weber seems convinced that it is here to stay. The famous Weberian metaphor of the "iron cage" indicates that, structurally, there is no turning away from the achievements of rationalization.[52] But as Alkis Kontos points out, "the iron cage is not hermetically sealed."[53] There appears to be room for "reenchantment." The key to reenchantment is in recovering the existential space for meaningful action. This means for Weber the making of "a series of ultimate decisions."[54] The concept of "vocation" is where Weber turns for such possibility. Obviously, Weber's two well-known essays, "Science as a Vocation" and "Politics as a Vocation," will be the basis of our discussion.[55] Weber sees the scientist with a calling and the politician with a calling as individuals who are able to engage in meaningful action in their respective roles despite living in a disenchanted world. More interesting, however, is the fact that Weber sees the scientist and the politician as partners in preserving what may be the last bulwark against disenchantment—politics.

"Science as a Vocation"

In "Science as a Vocation," Weber compares the scientist to the artist.[56] He says that for both, inspiration is required. Like the artist, the scientist is required to have an "inner" "passionate" devotion to one's work. Without such a kind of "inward calling," it will not be possible to sustain the rigor that scientific work requires. However, in another sense, scientific work is even more demanding. For a work of art will never be outdated, yet scientific work, being tied to the chain of progress, will be surpassed. In fact, it is in the very nature of scientific work to be "outdated."

In the essay "'Objectivity' in Social Science and Social Policy," social science is considered as part of this "*ad infinitum*" progress. There, Weber points out that the progress of social science occurs when there is a tension between old and new knowledge. The result of such a tension is the "perpetual reconstruction of those concepts through which we seek to comprehend reality."[57] Weber goes on to say that

> The history of the social sciences is and remains a continuous process passing from the attempt to order reality analytically through the construction of concepts—the dissolution of the analytical constructs so constructed through the expression and shift of the scientific horizon—and the reformulation anew of concepts on the foundations thus transformed. . . . The relationship between concept and reality in the cultural sciences involves the transitoriness of such synthesis.[58]

It is therefore clear that social scientists must endure the same fate as scientists in that for both, knowledge is by definition in a constant state of flux.

Given the nature of scientific work, it is undoubtedly an illusion for a scientist to hope for the attainment of some transcendental truth and ultimate knowledge that will defy historicity. Indeed, if Nietzsche had any influence on Weber, it is perhaps most obvious in his insistence that it is the very nature of scientific discovery to be constantly surpassed.[59] Thus, when looked at from the point of view of progress, scientific knowledge, which includes knowledge generated by the social sciences, has profound anti-Platonic and anti-Christian implications. The meaning of life for scientists cannot be derived from the same source as for a Platonic philosopher or a Christian believer. The meaning of scientific work will have to be sought elsewhere.

Weber's answer to this begins with what he considers to be the presupposition of all scientific work, which is that whatever is yielded by scientific work is also something that is "worth being known."[60] To assert that a particular aspect as opposed to another is "worth being known" is not a claim verifiable by "scientific means."[61] As Weber puts it, while "empirical data are always related to those evaluative ideas which alone make them worth knowing," these data themselves cannot be the "foundation for the empirically impossible proof of the validity of the evaluative ideas."[62] This suggests that what is "worth being known" is ultimately a question of choice which involves the making of a decision.[63] The relationship between the scientist and one's work thus creates a condition in which the meaning of life can be attained. We can now appreciate what is at stake for Weber to maintain that the social scientist, as knower, is fully responsible for what there is to know.

Although the world is no longer thought to be filled with unknown mysterious forces, Weber, speaking metaphorically, insists that "absolute polytheism" is the "only appropriate metaphysic."[64] Again, this assertion reminds one of the Nietzschean view that all claims to the absolute or the transcendental are ultimately ungrounded.[65] Since no value has absolute claim over the others, "different gods" will have to "struggle with one another," and "the various value spheres of the world" are in "irreconcilable conflict with each other."[66] Hence, the decision will be one that requires both "passion" and "perspective."[67] In the end, the relationship between scientists and their work cannot be a scientific one. It is precisely this nonscientific relationship that gives meaning to the work of scientists.

Rationalization and the Modern State

To appreciate the significance of politics as a vocation, we need to first look at how rationalization has impacted on politics. More specifically, Weber sees bureaucratization as an inherent aspect in the rise of the modern state. In Weber's words, if we regard "progress toward capitalism" as the "unequivocal criterion for the modernization of the economy since medieval times," then "progress toward bureaucratic officialdom" is the *"unambiguous yardstick for the modernization of the state."*[68] In fact, bureaucratism has become such an integral and defining feature of the modern state that power is no longer exercised through "parliamentary speeches nor monarchical enunciations." Instead, power in the modern state is exercised "through the routines of administration" to the point where "the actual ruler is necessarily and unavoidably the bureaucracy."[69] Bureaucracy is rightly a form of "domination" [*Herrschaft*], which is an *"authoritarian power of command,"* defined as

> The situation in which the manifested will (*command*) of the *ruler* or rulers is meant to influence the conduct of one or more others (*the ruled*) and actually does influence it in such a way that their conduct to a socially relevant degree occurs as if the ruled had made the content of the command the maxim of their conduct for its very own sake. Looked upon from the other end, this situation will be called *obedience*.[70]

As structure of domination, bureaucracy is being contrasted with patriarchism and charismatic structure of domination. The corresponding modes of legitimation of each of these structures of domination are rational rules, tradition, and personal charisma.[71]

On the surface, Weber's account of the rise of bureaucracy in the modern state seems banal enough. He notes that the development was in part demanded by "the increasing complexity of civilization" and the rising demand of a society "for order and protection ('police')." Moreover, the development of modern means of communication, like "public roads and water-ways, railroads, the telegraph, etc." helped facilitate the centralization of administration.[72] But what makes the bureaucratic state distinctly modern is Weber's claim that with the "leveling of economic and social differences," "bureaucracy inevitably accompanies modern *mass democracy*." That bureaucracy and mass democracy go hand in hand is due to the nature of bureaucratic domination, in which authority is executed with remarkable regularity. By exercising authority "without regard for persons," bureaucratic domination appears to be most suited to the demand of democracy for "'equality before the law'" as well as the "principled rejection of doing business 'from case to case.'"[73]

Thus, the welfare state becomes a particularly revealing instance of the modern "bureaucratic state apparatus" administering justice "'without regard to the person.'" To adhere to "the rational rules of the state order," the welfare state operates by way of dividing its citizens into different classes.[74] Yet these are not classes in the Marxian or even in the Weberian sense. Rather, the classifications of the welfare state are best described as "bureaucratic classes." The "bureaucratic class" is "a classification, a category defined by the application of *abstract criteria* which are designed to accentuate attributes deemed systemically useful rather than to emphasize the differences created by historical practices, institutions, and values."[75]

Bureaucracy is not just a different form of domination, it also means that a different type of people are in command. For bureaucracy is, as Fred Dallmayr notes, "rule through knowledge." More specifically, this knowledge is no "essential insight." Rather, it is "'technical' knowledge, that is, knowledge geared towards efficiency of goal attainment and predictability of results." In other words, the modern state is where science as a paradigm of knowledge and bureaucracy as a structure of domination converge. It is "bringing up to date Bacon's equation of knowledge and power."[76]

Thus, the modern "political 'master' always finds himself, vis-à-vis the trained official, in the position of a dilettante facing the expert."[77] Indeed, the "specialized knowledge of the expert" became the "foundation for the power of the officeholder."[78] Educational institutions are therefore "dominated and influenced by the need for the kind of 'education' which is bred by the system of specialized examinations or tests of expertise (*Fachprüfungwesen*) increasingly indispensable for modern bureaucracies." Bureaucratization in full scale brings with it a "system of rational examinations for expertise irresistbly to the fore."[79]

Such a system tends to produce "experts" rather than "cultivated" persons. Traditional education that aims at producing the "cultivated" consists in nurturing "a quality of life conduct which *was held to be* 'cultivated.'" However, growing bureaucratization leads to the replacement of the "cultivated" personality by the specialized "expert" as the educational ideal. Traditional and charismatic modes of domination consider the possession of more "*cultural quality*" as a "plus" for those who seek to be members of the ruling stratum; whereas bureaucratic domination regards the possession of more "expert knowledge" as the most relevant qualification.[80]

Given the "irresistible advance of bureaucratization" and its tremendous impact on political structure, Weber poses the following questions, which I shall quote extensively:

> 1. How can one possibly save *any remnants* of "individualist" freedom in any sense? . . .
> 2. . . . [H]ow can there be any guarantee that any powers will remain which can check and effectively control the tremendous influence of this stratum [that is, bureaucratic officialdom]? How will democracy even in this limited sense be *at all possible*?
> 3. A third question, and the most important of all, is raised by a consideration of the inherent limitations of bureaucracy proper. . . . The "directing mind," the "moving spirit" . . . of the politician . . . differs in substance from the civil-service mentality of the official. . . . If a man in a leading position is an "official" in the spirit of his performance, no matter how qualified—a man, that is, who works dutifully and honorably according to rules and instruction — then he is useless at the helm . . . of a government. . . .
> The difference lies . . . in the kind of *responsibility*. . . . An official who receives a directive which he considers wrong can and is supposed to object to it. If his superior insists on its execution, it is his duty and even his honor to carry it out as if it corresponded to his innermost conviction, and to demonstrate in this fashion that his sense of duty stands above his personal preference. . . . This is the ethos of *office*. A political leader acting in this way would deserve contempt. . . . "To be above parties"—in truth, to remain outside the realm of the struggle for power—is the official's role, while this struggle for personal power, and the resulting personal responsibility, is the lifeblood of the politician. . . .[81]

This set of questions indicates where Weber stands with regard to the question of rationalization and its relation to the structure of domination. In sum, the three things that concern him most are: 1) the possibility for "individualist freedom" in a rationalized world; 2) the effectiveness of democracy to counter the overpowering bureaucratic structure inherent in the modern state; and, perhaps most important of all, 3) the possibility for authentic political action—action that bears the stamp of "personal responsibility" and "moving spirit."

Plebiscitary Leadership versus Bureaucracy

In defending the right of parliamentary inquiry into bureaucracy, Weber points out the importance of politicians becoming "the countervailing force against bureaucratic domination."[82] It is against this comment that the role of charismatic leadership is considered here.

Politicians in the modern state are inevitably linked with party politics. Weber observes that political parties "are today the most important political vehicles for those ruled by bureaucracy—the citizens."[83] Thus, gaining party leadership is the first step toward becoming an effective politician in the modern era. In the age of "active mass democratization," it means that the political leader must first gain the "trust and the faith of the masses in him and his power with the means of mass demagogy." Weber calls this the "*caesarist* mode of selection," which is the direction that every democracy tends toward. Indeed, Weber maintains that ever since Pericles' times, successful mass democracy has been characterized by "major concessions to the caesarist principles of selecting leaders." "The specifically caesarist technique is the plebiscite," which is "not an ordinary vote or election, but a profession of faith in the calling of him who demands these acclamations."[84]

Plebiscitary leadership is in effect a form of charismatic leadership, although "the basically authoritarian principle of charismatic legitimation may be subject to an anti-authoritarian interpretation." In Weber's words:

> For the validity of charismatic authority rests entirely on recognition by the ruled. . . . But when the charismatic

organization undergoes progressive rationalization, it is readily possible that, instead of recognition being treated as a consequence of legitimacy, it is treated as the basis of legitimacy: *democratic legitimacy*.[85]

Accordingly, plebiscitary leadership, which is the legitimation of authority by plebiscite, is the most important transitional type. Modern party leaders constitute the most common example of this type of leadership.

Yet Weber's belief in the possibility of plebiscitary leadership in the context of modern democracy is not unqualified. In fact, Weber is skeptical of mass democracy because it is always subject to the danger of being dominated by "emotional elements." Weber maintains that it is in the nature of the "mass" to think only in "short-run terms" and to be vulnerable to "direct, purely emotional and irrational influence."[86] This distrust of the "mass" leaves one wondering how effective active mass democratization under "plebiscitary leadership" can be as a form of political resistance against bureaucratic domination.[87]

Perhaps more antidemocratic than his distrust of the "mass" is Weber's notion of political action, which is by definition elitist in that genuine political action is the heroic act of individuals who have a calling for politics. The politician who has a "calling for politics" is one who faces squarely the tension of balancing between means and ends through a sensitivity to the simultaneous but often contradictory demands of the "ethic of ultimate ends" and the "ethic of responsibility."[88] The truly *political* decision for Weber is precisely one that is made without recourse to supranatural resources or absolute values. One becomes totally responsible for one's choice and this is the politician who can say "'Here I stand; I can do no other.'"[89] It is clear from his critique of the modern bureaucratic state that politics for Weber is simultaneously an individual act of reason and passion which, by definition, defies the predictability and routinization of institutional structure of power.

Social Scientist and Politician

By now, it should be obvious that there is a certain parallel between science and politics.[90] It appears that both the scientist with a calling and the politician with a calling are individuals who, because of the nature of their professions, are somewhat in a privileged position to enagage in meaningful act. As Tracy Strong notes, "the ideal type is the scientific equivalent of the Lutheran '*Hier stehe ich.*'"[91] However, the scientist, because of one's expertise, may also be a bureaucrat and, as such, the antithesis of the politician with a calling for politics. It is thus important for us to examine Weber's thought on the relationship between expert knowledge and politics.

Despite his antifoundationalism, Weber believes that there are ethically neutral "facts" in the sciences that can be transmitted.[92] More specifically, social scientists can offer *technical* advice to politicians. Yet this relationship between social scientists and politicians is strictly professional, not political. Likewise, the state ought to ensure that social scientists are free to pursue their investigations. In discussing the issue of intellectual freedom in Germany, Weber points out that the state should not consider its financial control over universities as "a means of attaining a certain political obedience among university students." Rather, the state should take its obligation toward universities as "an assumption of a cultural responsibility." Otherwise "the interests of science and scholarship in such a 'state' are no better and indeed, in many respects, are worse served than they were in the earlier condition of dependence on the church."[93] With the strict division between scholarship and politics stipulated, Weber explains what social science can offer to politicians. In Weber's words,

> It may be asserted without the possibility of a doubt that as soon as one seeks to derive concrete directives from practical political (particularly economic and social-political) evaluations, (1) the indispensable means, and (2) the inevitable repercussions, and (3) the thus conditioned competition of numerous possible evaluations in their *practical* consequences, are all that an *empirical* discipline can demonstrate with the means at its disposal.[94]

Here, Weber reminds us that the social sciences, being "strictly empirical sciences," are "the least fitted to presume to save the individual the difficulty of making a choice, and they should therefore not create the impression that they can do so."[95]

The conception that social science is an "empirical" science and thus has its limits allows the passion of politics to be preserved from the onslaught of modern science. For Weber, there can never be a science of politics because politics, as noted, requires both passion and perspective. At best, the social scientist can provide empirical knowledge that informs the politician's decision. Hence, the social scientist cannot play God to the politician as if the power of science is unlimited.[96] Only then can the social scientist (or more generally, the specialist) be a specialist with spirit in order "to swim against the stream" and perform a truly political act in "a polar night of icy darkness and hardness."[97]

IV

Weber and the Political

What emerges from Weber's notion of vocation can be best described as a form of engaged individualism informed by perspectivism.[98] If resistance to rationalization is political for Weber, it is because such an effort helps to preserve the authenticity of being. Having a vocation is a quintessential form of resistance in an age where the context of meaningfulness is constantly being undermined by the obsession with predictability and calculability in modern capitalist society. As Scaff has suggested, the resistance constitutes for Weber "a 'subjectivist culture' in relation to politics, most importantly in the sense that it validated a standard of *judgment* based on the state of the 'inner' self, the life of the psyche, the authenticity of subjective experience."[99]

The "political" thus understood is highly personal. While political engagement is ultimately ontological for Weber, it is really quite limited in its goal.[100] First of all, it is unclear how ordinary individuals, faced with mundane everyday decision making, can live and relive passion. But perhaps more disturbing is the fact that Weber's revolt has nothing to do with institutional or structural changes that may have alleviated the undesirable conditions in the "iron cage." Rather than attribute this somewhat fatalistic stance to Weber's pessimism, I want to suggest that there is good reason to locate this impasse in Weber's distrust of the state as a venue for political engagement. In this regard, Weber appears to share a basic feature with the postmodernists. What we find in Weber is a form of politics that emerges in the post-Nietzschean world; one in which the possibility of any foundational act executed in the name of universality and totality has been categorically denied.

But to note that Weber does not have any plan for foundational political action is not the same as saying that Weber has no principled political stance. In defining the relationship between the social scientist and the politician, Weber's effort in grappling with the issue of the limitation of specialization vis-à-vis the nonscientific aspects of life is clearly revealed. As argued, Weber wants to sustain the tension between the scientific and the nonscientific as he sees this to be the only way to preserve a space for politics or more specifically, the passion of politics. Hence, when we reconsider what politics is for Weber, we can hardly say that Weber does not have a clearly defined political stance. Politics for Weber is the appropriate domain for restoring meaning in action. This kind of politics may be anti-statist. But it is so not because of Weber's antifoundationalism. Rather, Weber's distrust of the state has to do with his view that the modern state, as an institution, has already been "rationalized."

Where then does the preceding discussion lead us with regard to the relationship between truth and politics in Weber? It is clear that Weber's philosophy of social science is antifoundationalist. Moreover, we can even say that Weber's politics is informed by his antifoundationalism in that unlike Plato, Weber does not provide us with an alternative vision in which our ontological predicament can be resolved. Yet I think it will be wrong to treat Weber as a precursor of postmodernist politics as it is defined in this book. For what Weber is saying is that unless there is passion, engagement in politics is simply meaningless. Truth, even when it is antifoundationalist, must know its limits.

CHAPTER FIVE

Foucault: Discursive Politics and the Modern State

OF THE THINKERS CONSIDERED IN THIS BOOK, Michel Foucault has perhaps written most extensively on the relationship between truth and power. More specifically, in North America Foucault's major impact on the Anglo-American academic world is that of a radical who was instrumental in the politicization of knowledge. As noted in chapter 1, the restructuring of university curriculum has become the latest political arena, in which the fight for an "inclusive" curriculum is considered to be the key to a more inclusive polity. Coupled with identity politics, the politicization of knowledge amounts to a crude postmodernist rendition of Bacon's old dictum that "knowledge is power."[1] The common ground between politicized knowledge and identity politics is their shared skepticism of the principle of universality. Both want to counter the abstract universalism of the Enlightenment and liberalism with the concreteness of existential particularities by making experience the basis for the validation of truth and of political action.

Having now dominated the academic world for more than a decade, postmodernism is undoubtedly a major intellectual movement that puts traditional scholarship on the defense. Yet it is also becoming clear that postmodernism as it evolves in the academy has important political implications. First is the receptiveness with which knowledge is engaged as battleground in the name of political progressiveness. This is no minor impact when we consider that it represents a complete reversal of a political tradition that used to take pride in condemning the politicization of knowledge as an indicator of authoritarianism. The second political message of postmodernism is that power is a much more insidious thing than what liberalism and Marxism would have us believe, because "power is everywhere." Indeed, there is no such thing as relation without power, be this between individuals, between individual and group, individual and institution, and all other relationships. "Local" struggles thus take on new political significance. This is how "knowledge" becomes a major site of political struggle.

Can Foucault be held responsible for the so-called cultural warfare outlined above? This is no trivial question as many see that what we are dealing with is in fact the symptom of a more fundamental crisis, which is the crisis of legitimation.[2] We begin with the much-cited exchange between Charles Taylor and William Connolly between 1984 and 1985, which can be taken as a major watershed in the way the English-speaking world has understood Foucault.[3] Taylor claims that Foucault is basically incoherent in that one cannot engage in a critique of humanity without the assumption of "some notion of a good unrealized or repressed." But "Nietzschean relativism" keeps Foucault from recognizing the obvious.[4] Connolly's defense is that Foucault may be Nietzschean, but this by no means renders Foucault ineffectual as a political thinker. In fact, Connolly maintains that Foucault points us toward a new kind of contructive politics—a politics that is uniquely suited to the reality of the late twentieth century. As noted in chapter 1, central to Connolly's vision of "agonistic democracy" is a notion of individual identity built on differences rather than homogeneities. The state as such becomes an anachronistic venue for political action, since state legitimacy requires a collective identity that all individuals are supposed to share. This new form of democratic politics will be issue-driven and politics will no longer need the discourse of universality to justify itself.

What is important for our consideration here is that the exchange is instrumental in shaping the Anglo-American reception of Foucault, which focuses almost exclusively on the Nietzschean aspects of Foucault. This means that what gets emphasized is indeed the postmodernist thrust of Foucault's works, which is a relentless critique of the Western philosophical tradition and its political implications.

But the Nietzschean Foucault is based on only a partial reading of the man. In this chapter I propose to look at other aspects of Foucault, aspects that are Kantian rather than Nietzschean.

Moreover, I will also explore Foucault's writing on modern liberalism, which constituted a significant portion of his research following the publication of Volume One of *The History of Sexuality*. I argue that no reading of Foucault as a political thinker can afford to ignore these works of his. Of course, Foucault's political writing is the work of Foucault the philosopher engaged in the quintessential postmodernist project of dismantling "metanarratives." Hence, it is important to place Foucault's political work in its proper philosophical context. Philosophy for Foucault is first and foremost a critical engagement of the self with the self. If Foucault's political analysis has any practical implication, it is in exposing the inadequacy of the liberal program of "containing" the power of the state by way of what Foucault regards as a political history of the self. However, Foucault does not really have a "postmodernist" political agenda. Against this observation, I argue that if we want to draw any guidance for political action from Foucault, we need to bear in mind that Foucault's postmodernism is really meant to enhance, rather than to displace, liberalism as it is practiced. This is why the postmodernist Foucault shows such incredible political naiveté when he fails to address what both Plato and Hobbes see as the key to political power—that the "sovereign definer" must coincide with the sovereign.

I

Philosophy and Modernity

There are two good reasons to support the case that Foucault's philosophical works are responsible for the politicization of knowledge on campuses in the late twentieth century. One is Foucault's claim that not only is there no objective truth that transcends historical specificities, but that intellectuals pursuing such a goal only propagate a "global," "totalitarian" discourse meant to suppress "local," "popular" knowledge.[5] Second is Foucault's assertion that power is insidious and all-pervasive. Thus, we must not delude ourselves into thinking that politics is something "out there" that has nothing to do with our everyday life. What leads Foucault to these observations is presumably genealogy. But what exactly is genealogy and how does Foucault come to adopt such a project?

In an interview conducted in 1977, a year after the first volume of *The History of Sexuality* was published, Foucault was asked why he considered himself a historian rather than a philosopher. His response was that the two roles are in fact inseparable:

> Since the 19th century, philosophy has never stopped raising the same question: "What is happening right now, and *what are we*, we who are perhaps nothing more than what is happening at this moment?" Philosophy's question therefore is the question as to what we ourselves are. That is why contemporary philosophy is entirely political and entirely historical. It is the politics immanent in history and the history indispensable for politics."[6]

In 1983, Foucault said that the investigation of "what we are" had led him to conclude that power is constitutive of the self and that "a society without power relations can only be an abstraction."[7] As Thomas McCarthy puts it, Foucault has given the notion of power an "ontological twist": subjection is being.[8]

Before we explore the implications of this claim, I want to consider *how* Foucault himself accounted for his philosophical agenda. In a lecture delivered at the Collège de France in 1983, Foucault presented Kant as having founded the two great critical traditions that characterize modern philosophy. One is the "analytic of truth," in which Kant's fundamental purpose is in identifying and defining "the conditions under which a true knowledge is possible." The other critical tradition is concerned with "an ontology of ourselves" based on an "ontology of the present." It is in the latter tradition that Foucault places himself.[9]

More specifically, this latter tradition is built on Kant's interpretation of modernity as "an attitude" rather than as "a period of history."[10] This was Kant, the philosopher, who reflected on the historic Enlightenment with a distinctively modern ethos. According to Foucault, in Kant's text, *What is Enlightenment?*, one encounters "for the first time" a distinctive critical posture, whereby philosophy problematizes its own "discursive present-ness." This means the capacity of philosophy to question itself "as an event, an event whose meaning, value and philosophical singularity it is required to state, and in which it is to elicit at once its own *raison d'etre* and the foundation of what it has to say."[11] Thus, philosophy, "as a discourse of and upon modernity," is "the problematisation of a present-ness of which it is part and relative to which it is obliged to locate itself . . ."[12]

On this reading, the Enlightenment represents a "philosophical ethos" that demands "a permanent critique of our historical era." Informed by such an ethos, criticism no longer sets out to search for some "formal structures with universal value." Rather, the purpose of criticism, defined as "a historical investigation into the events" that have contributed to the constitution of the self, is to transgress these contingently imposed historical limits.[13] In sum, the Enlightenment, as "an ethos," represents

> A philosophical life in which the critique of what we are is at one and the same time the historical analysis of the limits that are imposed on us and an experiment with the possibility of going beyond them.[14]

As Colin Gordon aptly points out, "Foucault distinguishes between an Enlightenment of sure identity, conviction and destiny, and an Enlightenment which is question and questioning, which is commitment to uncertainty."[15] By identifying contemporary philosophy with the latter tradition, Foucault has undoubtedly transformed philosophy into a form of critical engagement with subversive purpose.

It may seem odd that Foucault should choose to present his philosophical project at the end of his life as a critical project of the self informed by Kant.[16] Yet in terms of Foucault's intellectual development, he had simply come full circle from his first major engagement with Kant. Foucault's earliest work on Kant is a translation of his *Anthropology from a Pragmatic Point of View* with an extensive interpretive essay as introduction.[17] The text is a collection of Kant's lectures on the empirical study of man, which he sometimes referred to as "empirical psychology." Foucault notes that the obstinacy with which Kant pursues the subject "is linked to the very structure of the Kantian problem." The problem as defined by Foucault is as follows: "how to think, to analyze, to justify and to ground the finitude in a reflexion that does not resort to an ontology of the infinite and does not justify itself by a philosophy of the absolute?"[18] Indeed, early in Foucault's academic career, he saw Kant as having posed the question of "what is man?" in a distinctly secular manner. Foucault's later treatment of Kant as noted above is undoubtedly informed by this reading.

Philosophy as Genealogy

Against this interpretation of Kant, Foucault sees Nietzsche as a key figure in taking up the Kantian project of engaging in a critical ontology of the self.[19] More precisely, if a critical ontology of the self implies a political history of the self, it is in Nietzsche that Foucault discovers genealogy as a way of constructing this history. For genealogy demands that its practitioners write "effective history," as opposed to "traditional" history. It distinguishes itself from "traditional" history by starting from the radical premise that "nothing in man—not even his body—is sufficiently stable to serve as the basis for self-recognition or for understanding other men." There are no necessary elements or structures waiting to be realized or unfolded in history. In short, history becomes "effective" by introducing "discontinuity" into being.[20]

The concept of discontinuity is profoundly political for Foucault because it facilitates an understanding of history as a struggle for domination by the displacement of discursive rules. History becomes a series of "interpretations," defined as the "violent or surreptitious appropriation of a system of rules" for the purpose of imposing a new direction in domination."[21] The moment when a particular interpretation emerges is also the moment when a particular system of rules becomes *privileged*. Or to put it differently, interpretation is when certain rules of exclusion are replaced by others. Accordingly, there are three categories of such rules. They include "prohibition," "division" and "rejection," and lastly, but most importantly, "the opposition between true and false." It is this opposition that constitutes the "true discourse," which is the most dominant discourse since Plato.[22]

Genealogy and Power

Not only does genealogy aim to displace traditional history, it also targets "traditional" political theory, which characteristically employs the "juridical" model of power. Hobbes in particular is noted for the use of the "juridical" model that focuses on the problem of sovereignty and the related notions of law and prohibition.[23] On Foucault's reading, the "juridical" model conceives of power only negatively—it is that which says no; that which prohibits by imposing limits.[24] Moreover, the juridical notion of power treats power as an entity similar to a "commodity." Power thus becomes something to be possessed, something that one may or may not have a right to.[25]

Foucault challenges the juridical model by counselling political theorists "to cut off the King's head."[26] Using Hobbes as his foil, Foucault suggests that we abandon the "scheme of Leviathan," which is the embodiment of undivided and ultimate power—sovereignty. In Foucault's words,

> Rather than worry about the problem of the central spirit, I believe that we must attempt to study the myriad of bodies which are constituted as peripheral *subjects* as a result of the effects of power.[27]

Unlike traditional political theory, the genealogical analysis of power is therefore always expressed in the "how" of power: "'How,'" not in the sense of 'How does it manifest itself?' but 'By what means is it exercised?'"[28] As Foucault sees it, the former question necessarily entails "a theory of power" that "assumes a prior objectification"; whereas, the latter question is more suited to the kind of "analytical work" that proceeds by way of an "ongoing conceptualization." "This conceptualization implies critical thought—a constant checking," which includes "the historical conditions which motivate our conceptualization."[29] Hence, Foucault's critique of the juridical model is ultimately a *political* critique. By confining the analysis of power to what is prohibited and denied of us, the juridical model helps to mask the actual operation of power. Foucault states:

Power is tolerable on condition that it masks a substantial part of itself. Its success is proportional to its ability to hide its own mechanisms.[30]

To sum up, if Foucault were a postmodernist, then genealogy is critical philosophy without a "metanarrative." This is why genealogy is methodology, a critical mode, not a truth discourse.[31] That Foucault should keep insisting that his readers get him "right" on the nature of genealogy is revealing in this regard.[32] For all truth discourse, be it foundationalist or antifoundationalist, necessarily entails a "regime of truth."[33] Thus, genealogy is, by definition, "knowledge of details."[34]

II

Power and Government

Genealogy as outlined above provides us with the appropriate analytical framework for understanding the concept of "government," a term that Foucault uses increasingly in his later works. The concept is about power as relations, vis-a'-vis the self and others. Government is defined as "the contact point, where individuals are driven by others is tied to the way they conduct themselves." "Governing people" does not mean forcing "people to do what the governor wants." Rather, it is always a "versatile equilibrium" between the governor and the governed. Understood in this sense, "government" is the condition of the self as "subject."[35] For subjugation entails "a form of power which subjugates and makes subject to."[36]

Most importantly, the concept of government enables us to appreciate why Foucault considers philosophy to be the critical engagement with the question of "what we are." To be governed is to be a subject, which necessarily entails self-knowledge. Yet this knowledge of the self has nothing to do with the "authentic self." While men do "*govern (themselves and others) by the production of truth*," Foucault insists that this has nothing to do with "true utterances."[37] It is interesting to note how Foucault compares himself with Weber in this regard. Weber's question, according to

Foucault, is this: "If one wants to behave rationally and regulate one's action according to true principles, what part of one's self should one renounce?" In contrast, Foucault does not presuppose that there is a self to be renounced. Instead, Foucault poses his question as follows: "How have certain kinds of interdictions required the price of certain kinds of knowledge about oneself? What must one know about oneself in order to be willing to renounce anything?"[38]

Genealogy and Sexuality

The concept of government therefore provides the key to explaining the centrality of sexuality in Foucault's analysis of power. Defined as *dispositif*, sexuality embodies "a thoroughly heterogeneous ensemble" of "discourses, institutions, architectural forms, regulatory decisions, laws, administrative measures, scientific statements, philosophical, moral and philanthropic propositions."[39] Accordingly, two characteristics of the operation of power are identified. First, we find in modern sexuality the dynamics of power as captured by Foucault's concept of "government." For sex "was tied to the disciplines of the body" on the one hand and "on the other hand . . . to the regulation of populations."[40] In other words, sex is where the "techniques of domination" over others and the "techniques of the self" converge.[41] Second, sexuality illustrates that even though power is exercised with "a series of aims and objectives," it does not need to come from "the choice or decision of an individual subject" nor "the caste which governs." Sexuality, taken as *dispositif*, demonstrates those "great anonymous, almost unspoken strategies" of power which turn individuals into "subjects."[42] Thus sexuality, when genealogically construed, serves as a perfect illustration of the inadequacy of the juridical model of power.

Hence, Foucault's concept of "government" aims at exploring power relations that exist outside a formal political institutional framework. The concept of "government," engaged analytically, implies the analysis of the self as "subject." Moreover, what is at stake is not simply to prove that we are "subjects," but that we are a specific kind of subject under specific mode of subjection. In the second and third volumes of *The History of Sexuality*, we find Foucault's growing interest in the technology of the self as an aspect of "government" in the classical era. By investigating Greek and Roman problematizations of sex, Foucault turns his attention to "the history of the forms of moral subjectivation, to how we constitute ourselves as moral subjects of our own actions."[43] This project is more specifically labelled as "ethics," which is the "relationship of self with self."[44]

The genealogical analysis of sexuality point to two more general and interrelated conclusions that emerge from Foucault's notion of power. The first is that the state can no longer be the focal point for the analysis of power. For intrinsic in the concept of the state is the juridical model of power.[45] The state, however, simply cannot account for all the actual power relations in our society. More precisely, the state needs "other, already existing power relations," as it is these relations, that "often sustain the State more effectively than its own institutions, enlarging and maximizing its effectiveness."[46]

The second, and indeed more disturbing, conclusion follows from the first in that according to Foucault, the conventional distinction between totalitarianism and liberal democracy in effect disguises the important similarities that exist in both. Speaking in the midst of the Cold War, Foucault insisted that while the Soviet Union had a socialist "State apparatus," the "social hierarchies, family life, sexuality and the body" remained "more or less as they were in capitalist society." Hence, in Foucault's view, one was simply deluded to think that there were significant differences between "the mechanisms of power" that operate among "technicians, foremen and workers" here and in the Soviet Union.[47]

In fact, both fascism and Stalinism were really not "quite original," as they employed "mechanisms already present in most other societies" and relied on "the ideas and the devices of our political rationality" extensively.[48] For example, Foucault points out that there is nothing unique about the role of psychiatry in the former Soviet Union, as psychiatrists have always been "*the* functionaries of social order."[49] What happened in the Soviet Union was "not the monstrous coupling of a medical function and a police function. . . . It is simply the intensification, the ossificaton of a kinship structure that has never ceased to function."[50] Here, Foucault is obviously on slippery moral ground—a stance that accounts for Taylor's criticism. Foucault seemed not to realize that the Soviet imprisonment of political dissenters had nothing to do with psychiatry as therapy, although this fact does not necessarily undercut Foucault's insight, which is that clinical therapy is a form of disciplinary power.

The State and Modernity

Thus far we have covered works of Foucault that are most commonly referred to by those who associate postmodernism with radical left politics. Yet there are other writings that point to Foucault's alternative use of the term "government" to capture a unique historical phenomenon. The works that I have in mind are the closing pages of Volume One of *The History of Sexuality* (1976); two series of lectures, titled "Security, territory and population," and "The birth of biopolitics," delivered at the Collège de France between 1978 and 1979;[51] and the Tanner Lecture, titled "Omnes et Singulatim: Towards a Criticism of 'Political Reason,'" delivered at Stanford University in 1979.[52] In these analyses, "government" comes to denote a specific form of political power that evolved with the emergence of the modern state and shaped it distinctively.[53] As we shall see, the narration of the history of this form of power turns out to be an analysis of the evolution of the modern liberal state in the West.

Two phenomena occurred in the eighteenth century that contributed to the emergence of the modern state. First was the emergence of "the idea of *society*" in the realm of political discourse, understood as "a complex and independent reality" that is distinct from "a territory," "a domain," and "its subjects." "This new reality" has its own "laws and mechanisms of reaction, its regulations as well as its possibilities of disturbance."[54] Second, and no doubt related to the first, is the politicization of life itself. More specifically, society marks "the entry of life into history, that is, the entry of phenomena peculiar to the life of the human species into the order of knowledge and power," and with this, life itself enters "the sphere of political techniques." The entry of life into history implies that our "biological existence" is henceforth reflected in "political existence" and that the object of power is no longer constituted by "legal subjects" but by "living beings."[55] Individuals, as living beings rather than legal subjects, come to form a "population."

Foucault calls this phenomenon the "governmentalisation of the State," which is meant to capture the evolution of the state apparatus as it struggled to define its competence to rule over individuals. More precisely, there was a specific tactic for the survival of the state as it evolved in the eighteenth century, and that tactic is termed "governmentality."[56] The "governmental State" is distinctive not only because of its object of rule but because of the form of power it wields. In "Omnes et Singulatim: Towards a Criticism of 'Political Reason,'" Foucault's main objective is to show that the modern state is the convergence of two techniques of power—one "individualizing" and the other "totalizing."

"Individualizing power" is "pastoral power." The concept of pastorship is unique to "ancient Oriental societies: Egypt, Assyria, Judaea," where the relationship between the king and his people is conceptualized metaphorically as one between the shepherd and his flock. But it was "the Hebrews who developed and intensified the pastoral theme," postulating God as the people's shepherd. Using Hebrew texts as guide, Foucault highlights the following characteristics of pastorship. The shepherd, in wielding the pastoral form of power, performs one's duty with "devotedness." The shepherd is constantly "keeping watch" over the flock. And when the shepherd watches over the flock, "he pays attention to them all and scans each one of them." This is how the shepherd gets to know his flock in great detail. Thus, pastoral power, as understood by Foucault, is a form of concrete power that treats individuals as living individuals. The power is exercised through a highly structured routine which organizes the everyday activities of each person. This is how power achieves its pervasiveness.[57]

The other form of power is what Foucault calls "totalizing" power. It is totalizing in that it is exercised over a polity rather than an individual. Embodied in the "state," this power is at once "centralized and centralizing."[58] Foucault claims that this form of power can be traced to the "city-citizen" relationship in Plato's conception of statesmanship. Plato's main intention in the *Statesman* is to impugn the association of political power with pastoral power:

> Situated between the two—the gods and the swains—the men who hold political power are not to be shepherds. Their task doesn't consist in fostering the life of a group of

individuals. It consists in forming and assuring the city's unity. In short, the political problem is that of the relation between the one and the many in the framework of the city and its citizens. The pastoral problem concerns the lives of individuals.[59]

The contrast that Foucault wants to draw between the Platonic statesman and the Hebrew shepherd is that one deals with the human person as citizen and the other as living being.

Foucault claims that these two forms of power converged historically in the formation of the modern state. As he puts it, our societies are "really demonic" since they combine "those two games—the city-citizen game and the shepherd-flock game—in what we call the modern states."[60] On this reading, the "'welfare state problem'" is "one of the extremely numerous reappearances of the tricky adjustment between political power wielded over legal subjects and pastoral power wielded over live individuals."[61]

Prior to the rise of the modern state as we know it, sovereign power was symbolized by the "right to *take* life or *let* live." In contrast, the modern sovereign power is "a power to *foster* life or *disallow* it to the point of death." As "power over life," modern sovereignty is characterized by "the administration of bodies and the calculated management of life." At one level, the "power over life" conducts itself through the "anatomo-politics of the human body" to discipline the individual. At yet another level, the "power over life," in the form of "bio-politics" of the population, exerts itself over the human species through "regulatory controls." Together, "the disciplines of the body and the regulations of the population constituted the two poles around which the organization of power over life was deployed." A "normalizing society" is the "historical outcome" of an all-encompassing "technology of power centered on life."[62]

Hence, the relevance of sexuality as a political issue. But this time we are given the specific *historical* circumstances that accounted for the political importance of sexuality. Sexuality was the logical and "crucial target of a power organized around the management of life rather than the menace of death." For sex offered a convenient "means of access both to the life of the body and the life of the species." It was by no means accidental that in the nineteenth century "sexuality was sought out in the smallest details of individual existences."[63]

It is against the background of this uniquely modern "political technology of life" that Foucault situates liberalism. In his words:

> Liberalism ... is to be analyzed as a principle and method of rationalizing the exercise of government.... [G]overnment is not to be understood as an institution but, rather, as the activity which consists in directing human conduct within the setting and with the instruments of a state....
>
> Liberalism is permeated by the principle that "there is always too much government." ... The suspicion that there is always a risk of too much governing is tied to the question: why is it necessary to govern at all? With this interrogation, the liberal critique is hardly separable from the problematic of "society."[64]

For Foucault to say that liberalism is "permeated by the principle that 'there is always too much government'" may strike us as rather banal. However, like Foucault's appropriation of the Enlightenment, his liberalism is both "question and questioning." Thus, liberalism, in contrast to "reason of State" that justifies the "growing exercise of government," is at once "an instrument for the criticism of reality."[65] Placed in this context, Foucault's genealogical analysis of biopolitics as a unique form of modern state power is by no means a random subject of analysis. It is Foucault's engagement with the liberal project, which is being constantly watchful of "too much government."[66] Philosophy in this sense does have a historically defined political role. Foucault notes:

> Since Kant, the role of philosophy has been to prevent reason going beyond the limits of what is given in experience; but from the same moment—that is, from the development of modern states and political management of society—the role of philosophy has also been to keep watch over the excessive powers of political rationality ... [67]

III

Truth and Power

I began the chapter by situating Foucault as a major postmodernist thinker who has a hand in what many see as a crisis of legitimation. What I have done so far is to present two aspects of Foucault that are absent in the popular rendition of him. One aspect can be considered "Kantian" and the other "liberal." Moreover, I argue that both are central to understanding Foucault's works despite the fact that neither fits into what is generally considered to be Kantian or liberal. Having said this, where then should we place Foucault the radical thinker politically? Is Foucault "normatively confused," in Nancy Fraser's words, or is Foucault a "colonizer who refuses," as Nancy Hartsock notes?[68] I think not. For whatever is taken to be Foucault's "postmodernism," it is certainly not intended to be a "global" theory (to borrow Foucault's parlance), either for himself or for others. Genealogy, properly understood, is Foucault's way of answering the Kantian question of "what is man?"

But why is it important to read Foucault as someone who regards himself as being informed by Kant's critical ethos? And what are we to make of Foucault's "liberalism"? Among critics of postmodernism, Christopher Norris belongs to a tiny handful of scholars in the English-speaking world who takes Foucault's reading of Kant seriously.[69] Norris argues that Foucault is not an ethical relativist totally absorbed with the project of self-invention. Rather, Foucault is a politically responsible philosopher committed to the Kantian ethical ideals.[70] In the end, Foucault is a true child of the Enlightenment who takes the motto "Dare to Know!" to heart.

Indeed, no one can fault Foucault for not taking the motto "Dare to Know!" seriously. However, how plausible is the claim that Foucault is a politically responsible philosopher committed to the Kantian ethical ideals?[71] To answer this question, I want to return to the essay "What is Enlightenment?" in which Foucault notes that Kant had effectively made the political question of the

Enlightenment one of assuring the "public and free use of autonomous reason." Here Foucault addresses specifically Kant's distinction between the "private use" of reason and the "public use" of reason. Private use of reason is reasoning for a particular end. Public use of reason is reasoning for reasoning's sake, that is, "when one is reasoning as a member of reasonable humanity."[72] With this distinction, Foucault notes that the Enlightenment is more than "the process by which individuals would see their own personal freedom of thought guaranteed." Rather, the Enlightenment is importantly defined as the moment "when the universal, the free, and the public uses of reason are superimposed on one another."[73] On this ground, Kant proclaims that "the public use of one's reason must always be free, and it alone can bring about enlightenment among men."[74] As Hannah Arendt notes in her lectures on Kant, "for Kant, the moment to rebel is the moment when freedom of opinion is abolished."[75]

Does Foucault have a comparable concept of the "public use of reason"? Foucault once remarked that each of his books constituted "an experience" for him. As such, a book changes the "terms of thinking" by giving us an opportunity to experience a "determinate historical content." Foucault continues by saying:

> Starting from experience, it is necessary to clear the way for a transformation, a metamorphorsis which isn't simply individual but which *has a character accessible to others: that is, this experience must be linkable . . . to a collective practice and to a way of thinking.* That is how it happened, for example, for such movements as anti-psychiatry, or the prisoners' movement in France.[76]

Disclosing alternative modes of discourse that have previously been excluded or subjugated is thus a major task for the genealogist. If genealogy has concrete political implications, it is to create the possibility and the condition for "counter-discourse" so that a multiplicity of voices can be achieved.[77]

Nonetheless, since Foucault repeatedly denied that he had any political prescription, how would Foucault go about ensuring the "public use of reason"? This question is particularly pressing given Foucault's claim that discourse is an ensemble of "discursive events."[78] Since there is no such thing as an "immaterial" event, an event always "takes effect, becomes effect, always on the level of materiality."[79] Words are as "real" as anything else. Indeed, Foucault is fully aware that when discourse is treated as event, what happens at the "level of materiality" is nothing short of politics. Thus, Foucault raises the following questions with regard to the appropriation of discursive rules:

> What individuals, what groups or classes have access to a particular kind of discourse? How is the relationship institutionalized between the discourse, speakers and its destined audience? How is the relationship of the discourse to its author indicated and defined? How is struggle for control of discourses conducted between classes, nations, linguistic, cultural or ethnic collectivities?[80]

Yet we all know that when it comes to answering these strategic questions, Foucault does not have much to offer. This silence is often nullified by Foucault's postmodernist rhetoric, which says that "what I write does not prescribe anything, neither to myself nor to others."[81] For "as soon as one 'proposes'—one proposes a vocabulary, an ideology, which can only have effects of domination."[82]

But perhaps there is more to this silence than just the postmodernist refusal to prescribe. What I want to suggest is that Foucault's silence on the question of the appropriation of discourse is linked to his concern about the political role of intellectuals rather than Foucault's alleged "Nietzschean relativism."[83] To tackle this controversial issue of Foucault's view on the political responsibility of intellectuals, I suggest that we turn to his distinction between the "universal" and "specific" intellectual. Most often, the distinction is interpreted as Foucault's way to discredit all "global, *totalitarian theories*" and thereby facilitate the "*insurrection of subjugated knowledges.*"[84] I shall argue that this distinction in fact has more profound implication. Ultimately, Foucault's refusal to prescribe is his attempt to sever the claim that knowledge, be it "global" or "local," justifies power. This, however, does not necessarily entail the abnegation of the intellectual's responsibility to others.

Specialization and Political Commitment

The universal intellectual is derived from the model of "jurist or notable" whose critical stance is grounded on invoking the "universality of justice and the equity of an ideal law." When the universal intellectual speaks, he/she is considered as expressing a kind of "universal consciousness." But for Foucault, any claim to universality is totalizing. He notes scathingly that intellectuals in fact serve as "agents" of totalizing power if they believe that it is their responsibility to speak on behalf of the "consciousness" of humanity. Hence, according to Foucault, an intellectual should no longer "place himself 'somewhat ahead and to the side' in order to express the stifled truth of the collectivity."[85]

Against this critique, the specific intellectual emerges as the model that Foucault commends. The atomic scientist is the prototypical specific intellectual for he/she is an intellectual by virtue of his/her possession of highly technical and specialized knowledge. Oppenheimer, who has been singled out as the atomic scientist *par excellence*, has likened science to a "vast house," which is not "built upon any plan" and has "no central chamber, no one corridor from which all others debouch."[86] For science has rendered "the notion of universal knowledge" "an illusion."[87] The political power of the atomic scientist lies not in one's ability to produce a general discourse. Rather, it lies precisely in one's specialized knowledge. As Foucault points out, the kind of "political threat" posed by the atomic scientist was a major historical breakthrough. For it was simply unprecedented that "the intellectual was hounded by political powers, no longer on account of a general discourse which he conducted, but because of the knowledge at his disposal . . . "[88]

It is odd for Foucault to advocate that being a specialist is an indispensable step in being a political intellectual. For what can be more exclusive than the expert knowledge that sustains all advanced industrialized societies?[89] Indeed, it does not look like that specialization by itself is a sufficient condition. There is, after all, a gap between specializing in one's area of research and performing the political act of "revealing and undermining power where it is most invisible and insidious."[90] Again, Oppenheimer can be illuminating in this regard. For he clearly believed that the scientist has moral and political obligations to the human community:

> It is not possible to be a scientist unless you believe that the knowledge of the world, and the power which this gives, is a thing which is of intrinsic value to humanity, and that you are using it to help in the spread of knowledge, and are willing to take the consequences.[91]

Oppenheimer maintained that scientific work must be made relevant to the well-being of humanity. But this is in the end a matter of one's conviction, which was what Oppenheimer was attempting to invoke among his fellow scientists.

Likewise, Foucault believes that intellectuals are responsible to their society:

> His [the intellectual's] role, precisely because he works within the order of thought, is to see to what extent the liberation of thought can succeed in rendering ... transformations so urgent that one longs to make them, and so difficult that they're profoundly inscribed in the real.[92]

To perform this political role an intellectual must be engaged in criticism, which is to show that "things are not as obvious as we might believe" and to render "the too-easy gestures difficult."[93]

Criticism as defined is possible because of the unique independence of thought from "the set of representations that underlies a certain behavior" and "from the domain of attitudes that can determine this behavior." In short, thought is not "what inhabits a certain conduct and gives it its meaning." Rather, thought is what enables us to retain a critical distance so that we can "step back from this way of acting or reacting" and "present it to oneself as an object of thought." This entails questioning the meaning, the conditions, and the goals of actions. Thought is thus "freedom in relation to what one does, the motion of which one detaches oneself from it."[94] Presumably, the autonomous capacity to think makes the philosopher's engagement in a critical ontology possible and meaningful. In the end, Foucault is far from being deterministic in the creative role of the self as an inquisitor.

To appreciate Foucault's distinction between universal and specific intellectuals is crucial to understanding his view on the relationship between knowledge and politics. Intellectuals have an obligation to humanity, which is to think critically. But knowledge, whether foundationalist or antifoundationalist, does not make us superior political actors. Thus, philosophers should not be king nor should intellectuals appoint themselves as voices of the oppressed. Foucault's stance on this is clear: "there is always something ludicrous in philosophical discourse when it tries, from the outside, to dictate to others, to tell them where their truth is and how to find it. . . ."[95] If we act politically, it is because we care about others as human beings.[96] Foucault's lifelong political engagement to various causes was testimony to his sense of commitment to the world around him.

Among Foucault's last political actions was his plea for international support in light of the plight of the Vietnamese boat people. At a press conference in Geneva in 1981, Foucault invoked both the obligations and rights of all private individuals, as members of an "international citizenry," to urge their governments not to remain silent to the suffering of displaced people. Foucault's call for solidarity is extended to all, as we are united by the simple fact that "we are all governed." Thus, we must be ever watchful of governments and ensure that there is no abuse of power.[97] Critics such as Tom Keenan aptly note that it is rather odd, to say the least, for Foucault to use the language of right.[98] But Foucault once made the claim that we need "a new form of right"—a right that is at once "anti-disciplinarian" and "liberated from the principle of sovereignty."[99] I take Foucault's use of the language of right in this instance to be "anti-disciplinarian" to the extent that he was under no illusion that by invoking right, we can thereby circumvent the power of the modern state.[100]

Having said this, I suspect that Foucault the citizen, when acting politically, was likely to be shaped by the liberal sentiment that there is always "too much governing."[101] Foucault's own intellectual works would have supported such a suspicion. In a 1982 interview, Foucault said that "if I were younger, I would have immigrated to the United States."[102] When asked to explain, he replied:

> I see possibilities. You don't have a homogenous intellectual and cultural life. As a foreigner, I don't have to be integrated. There is no pressure upon me.[103]

This statement is more likely Foucault's courteous response to his host rather than a political statement. Yet it is still worth noting that the characteristics that Foucault regards as distinctive of the American intellectual and cultural milieu are precisely those that go into constituting that liberal "land of opportunity," where pluralism and diversity are meant to strive.

IV

Foucault the Radical: A Reassessment

The conclusion that Foucault's "postmodernism" is in fact informed by a modernist critical ethos à la Kant must leave those who regard Foucault as some kind of radical rather dissatisfied and uncomfortable. But what can be more radical than to challenge the age-old linkage between truth and legitimation that began with Plato? Foucault is first and foremost an intellectual interested in the question of thought.[104] The mature Foucault defines philosophy as a way of life—"an exercise of oneself in the activity of thought."[105] As Gilles Deleuze notes, Foucault's unique contribution lies in historicizing Kantian skepticism by translating all conditions of knowledge into questions of historical conditions.[106]

Thus considered, Foucault becomes a political thinker only accidentally in that as he sets out to investigate the self as the inquisitive self, he discovers a history that has systematically disguised historicity by a discourse of universality. The postmodernist Foucault aims at undermining the notion of "Truth" that has haunted the Western philosophical tradition since Plato. If Foucault's philosophical project has political implication, it is in pointing to the failure of that tradition to engage our critical capacity. Moreover, the political force of this message is undoubtedly enhanced by Foucault's relentless insistence that indeed nothing, not even our critical capacity, should be taken for granted. The last public lecture that Foucault delivered at the University of California at Berkeley in 1983 dealt with the "genealogy of the critical attitude in Western philosophy," which is "concerned with the question of the importance of telling the truth."[107] This genealogical task takes Foucault back to pre-Socratic philosophy and the concept of *parrhesia*, which denotes "truth-telling as a specific activity." What Foucault wants to analyze is "how the truth-teller's role was variously problematized in Greek philosophy."[108]

Perhaps in the end Foucault is less of a political thinker than he is often thought to be. This, I think, is a more convincing explanation than, say, "Nietzschean relativism" for why Foucault was not as politically astute as he ought to have been. Among the things he said that many find unconvincing and indeed outrageous is the claim that there is no substantive difference between a totalitarian state and a liberal democracy when both are subject to genealogical analysis. In the closing pages of Volume One of *The History of Sexuality*, Foucault makes the point that genocide in its twentieth-century form is possible precisely because life has become an object of state power. In his words, "if genocide is indeed the dream of modern powers . . . it is because power is situated and exercised at the level of life, the species, the race and the large-scale phenomena of population."[109] However, all the major incidents of genocide of this century can be tied to totalitarian regimes, as in the extermination of the Jews under the Nazis or the massive killing of intelligentsia and city dwellers under the Pol Pot regime in Cambodia. It seems clear that the "governmental State" is a necessary but not sufficient condition for the occurrence of state-sponsored genocide.[110]

How can someone of Foucault's penetrating analytical skills be blind to such a basic distinction? Setting aside the postmodernist rhetoric, I believe that Foucault simply fails in his critical work to consider the state's monopolization of the production of truth. As discussed earlier, Foucault treats discourses as "real" events. Yet ironically, Foucault treats them as "apolitical" events. In short, the "sovereign definer" for Foucault is Truth. Once removed, the discursive space is one that Foucault characterizes as "an autonomous, non-centralized kind of theoretical production."[111] This is literally Foucault's idea of a "revolution."

To illustrate my point, let us take a look at how Foucault justifies the use of Bentham's *Panopticon*, a text that demonstrates the rationality of the "normalizing" society in its most ideal form. As Foucault himself acknowledged, in choosing Bentham he was not concerned with describing "'real life'" as it was experienced in the prisons. Foucault seemed to be fully aware of the gap that existed between Bentham's schema and the real prison life. But he added, "the fact that this real life isn't the same thing as the theoreticians' schemas doesn't entail that these schemas are therefore Utopian, imaginary, etc." To draw such a conclusion is to subscribe to a "very impoverished notion of the real." Instead of treating Bentham's proposals as "abortive schemas for the creation of a reality," Foucault interpreted these proposals as "fragments of reality which induce such particular effects in the real as the distinction between true and false implicit in the ways men 'direct', 'govern' and 'conduct' themselves and others." What this amounts to is that Bentham's *Panopticon* itself was a "historical event" that had implications for the "question of truth."[112]

If a utopian text of this nature is selected in order that we can have a more enriched picture of the "real," then it reveals Foucault's assumption that we are free to think (in the way he defines the term, as discussed earlier), both philosophically and politically. It will be rather pointless to take Bentham seriously if he was simply a mouthpiece of some "sovereign definer," be this the Platonic Truth or the Orwellian Newspeak. It is in this rather odd way then that truth is insulated from politics. The "sovereign definer" and the sovereign for Foucault are, after all, not identical and should not be identical. In other words, Foucault's philosophical project simply takes for granted a liberal political framework that is constantly on guard against "too much government." If Foucault has any practical political insight to offer, it is in pointing out that liberal democratic states are more "totalitarian" than we think them to be and that, more importantly, their "totalitarian" nature is not necessarily supported by what we regard as the most obvious nexuses of power.

Having considered Foucault's stance on the relationship between truth and politics, let us recall an issue raised originally in chapter 1. I note that during the decade of the 1980s there developed a set of contrasting developments regarding the relationship between knowledge and power. While the West was preoccupied with the politicization of knowledge, those living in the Communist Bloc fought to dissociate knowledge from politics. Although the breakdown of the Cold War ideological division means that we can no longer set up such a sharp contrast, the same set of opposing developments is in fact still happening among democratic and non-democratic regimes. In the context of this chapter, the logical question that emerges from the observation is thus as follows:

would Foucault care to make a distinction between these two forms of struggle? I suspect that Foucault, the postmodernist, would likely say that to the extent that both developments were instances of "subjugated knowledges" fighting against "totalitarian theories" (that is, theories that claim to have *the* truth), both forms of struggle are equally political.

Yet if we pose the contrast in terms of the role of the state in the circulation of knowledge, then the distinction between the two forms of struggle seems obvious. One happens without the direct involvement of the state while the other happens with either the direct participation or at least the acquiescence of the state. Surely there is a difference. If the state has absolute power over the possibility of making a "fictional discourse" inducing the effects of "truth" (to borrow Foucault's postmodernist parlance), then clearly the state does matter.[113] But can Foucault articulate the difference? I surmise that the situation does pose a significant conundrum to Foucault, one that he simply cannot resolve. It is against this problematic that we turn to Hannah Arendt.

CHAPTER SIX

Arendt: Totalitarianism and the Human Condition

THE ORIGINS OF TOTALITARIANISM, WHICH WAS PUBLISHED in 1951, was Arendt's first book in America. Arendt made two sweeping claims regarding the significance of this uniquely twentieth-century political phenomenon. One is that the victory of totalitarianism will mean the "destruction of humanity."[1] The other is that understanding the "nature of totalitarianism" is the key to "understanding the very heart of our own century."[2] Against these claims, Margaret Canovan's reinterpretation of Arendt's political thought seems formidable. Canovan argues that "not only is *The Human Condition* itself much more closely related to *The Origins of Totalitarianism* than it appears to be, but virtually the entire agenda of Arendt's political thought was set by her reflections on the political catastrophes of the mid-century."[3] As Canovan notes in the preface, her book is a "*re*interpretation" in two senses. By systematically incorporating the unpublished writings of Arendt in the study of her thought, Canovan sees the need to revise her own earlier reading of Arendt. But more importantly, the work is an effort to persuade scholars that they "cannot afford to concentrate on *The Human Condition* to the point of ignoring her earlier work."[4]

I am generally sympathetic to Canovan's claim about the centrality of *The Origins of Totalitarianism*.[5] Moreover, what I want to emphasize is that Arendt's analysis of totalitarianism is a profound indictment of the role of philosophy in politics. As we shall see, Arendt's argument hinges on one important point, and that is the significance of immateriality in a totalitarian system. By immateriality, I have in mind Arendt's observation that totalitarianism is first and foremost an ideological system that is virtually a self-contained system of ideas.[6] The thrust of this argument is that totalitarianism can only sustain itself in a fabricated reality perpetuated by a complete defiance of experience. That is to say, totalitarianism is a form of radical idealism.

What is it about this metaphysical position that lends itself to a political movement that represents for Arendt a diabolic force of unprecedented scale? What does Arendt mean when she declares that the victory of totalitarianism will mean the "destruction of humanity"? And how can an analysis of totalitarianism shed light on the "very heart of our own century"?

In what follows, I will argue that even before the theory of political action was first systematically laid out in *The Human Condition*, we can already see in Arendt's analysis of totalitarianism that what defines humanity is the condition of plurality. Thus considered, Arendt's insight in *The Origins of Totalitarianism* is not simply in pointing out that idealism facilitates the illusion that "everything is possible," which is eventually self-destructive and self-defeating. More profoundly, the triumph of idealism means that the human condition is one characterized by singularity rather than plurality, rendering debate, the "very essence of political life," superfluous.[7] In other words, what is most disturbing in Arendt's analysis is not only the claim that idealism is inherently antipolitical, but that there exists a human condition that is receptive to substituting politics with a certain metaphysical posture which, by definition, precludes politics.

However, as I will also argue, while Arendt maintains that there is no place for philosophy in politics, she by no means thinks that truth is irrelevant to politics. Here what Arendt has to say about Machiavelli is illuminating. As she puts it, "*virtù* is the response, summoned up by man, to the world, or rather to the constellation of *fortuna*.... There is no *virtù* without *fortuna* and no *fortuna* without *virtù*...."[8] Like Machiavelli, Arendt sees the dynamics of politics as the act of endeavoring within the realm of the possible. The boundary of the possible, however, is not set by the struggle between *virtù* and *fortuna*. It is rather the categories of truth and falsehood.

I

Totalitarianism and Idealism

In this section, we shall examine the key arguments in *The Origins of Totalitarianism* to ascertain why the work is central to Arendt's thought. I will be using the 1973 edition, which contains the chapter "Ideology and Terror: A Novel Form of Government" and new prefaces to all three parts of the book. The chapter, which was first added to the book in 1958, is important as it does serve as a more succinct conclusion to Arendt's study of totalitarianism than the original "Concluding Remarks" in the first edition. In accounting for this particular change between the 1951 and the 1958 editions, Arendt noted, "there were certain insights of a more general and theoretical nature which now appear to me to grow *directly* out of the analysis of the elements of total domination in the third part of the book, but which I did not possess when I finished the original manuscript in 1949."[9] But even in the original "Concluding Remarks," Arendt notes that the destructiveness of totalitarianism is closely tied to the conviction that "everything is possible" and that the essence of politics lies in the fact that "not a single man but Men inhabit the earth."[10] As we shall see, both observations are essential to Arendt's more definitive view stated in "Ideology and Terror."

The two examples of the totalitarian system that Arendt discusses at length are Nazism and Stalinism. Arendt regards these two movements as more than just radical ways of conducting racial conflict or class struggle. For the important point is not what these two movements have to say about race or class. Rather, as Arendt puts it,

> Totalitarian politics—far from being simply antisemitic or racist or imperialist or communist—use and abuse their own ideological and political elements until the basis of factual reality, from which the ideologies originally derived their strength and their propaganda value—the value of class struggle, for instance, or the interest conflicts between Jews and their neighbours—have all but disappeared.[11]

In other words, what makes totalitarianism characteristically totalitarian is its radical disjunction from what Arendt calls "factual reality." As such, totalitarianism operates by way of "ideology," which distinguishes this system of politics from previous forms of "political oppression" like despotism, tyranny and dictatorship.[12]

Ideology is the "logic of an idea," which is marked by a mode of reasoning called "ideological thinking." Ideological thinking is a distinctive mode of political reasoning defined by three characteristics. The first is the claim to "total explanation" of all historical happenings. This claim to totality is meant to include the entire historical spectrum, that is, the past, the present, and the future. Secondly, while ideological thinking is an attempt to account for "factual reality" in its totality, this mode of thinking is in fact completely divorced from reality and experience. For experience, being rooted in specificity, is clearly limited in its claim to totality. Indeed, and this brings us to the third characteristic, ideological thinking tries to achieve the "emancipation of thought" from the limitation imposed by experience through a specific method of demonstration. This is achieved by arranging facts into an "absolutely logical procedure" that starts from an "axiomatically accepted premise." It is, in short, a "process of deduction from a premise," which is the only possible movement in the realm of logic. It is this "logicality of ideological thinking" that provides the basis for total explanation and the "principle of action" for totalitarian movement.[13]

Arendt's contention is that the kind of consistency offered by totalitarian thinking is appealing especially to those who have lost a sense of bearing in the real world (that is, the world that we inhabit).[14] As Arendt notes,

> The ideal subject of totalitarian rule is not the convinced Nazi or the convinced Communist, but people for whom the distinction between fact and fiction (i.e., the reality of experience) and the distinction between true and false (i.e., the standards of thought) no longer exist.[15]

Accordingly, the kind of "subject" that fits into this description is the "mass man," a highly isolated and atomized individual.[16] Masses exist where people are "superfluous or can be spared without disastrous results of depopulation." Moreover, these are people who otherwise "cannot be integrated into any organization based on common interest." Arendt maintains that by the end of the First World War, "the breakdown of class society," coupled with massive unemployment and displacement of population, facilitated the development of "the psychology of the European mass man."[17]

Whether or not one agrees with the historical accuracy of Arendt's analysis of the socioeconomic conditions in Europe between the two world wars is a subject beyond the scope of this book. What is important for our purpose here is Arendt's insight that the mass man is someone who is "obsessed by a desire to escape from reality." For in his "essential homelessness," the mass man can "no longer bear its accidental, incomprehensible aspects." This longing for escape from reality is a "verdict against the world" in which one is "forced to live" but "cannot exist." Such a situation is ripe for the "revolt of the masses" against "common sense," which is "the result of their atomization, of their loss of social status," and with it, the "whole sector of communal relationships in whose framework common sense makes sense."[18]

The collapse of common sense is significant because it is necessary for the effectiveness of totalitarian propaganda. By offering the masses a substitute reality validated by the "logic of an idea" rather than by experience, totalitarianism makes it possible for the masses to live in a world that has denied the condition of plurality. Thus, between "facing the anarchic growth and total arbitrariness of decay" and "bowing down before the most rigid, fantastically fictitious consistency of an ideology," the masses will likely "choose the latter." A world created by ideology is more attractive to the masses not because "they are stupid and wicked, but because in the general disaster this escape grants them a minimum of self-respect" by conjuring up "a lying world of consistency which is more adequate to the needs of the human mind than reality itself." And it is precisely this ability to guarantee consistency that makes it possible for the regime to demand "total, unrestricted, unconditional, and unalterable loyalty" from its followers.[19]

Where does the originality of Arendt's analysis lie? For one thing, the more skeptical reader may now impatiently point out that Arendt's understanding of totalitarian ideology is just an elaborate way of saying that it is one big lie. Indeed, Arendt does equate totalitarian ideology with lying. More specifically, the kind of lie that is characterisitic of totalitarianism is "modern lie," in contrast with "traditional lie." On this view, traditional lie is restricted by two conditions: that it is a lie about the "particulars" and that it deceives only the "enemy," which means that the liar is not engaged in self-deception. Modern lie, however, involves a "complete rearrangement of the whole factual texture." It also intends to deceive everyone alike, to the extent that those who initiate the lie eventually "fall victims to their own falsehoods."[20]

This distinction between traditional and modern lie is important. It indicates that not only is totalitarianism a lie, but in fact the lie is literally so "big" that we can no longer call it a lie. For the distinction between truth and lie requires a common standard. In the case of traditional lie, the common standard between truth and lie is "the fabric of factuality." As such, the lie always appears as a "tear" in the fabric. On the other hand, modern lies are "so big that they require a complete rearrangement of the whole factual texture—the making of another reality, as it were. . . . " This surrogate reality provides a completely different context for facts to fit "without seam, crack, or fissure, exactly as the facts fitted into their original context." Arendt notes critically that as long as those who concoct the surrogate reality are prepared to engage in self-deception to "create a semblance of truthfulness," there is nothing to prevent "these new stories, images, and non-facts from becoming an adequate substitute for reality and factuality."[21]

To judge totalitarianism therefore requires one to stand outside of the system itself. Arendt points out that it is futile for us to argue with a Nazi or a Stalinist on what he or she has to say about race or class. To confront totalitarianism requires more than just a confrontation with facts, which are specific. Rather, it is a more fundamental confrontation—it is about whether ideas alone, to the point of defying facts, should serve as guide for politics.

Truth: Rational and Factual

What is wrong with engaging "idealism" as the basis for politics? To answer this question, we turn to the essay "Truth and Politics," which was written in response to the controversy caused by the publication of *Eichmann in Jerusalem*.[22] Here, Arendt defines truth in the following manner:

> Conceptually, we may call truth what we cannot change; metaphorically, it is the ground on which we stand and the sky that stretches above us.[23]

In other words, truth is what gives us a sense of bearing. Yet not all truth is the same. Accordingly, there are two forms of truth. One is "rational truth," and it is constituted by axioms and theories. This is the kind of truth that mathematics, science, and philosophy pursue. The other is "factual truth," which is found in "facts and events." Unlike rational truth, factual truth has nothing to do with intellectual pursuit. It is simply what happens when men are "living and acting together."[24]

This distinction between rational and factual truth is crucial to understanding Arendt's view on the relationship between truth and politics. The main reason being that Arendt sees important political implications in the respective modes of validation for both rational and factual truth. More specifically, each mode of validation is reflective of the relationship between the individual and the collective. Rational truth is the product of the "relative permanence of the human mind's structure."[25] Consequently, such truth is meant to transcend both particularity and temporality. Moreover, being a product of the "speculative mind," rational truth has to do with the individual in his or her singularity rather than in his or her relations with the community. Rational truth is thus "unpolitical by nature."[26] On the other hand, factual truth always occurs in the midst of the "ever-changing affairs of men."[27] It is therefore particular and temporal by definition. Factual truth is also "political by nature" because it can only be validated in the context of the human community.[28] In other words, factual truth presupposes the human condition of plurality.

However, this contrast between rational and factual truth points to a more fundamental conflict. Indeed, Arendt's basis for making the distinction brings us back to the issue discussed in the earlier chapter on Plato. It is the conflict between philosophy and politics. As we shall see, what Arendt has to say about the issue is important because it shows the anti-Platonic strand of her thoughts while reaffirming the centrality of truth in politics.

II

Politics and Philosophy

In Arendt's analysis of the history of Western philosophy, Socrates and Plato represent two radically different approaches to knowledge.[29] The critical turning point in the development of Plato's political philosophy was the trial of Socrates. Plato's reflection on the trial turns out to be of profound impact on the relationship between philosophy and politics in the history of Western thought. As Arendt puts it, "the gulf between philosophy and politics opened historically with the trial and condemnation of Socrates."[30]

The key issue at stake in the trial of Socrates is the role of opinion (*doxa*) in politics. This problem is clearly related to the fact that the Athenians prided themselves for being able to conduct political affairs in the form of speech. Its objective is to persuade (*peithein*). Thus, persuasion is considered to be "the specifically political form of speech," and what is being persuaded is opinion (*doxa*).[31] More significant is the way in which opinion is persuaded, thereby defining persuasion's political nature. Accordingly, the word *doxa* means "not only opinion but also splendor and fame." The delivery of *doxa* requires one to situate oneself in the "public sphere" so that asserting one's own opinion amounts to showing oneself (to others) and being seen and heard (by others). The Greeks considered this public display of oneself as among the great privileges that came with public life. In contrast, "one is neither seen nor heard by others" in the privacy of one's household. Thus, persuasion is by definition directed toward a multitude. Moreover, what is being persuaded, that is, opinion, is relative because every person who speaks in the public arena is entitled to an opinion.[32]

However, the historic trial of Socrates led Plato to question the effectiveness of persuasion and the viability of opinion for conducting human affairs. As Plato saw it, the condemnation of Socrates was the result of Socrates "submitting his own *doxa* to the irresponsible opinions of the Athenians." The catastrophic incident "made Plato despise opinions and yearn for absolute standards" even in the realm of human affairs. It was this that prompted Plato to argue that philosophy should rule over politics. From then on, Plato was convinced that unless "transcending standards" are imposed on the realm of human affairs, everything will remain "relative." With this, the Platonic notion of truth was construed as the "very opposite of opinion." This opposition of truth and opinion "was certainly the most anti-Socratic conclusion that Plato drew from Socrates' trial."[33]

A new discursive mode was therefore deemed necessary to convey the truth. Dialectic (*dialegesthai*), understood as the very "opposite of persuasion," became Plato's notion of a "specifically philosophical form of speech." "Dialectic is possible only as a dialogue between two" whereas persuasion addresses the multitude, of whom Plato was suspicious. With truth and dialectic posed as complete contrasts to opinion and persuasion, Plato establishes what Arendt calls the "tyranny of truth, in which it is not what is temporally good, of which men can be persuaded, but eternal truth, of which men cannot be persuaded, that is to rule the city." Truth in the Platonic sense is meant to destroy *doxa*, which constitutes "the specific political reality of the citizens."[34]

In the earlier chapter on Plato, I pointed out that he wants to convince us that not only should those who possess the truth rule, it is also just for them to rule. For the philosopher is both wise and just. We recall that the just man is defined by Plato as one who is able to keep all bodily appetites under the control of reason. On Arendt's reading, the hierarchical relationship between the soul (the reasoning part) and the body (the appetitive part) reflects an even "deeper contradiction between philosophy and politics." For the philosopher remains a man despite the claim that he "perceives something that is more than human, that is divine (*theion ti*)" in his capacity as a philosopher. Consequently,

> The conflict between philosophy and the affairs of men is ultimately a conflict within the philosopher himself. It is this conflict which Plato rationalized and generalized into a conflict between body and soul: whereas the body inhabits the city of men, the divine thing which philosophy perceives is seen by something itself divine—the soul—which somehow is separate from the affairs of men. The more a philosopher becomes a true philosopher, the more he will separate himself from his body. . . . If the philosopher

attains rulership over the city, he will do no more to its inhabitants than he has already done to his body. His tyranny will be justified both in the sense of best government and in the sense of personal legitimacy, that is, by his prior obedience, as a mortal man, to the commands of his soul, as a philosopher.[35]

The fundamental contradiction between philosophy and politics is again captured in the allegory of the cave. Arendt argues that the allegory is meant to depict "how politics, the realm of human affairs, looks from the viewpoint of philosophy" rather than "how philosophy looks from the viewpoint of politics." For the returning philosopher is one who no longer has "the common sense needed to orient himself in a world common to all, and, moreover, because what he harbors in his thought contradicts the common sense of the world."[36]

This discussion on the self-alienation of the philosopher is significant. Not only is philosophical truth antagonistic to the human community, it also alienates the philosopher from one's own humanness. Arendt notes that in his quest for truth, the philosopher needs "to be left alone" and "freed from all possible disturbances." This poses a "professional risk" to the philosopher as "the danger in solitude is of losing one's own self."[37] Thus, to apply rational truth in the realm of human affairs is an assault on our being, that is, an ontological assault. What happens in totalitarian politics is precisely an attempt to put rational truth into practice. By imposing standards of thought that transcend the limits of experiences, totalitarianism is a form of "Platonic tyranny of truth." How this tyranny mutilates the nature of our being is the subject of the next section.

Factual Truth, Opinion, and Judgment

We should not conclude from the inevitable conflict between philosophy and politics that truth, regardless of its nature, is always incompatible with the demands of politics. As pointed out earlier, factual truth is, by definition, "political" in that such truth is validated by "men living and acting together," that is, the condition of human plurality. But more importantly, Arendt maintains that factual truth is essential to the viability of politics. To appreciate the claim, we need to turn to Arendt's theory of political action.[38]

Inspired by the ancient Greeks, Arendt sees speech as the prototype of *human* action. "Action" as such is the only form of human activity that occurs "*directly* between men without the intermediary of things or matter," and thus corresponds to the "human condition of plurality, to the fact that men, not Man, live on the earth and inhabit the world."[39] This is why "speech is what makes man a political being."[40] As Dana Villa notes, since speech for Arendt is always "speech with others," "genuine political action is nothing other than a certain kind of talk,"[41] a variety of conversation or argument about public matters. It is the process, as opposed to the end result, that matters. On this ground, Villa argues that "*Arendt's theory of political action should be read as the sustained attempt to think of praxis outside the teleological framework.*"[42]

More precisely, the form of talk is debate, which constitutes the "very essence of political life." What is being exchanged in a debate is "opinion," which requires a kind of "political thinking" that is characteristically "representative." This means that one forms one's opinion "by considering a given issue from different viewpoints, by making present . . . the standpoints of those who are absent" in one's mind. Yet in representing those who are "absent," one "does not blindly adopt the actual views of those who stand somewhere else". Therefore, representative thinking is a "question neither of empathy, as though I tried to be or to feel like somebody else, nor of counting noses and joining a majority but of being and thinking in my own identity where actually I am not." To meet such a challenge, representative thinking requires an "'enlarged mentality,'" which means situating oneself in a world of "universal interdependence" while suspending "one's own private interests."[43] As Lisa Disch notes appropriately, what Arendt demands is nothing short of "'situated impartiality,'" defined as a "critical decision that is not justified with reference to an abstract standard of right but by visiting a plurality of diverging public standpoints."[44]

Drawing from Kant, Arendt regards "this capacity for an 'enlarged mentality'" as enabling individuals to make judgments.[45] Insofar as it is the individual who makes a judgment in the form of one's opinion, the act of judgment is highly personal and subjective. But to the extent that to judge is to disclose oneself to others, judgment presupposes the "sharing-the-world-with-others."[46] Thus, judgment is, by definition, intersubjective. In short, "when one judges, one judges as a member of a community." "Common sense is community sense, *sensus communis*."[47] As Ronald Beiner notes, by linking opinion with judgment, Arendt's aim is "to bolster the 'rank and dignity' of opinion." Judgment lends opinion a "measure of respectability when it is weighed against [rational] truth."[48]

One of the guides that give the mind engaged in judgment a sense of bearing is, of course, factual truth. For facts and events "constitute the very texture of the political realm."[49] However, Arendt maintains that there has to be a strict distinction between fact, on the one hand, and opinion on the other. For "factual truth," to be qualified as truth, has a "despotic character" that preempts debate. Yet factual truth does have a proper role in politics, which is to inform opinion. In Arendt's words:

> Facts and opinion, though they must be kept apart, are not antagonistic to each other; they belong to the same realm. Facts inform opinions, and opinions, inspired by different interests and passions, can differ widely and still be legitimate as long as they respect factual truth. . . . [F]actual truth informs political thought just as rational truth informs philosophical speculation.[50]

Moreover, Villa notes that the "'despotism'" of factual truth is of "a different order from that exercised by truths of reason or religion." Factual truth provides "nonpolitical boundaries" to opinion and persuasion; whereas rational truth "invariably quash[es] the plurality of perspectives that generates the 'incessant discourse' Arendt cherishes."[51]

Totalitarianism and the Displacement of Politics

With the relationship between factual truth and opinion established, we are now in a better position to understand why totalitarian thinking is destructive of politics. Under a totalitarian system, no formation of opinion is possible because of a "consistent and total substitution of lies for factual truth."[52] As noted, ideology operates by way of substituting concrete experiences with abstract ideas and thereby takes away the political context needed for the formation of opinion. For Arendt, the issue is not simply that we are not "free" to make opinion under totalitarianism. Rather, what is at stake in totalitarianism is that the political context that makes opinions matter is being completely mutilated. This is what Arendt has in mind when she says that "the fundamental deprivation of human rights is manifested first and above all in the deprivation of a place in the world which makes opinions significant and actions effective."[53]

The indispensable role played by factual truth in politics also helps to explain why Arendt claims that totalitarianism requires a breakdown of community and at the same time reinforces the breakdown. As in the case of "rational" and "factual" truth, Arendt relates the ideological mode of thought to the human condition. Logical reasoning, which is the essence of the ideological mode of thought, is characteristic of the human mind in loneliness—the human mind that is devoid of the self, the other, and the world.[54]

Thus far we have only established why rational truth is antipolitical when it is applied to human affairs. We have yet to account for the sense of omnipotence that totalitarianism entails. More specifically, how does rational truth support the conviction that "everything is possible"? To answer this question, we need to take into account Arendt's view on modern science, which represents to her a kind of perverted idealism as well.

In a 1968 lecture, "The Archimedean Point," Arendt identifes Archimedes as having established a model of science in which knowledge of things on earth requires a self-conscious withdrawal from the things under study on the part of the knower. Moreover, there is a conviction that "our power over things grows in proportion to our distance from them."[55] The Archimedean point is thus defined as the "point far enough removed from things of the earth to give power over them and perhaps to unhinge the earth."[56] Accordingly, modern science represents a radical withdrawal from the earth, so radical that all "anthropomorphic elements and principles" have to be eliminated to the point that "the goal of modern science . . . is no longer to 'to augment and order' human experiences. . . ."[57] In fact, there is a sense that earthbound human beings are actually standing in the way of knowledge.

Modern science is therefore a revealing instance of "modern truth," in which the "sheer force of abstraction and imagination" contributes to the conviction that "everything is possible." The assumption is that the knower, once liberated from the constraints of reality, can have more knowledge and, with it, more power over what there is to know. In short, "the modern scientific enterprise began with thoughts never thought before (Copernicus imagined he was 'standing in the sun . . . overlooking the planets') and with things never seen before," as in Galileo's telescope.[58] It is ironic that science, which sets out to understand nature, should regard the senses that give us our first-hand experience with the physical world as distrustful. As Arendt puts it, the scientists, "in their search for 'true reality,' lost confidence in the world of 'mere' appearances." They began to invent instruments to "refine the coarseness of our senses and they ended up with instruments designed to deal with data which strictly speaking do not appear at all. . . . " These data make themselves known "only because they affect our measuring instruments in certain ways." Quoting Eddington, Arendt notes that these data "may 'have as little resemblance'" to the "'true reality'" as "'a telephone number has to a subscriber.'" Yet there seems to be no doubt that the world behind mere appearances is the "'true reality.'"[59]

Arendt argues that this so-called increase of human power over things in the end diminishes one's respect for oneself. This can be seen in scientists' lack of hesitation to engage in the constuction of a power strong enough to kill "all organic life" on the planet. It is, moreover, an illusion to think that we have ultimate control over nature when the "coincidence of the population explosion with the invention of nuclear weapons" is perhaps nothing but a "'large-scale biological process' to prevent life on earth from being thrown out of balance."[60] Arendt urges for the need to recognize that there is indeed limit to "what we *can* discover and *can* make."[61] In the end, the location of the "Archimedean point with respect to earth" can only be an ad infinitum chase. "Man can only get lost in the immensity of the universe, for the only true Archimedean point would be the absolute void behind the universe."[62]

Like modern science, totalitarianism, by invoking the "sheer force of abstraction and imagination," is a form of radical idealism that knows no limit to its power. More precisely, totalitarianism is *"the specifically technological form of politics as plastic art."*[63]

The challenge faced by all totalitarian regimes is nothing short of the refabrication of mankind in accordance with "the law of Nature" or "the law of History." Under totalitarianism, all laws become "laws of movements" to which all of humanity is subject.[64] Nothing can be spared, not even oneself, in the quest for the Archimedean point.

III

Evil and Thoughtlessness

In the preceding sections, I have accounted for why Arendt thinks that the victory of totalitarianism will mean the "destruction of humanity" and why understanding the nature of totalitarianism amounts to understanding the "very heart of our own century." To sum up, the triumph of totalitarianism means that the human condition of plurality is mutilated. As discussed, at the very core of totalitarianism is radical idealism, which is manifested by way of molding human affairs after rational truth. For Arendt, understanding totalitarianism therefore necessarily entails the need to renegotiate the boundary between truth and politics, in order that neither oversteps the domain of the other. The key to the renegotiation lies in Arendt's thought on what we can rely on to fight against totalitarianism. While in Arendt's view truth is, by definition, antipolitical, she believes that "truth has the obligation . . . to check power."[65] Here Arendt obviously means the domain of factual truth. There are those whose profession is to "make sense" of human events, a point that I will return to later. But Arendt also maintains that the construction of these events is everyone's business. Her last work, *The Life of the Mind*, is undoubtedly an attempt to deal with the issue. Critics have suggested that Arendt's answer lies generally in her view that there is in all of us the capacity to think for ourselves critically and independently in each circumstance that demands judgment.[66]

This interpretation relies mainly on the impact of the trial of Eichmann, a former Gestapo officer, on Arendt. Indeed, if the trial of Socrates convinced Plato of the need to make thinking exclusive, then the trial of Eichmann convinced Arendt of the urgency of making thinking everyone's business. As Arendt puts it:

> Reason itself, the thinking ability which we have, has the need to actualize itself. The philosophers and the metaphysicians have monopolized this capability. . . . [W]e have forgotten that *every* human being has a need to think. . . . And he does it constantly.[67]

So what is it about the trial of Eichmann that prompted Arendt to believe that thinking ought not to be the "monopoly" of "professional thinkers"?[68]

As is well known, the "banality of evil" is the culminating theme of the series of reports written by Arendt on the trial, which began in 1961. It was a shocking claim that led to much controversy at the time. The observation that evil is banal states the disturbing fact that Eichmann was no Mephistopheles or Faust. In fact, this notorious war criminal displayed none of the base motives or aggressiveness that we would tend to associate with crime of such a scale. In Arendt's words, "he *merely*, to put the matter colloquially, *never realized what he was doing*. . . . It was sheer thoughtlessness . . . that predisposed him to become one of the greatest criminals of that period."[69]

What Arendt is in effect saying is that there is a "strange interdependence" between thoughtlessness (which is, as she reminds us, not to be confused with stupidity) and evil. This prompts Arendt to reconsider the nature of thinking in light of the moral challenge posed by totalitarianism. However, thinking cannot be philosophical thinking in the Platonic sense of quest for absolute truth. Not only does this way of thinking tend to exclude the ordinary people, the Platonic search for the absolute is profoundly inappropriate for human affairs. Arendt was known to have said that "if there still were ultimates," "this whole totalitarian catastrophe would not have happened." However, she certainly did not think that the way to fight against totalitarianism is by inventing another set of ultimates.[70] Indeed, if there is any lesson to be drawn from the historical experiences of totalitarianism, it is that we must learn to live without ultimates. For ultimates clearly lend themselves to justification by rational rather than factual truth. This was what totalitarianism did in delivering the ultimate promise for the purity of a "superior" race or a "classless" society.

Moreover, on Arendt's reading, it is in the very nature of totalitarian government "to make functionaries and mere cogs in the administrative machinery out of men, and thus to dehumanize them." In fact, Eichmann did attempt to excuse himself "on the ground that he acted not as a man but as a mere functionary whose functions could just as easily have been carried out by anyone else." In this sense, Arendt is dealing with the very issue that Weber attempts to address—"the rule of Nobody, which is what the political form known as bureau-cracy truly is."[71] Politics reduced to bureaucracy is politics without the stamp of individual responsibility. Such a form of politics will only deny the significance of human plurality in the end.

In the light of Arendt's view that there are no ultimates and that politics is threatened by the "rule of Nobody," the question posed by the Eichmann Trial is this:

> What we have demanded in these trials . . . is that human beings be capable of telling right from wrong even when all they have to guide them is their own judgment, which, moreover, happens to be completely at odds with what they must regard as the unanimous opinion of all those around them. . . . [T]here were no rules to be abided by, under which the particular cases with which they were confronted could be subsumed. They had to decide each instance as it arose, because no rules existed for the unprecedented.[72]

It is this demand that prompts Arendt to investigate the relationship between the ability to think and its moral consequences. She asks if the activity of thinking per se, regardless of its "results and contents," is actually capable of conditioning men against evil.[73]

What is Thinking?

To answer the question, Arendt turns to the "historical Socrates" as "an example of a thinker who was not a professional" and was able to move comfortably between "experiences in the world of appearances and the need for reflecting on them."[74] Thinking is "the two-in-one," that is, a *"duality* of myself with myself that makes thinking a true activity, in which I am both the one who asks and the one who answers." Thinking achieves its "dialectical and critical" potentials by way of "this questioning and answering process . . . the dialogue of *dialegesthai*," which is "a 'travelling through words,' . . . whereby we constantly raise the basic Socratic question: *What do you mean when you say* . . . ?" Truth is not the criterion of this "mental dialogue." Rather, "the only criterion of Socratic thinking is agreement," which is to be "consistent with oneself."[75] Indeed, the very use of the word "truth" can be misleading. Certainly, in Arendt's hands, Socrates is not concerned with truth as in abstract truth. He is instead concerned with truthfulness to oneself.

Hence, for Socrates, "the important thing is to make *doxa* truthful, to see in every *doxa* truth and to speak in such a way that the truth of one's opinion reveals itself to oneself and to others." For a "thinking being" is one "whose thought is manifest in the manner of speech." This identity of speech and thought is *logos*. Socrates maintains that "there are, or should be, as many different *logoi* as there are men." It is all these *logoi* together that constitute the human world, "insofar as men live together in the manner of speech."[76]

The identity of speech and thought as *logos* was of course not new to the Greeks. What was distinctive of Socrates' contribution (and hence, the beginning of his trouble) was the demand for "the dialogue of myself with myself as the primary condition of thought." For "in thought I am two-in-one." Socrates maintains that it is through this internal dialogue and thereby reaching an agreement with oneself that one can be truthful to one's *doxa*. Hence, "even if I were to live entirely by myself I would, as long as I am alive, live in the condition of plurality . . . and nowhere does this I-with-myself show more clearly than in pure thought, always a dialogue between the two who I am." This internal dialogue can assume a critical role because if "in thought I am two-in-one," then I can contradict myself potentially. It is this possibility of contradiction that ensures consistency within oneself. "The faculty of speech and the fact of human plurality" therefore always correspond to each other because at the minimum, I have to talk to myself.[77]

The idea of an internal dialogue enables Arendt to establish the important point that the human condition of plurality, which is the precondition for "political thought," can never simply disappear even "when the chips are down."[78] It is of great significance that Arendt ends the book *The Human Condition* with these words of Cato: "'Never is he more active than when he does nothing, never is he less alone than when he is by himself.'"[79]

More precisely, what Arendt means is that when there is a truthful internal dialogue, "the two-in-one" can only be friends and live in harmony. For to contradict oneself is to become one's "own adversary." Should one become a murderer, the other will quite naturally shun one's company for the simple reason that no one wants to be in the company of a murderer. Arendt claims that Kant's "Categorical Imperative" really amounts to the dictum "'Do not contradict yourself.'" By way of the basic rule of noncontradiction, what Arendt is arguing is that thinking generates its own "moral side effect," which is conscience. The "interconnectedness between non-thought and evil" is thereby established. This is how thinking helps to liberate the faculty of judgment, as manifested in "the ability to tell right from wrong, beautiful from ugly."[80]

According to Arendt, then, thinking is a "non-cognitive, non-specialized" activity, which is an "ever-present faculty in everyone." While thinking is a "natural need of human life" and not a "prerogative of the few," anyone can "come to shun that intercourse with oneself." In other words, no one should assume that "scientists, scholars, and other specialists in mental enterprises" can always "think." Likewise, no one can be excused for not "thinking" on the ground that one lacks "brain power."[81] Arendt aptly concludes her thought on thinking with these words:

> Thinking accompanies life and is itself the de-materialized quintessence of being alive; and since life is a process, its quintessence can only lie in the actual thinking process and not in any solid results or specific thoughts. *A life without thinking . . . fails to develop its own essence*—it is not merely meaningless; it is not fully alive. Unthinking men are like sleepwalkers.[82]

It is clear why Arendt has to make the point that thinking, in its "non-cognitive, non-specialized sense," is ontological. To characterize thinking as such is probably her way of coming up with the lowest common denominator without sacrificing the critical role that thinking is supposed to play "when all the chips are down." This particular understanding of thinking enables Arendt to say that "we must be able to 'demand' its exercise in every sane person no matter how erudite or ignorant, how intelligent or stupid he may prove to be."[83]

IV

Storytelling and Politics

What then is "the subject of our thought?" Arendt's answer is brief—"experience."[84] And what is the result of this "non-cognitive" and "non-specialized" way of thinking? Storytelling. With these further specifications, Arendt is making it even harder for anyone to deny that one can think. In her words,

> Everyone who tells a story of what happened to him half an hour ago on the street has got to put this story into shape. And this putting the story into shape is a form of thought.[85]

What Arendt means here is that in telling a story, we must make sense of facts. Hence, "who says what is . . . always tells a story, and in this story the particular facts lose their contingency and acquire some humanly comprehensible meaning."[86]

Drawing from Kant's distinction between "reason" and "intellect" (which is more commonly translated as "understanding"), Arendt notes that the former corresponds to "thinking" and the latter with "knowing." "Thinking" is concerned with "meaning," while "knowing" is concerned with "cognition."[87] In writing about the life of Isak Dinesen, Arendt explains why storytelling is significant and consistent with "thinking" as opposed to "knowing." It is that storytelling "reveals meaning without committing the error of defining it" and that it "brings about consent and reconciliation with things as they really are . . . "[88] This suggests that storytelling has the advantage of enabling us to be firmly rooted in experiences while "thinking." Storytelling as such is not about the abstract, and it prevents us from getting "into all kinds of theories" that have no place in thinking.[89]

But can storytelling really hold up when the chips are all down? I think not. After all, storytelling is about communication; about the sharing of the world with others. Arendt has already convincingly made the point that totalitarianism presupposes the breakdown of community and in turn reinforces the breakdown. Hence, in my view, the whole argument about the ontological status of thinking is more to account for why Eichmann had no excuse for what he did. For in refusing to think, one is refusing to be part of humanity. In equating thinking with storytelling, Arendt's main concern is in how we can make individuals responsible for their "thoughtless crime."

I believe that in the end, Arendt knows as well that storytelling alone is not enough to set the boundary against power. The last section of the essay "Truth and Politics" is revealing in this regard. There, Arendt talks about the relationship between the "Academe" and the "political realm" with respect to the political functions of "professional thinkers." Not surprisingly, Arendt says that their function is precisely to stand guard over factual truth:

> The political function of the storyteller—historian or novelist—is to teach acceptance of things as they are. Out of this acceptance, which can be called truthfulness, arises the faculty of judgment. . . .[90]

Elsewhere, Arendt notes that "to say the truth—that is the only responsibility of the intellectuals, insofar as they are intellectuals. The moment they stray from this path they are citizens, they are in politics and defend their opinions."[91] As Riley aptly points out, "for Arendt the custodians of truth must be extra-political, outside the *polis*; the guardians of truth are no longer Platonic guardians who rule (personally). . . ."[92]

"Storytelling" for the purpose of enriching the domain of factual truth must be done with "objectivity," which requires "noncommitment," "impartiality," "freedom from self-interest in thought and judgment" on the part of the storyteller.[93] To meet these demands, the storyteller has to "remove" oneself, "draw back as it were, from the object" to be studied. In short, storytelling requires an adoption of a moderate Archimedean point of sorts.

Arendt notes that Thyucydides' judgment, "such as that 'this was the greatest movement yet known in history,' would [not] have been possible without such withdrawal."[94]

As in the case of ordinary citizens, it is in "dark times" when the skills of "professional" storytellers to judge will be most tested and challenged. Beiner argues convincingly that this demand prompted Arendt to reconsider her earlier thoughts on a judgment.[95] Like the political actor who makes a judgment, the storyteller, as spectator of events, must also make a judgment. However, while the political actor makes a judgment as member of a political community, the spectator has to make a judgment by withdrawing from the community. This is, as Beiner suggests, where Kant's theory of aesthetic judgment comes into play for Arendt. For judgment as such entails judging the particular as particular, without "trying to subsume it under some universal scheme of interpretation or pre-given set of categories." This opens for Arendt the possibility of being a "theorist as judging critic" without assuming any political labels.[96] It also makes Arendt one of the most powerful critics of totalitarianism precisely because she did not think in terms of universals. In Arendt's words, "comprehension . . . does not mean denying the outrageous, deducing the unprecedented from precedents, or explaining phenomena by such analogies and generalities that the impact of reality and the shock of experience are no longer felt. . . ."[97]

There is one more aspect of Kant's theory of aesthetic judgment which is relevant and that is that a judgment of taste "must rest, as it were, on an autonomy of the subject who is making a judgment."[98] Arendt notes that the "Academe" as a whole has an important role to play because "the chances for truth to prevail in public are . . . greatly improved by the mere existence of such places. . . . " Arendt no doubt has the issue of autonomy in mind when she pleads for the support of the "political realm" in ensuring the independence of "places of higher learning." For unless the political realm recognizes that "it has a stake in the existence of men and institutions over which it has no power" even in times of conflict, these "men and institutions" certainly cannot guarantee their own existence.[99] As Arendt puts it, "the chances of factual truth surviving the onslaught of power are very slim indeed; it is always in danger of being maneuvered out of the world not only for a time but, potentially, forever."[100] The important point here is that in

Arendt's view, "at least in constitutionally ruled countries," the significance of having a nonpolitical realm to tell things as they are is being recognized by the political realm.[101] It seems to me this recognition has to be one major reason for her insistence that it is "the *fact* that liberals are not totalitarians."[102]

Arendt's remarks on the need to maintain a strict division of the respective domains of activities between the "Academe" and the "political realm" could indeed have come from Weber. Arendt undoubtedly believes that there are such things as "facts" to which we can attach some meaning by recounting them as stories. It is also equally clear that for these stories to be re-told with meaning, "facts" require protection from the onslaught of power precisely because of their vulnerability. By pointing out that "constitutionally ruled countries" recognize the need to protect truth from power, Arendt is able to provide us with some principled grounds to fight against totalitarianism. This political stance is something that is lacking in both Weber and Foucault.

Arendt's analysis of totalitarianism indicates that truth in its philosophical form is destructive of politics, and truth in its experiential (historical) form is vulnerable to power. This is a very important insight. It tells us that in the end, truth, in all forms, has political implications. Yet it also tells us why truth and power must be kept apart from each other. Nietzsche may say to Arendt that to think that truth is "what we cannot change" is a myth. It may be a myth, Arendt will probably answer, but it is a myth that we must hold on to. For we need a nonpolitical domain for "political" truth, if not for anything else.

Part III

CONCLUSION

CHAPTER SEVEN

The Politics of Truth in Context: The Case of China

IN EXPLAINING THE GENEALOGICAL APPROACH TO TRUTH as a "regime of truth," Foucault notes that truth is always "linked in a circular relation with systems of power which produce and sustain it, and to effects of power which it induces and which extend it." Along with this definition, stated in 1977, Foucault made a further claim—one can find the same regime in operation in both liberal and Leninist-socialist states, with perhaps one exception. As Foucault put it then, "I leave open here the question of China, about which I know little."[1]

As we shall see, the case of China does provide a significant qualification to Foucault's observation. The course of political development in China in the last thirty years poses important questions about the relationship between truth and politics. Granted that it would be naive not to recognize the importance of power struggle between individuals in the history of communist China, there are, however, some genuine political issues at stake when abstract ideas, in the name of truth, are imposed on experiential reality. In particular, the Cultural Revolution from 1966 to 1976 is relevant to my concern here in that it demonstrated the essential features that Arendt sees in totalitarianism. The starting premise of the Revolution, which the Chinese Communist Party now refers to as "ten bad years," was based on the conviction that history matters because the wrong class background leads one to have incorrect thoughts. However, the real theoretical breakthrough of the Revolution lies in its claim that a structurally classless society still requires a revolution of thought through the affirmation of proletarian consciousness. This is how the importance of history is paradoxically affirmed at the level of oppression but denied at the level of change. Indeed, had Mao taken history seriously, China might not even have had a Marxist-Leninist political agenda to begin with. With this denial of "historical constraints," the possibility of change became limitless, and hence the justification for the extremity of actions in the name of "thought reform."

The Cultural Revolution confirms Arendt's view on totalitarian movement in two important ways. First, the theoretical premise of the Cultural Revolution illustrates most clearly the totalitarian defiance of limits by way of a self-contained system of thought. Second, Arendt's point on the appeal of "ideological thinking" to isolated and atomized individuals can be usefully engaged to account for the scale of the movement and its most violent phase, which lasted from 1966 to 1969. The work of Lynn White shows insightfully that on the eve of the Cultural Revolution, Chinese society was basically a fragmented society, one in which people felt that they had not been treated fairly. More specifically, the use of class labels as an administrative device to allocate limited social and economic resources was a major cause of discontent.[2] When one reads the numerous biographical and autobiographical accounts of victims of the Cultural Revolution, the theme of ostracism, apart from the physical and mental torture, is predominant.[3] It was a time when children would testify against their own parents and spouses against one another in the name of class struggle. This was certainly a definitive indicator of the complete breakdown of the society, for the family is the most sacred social bond in the eyes of many Chinese people.[4]

What captures my attention is not simply the fact that the Cultural Revolution demonstrated Arendt's argument. It is rather the similarity between the post-Mao analysis of extreme leftism during the Cultural Revolution and Arendt's reading of totalitarianism which strikes me as even more pertinent to the problematic that this book sets out to explore. I have in mind the epistemological debate that occurred among China's political elites and intellectual circles in the late 1970s.

I

Ideology in Post-Mao China

The debate, which was about the nature of truth and its relation to politics, had to do with the broader need to reinterpret Marxism-Leninism-Mao Zedong Thought. This need emerged with the closing of what is now being regarded as the "leftist" era, that is, the period of the Cultural Revolution. Its end was first marked by the arrest of the Gang of Four in 1976, followed by the eventual defeat of the "Whatever" faction under the leadership of Mao's designated heir, Huo Guofeng. The "Whatever" faction, while denouncing the Gang of Four, was basically going to simply follow Mao's way. In fact, the faction got its label because of its slogan, which was, "whatever policies Chairman Mao devised we will resolutely support, and whatever directives Chairman Mao laid down we will forever observe." The defeat of the "Whateverists" was formally marked by the Third Plenum of the 11th Party Central Committee in December 1978, which ushered in the reform era of Deng Xiaoping.

Among the signs of change in the early years of Deng's rule, Deng's famous "cat" analogy was taken to mark the beginning of the age of "pragmatism" in China. As such, pragmatism means "liberation for the Chinese people from the heavy hand of doctrinal politics," which was characteristic of the Mao era.[5] Yet it would be mistaken, as Lucian Pye pointed out in 1985, to assume that a "pragmatic" China would be "less ideological and more practical," and thereby let "economic rationality" instead of political concerns be its guide.[6] Rather ironically, ideology has in some sense become more relevant than ever before because unlike the Mao era, theoretical formulations in post-Mao China actually "bear a significant relation" to the real problems that China is faced with.[7]

Indeed, when one looks at the works devoted to Marxism-Leninism-Mao Zedong Thought in post-Mao China, one is hard pressed to dismiss the continuing relevance of ideology in China.[8] In the period immediately following the death of Mao, the attempt to reinterpret Marxism-Leninism-Mao Zedong Thought had to serve two obvious political purposes. One was to explain why "leftism" is un-Marxist. The other was to provide an ideological guide to future socialist construction, this time in a truly "Marxist" manner. As we shall see, among the most politically significant set of discussions were those concerning the nature of Marxism-Leninism-Mao Zedong Thought as a theory, which revolved around the theme of truth. In the sections that follow, I will be comparing three views on how Marxism-Leninism-Mao Zedong Thought ought to be reinterpreted in this regard.[9] The time period covered is the first five years of the Deng era. I choose 1983 as the cutoff point not just because it was the centennial commemoration of Marx's death, which was a major occasion in China's intellectual circle, but more importantly, because 1983 was the year of the "anti-spiritual pollution" campaign, the year "when intellectuals went mute" for the first time since the Cultural Revolution.[10] We shall first look at the official view as explicated by Deng. The other two views are from the first two directors of the Institute of Marxism-Leninism-Mao Zedong Thought—Yu Guangyuan and Su Shaozhi. The Institute was founded in 1979 under the Chinese Academy of Social Sciences. Its mandate was "to study Marxism-Leninism-Mao Zedong Thought under the new situation in order to guide practice and provide reform with a theoretical basis."[11] As such, the Institute was an unofficial think tank for post-Mao China. Yet under progressive Marxists such as Yu and especially Su, the Institute was constantly putting forth ideas that advocated a more open and pluralistic China.

"Practice as the Sole Criterion for Testing Truth"

Deng's pragmatism was first captured in the phrase "practice is the sole criterion for testing truth," which was the title of a newspaper article published in *Guangming ribao* on 11 May 1978. The author was noted as "our paper's special commentator(s)." Sinologists had assumed throughout the 1980s that the author was Hu Fuming, a philosopher at the University of Nanjing, who did submit an article with a similar title to *Guangming ribao*.[12] But the more recent work of Michael Schoenhals has convincingly established that the published article was the work of Hu Yaobang, then the vice president of the Central Committee's Party School, and his "ghost writers," rather than of Hu Fuming.[13] Despite the fact that everything that made it into print had official sanction, it is significant to establish the authorship of the article. For the article represents a definitive turn toward the most thorough critique of ultra-leftism that China had ever seen.[14] It is therefore important to note how the article analyzes the nature of leftism.

The theme of the article is stated very clearly in the introduction. The article begins by pointing out that although the criterion for testing truth has long been settled by the "mentors of proletarian revolution," over the years the Gang of Four managed to confuse in everyone's mind what the criterion is. It is therefore "absolutely necessary" to correct the Gang's view on the matter. This is how the most in-depth critique of the Gang can be conducted and its pernicious influence countered. According to the author(s), from an epistemological standpoint, the Gang of Four had made two mistakes; both of which were un-Marxist and anti-Maoist. One was their "idealistic theory of apriorism," which rejected practice as the criterion for testing truth. The other mistake was the postulation of "unalterable truth." On this basis, the Gang had set up a number of "forbidden zones" that restricted the thinking of people. But any doctrine that claims to supercede practice and poses itself to be the absolute is a rejection of "science" and Marxism-Leninism-Mao Zedong Thought. Only "idealism" and "cultural dictatorship" endorse such "forbidden zones." Besides the criticism against the Gang of Four, there is of course a positive component in the article. The central claim here is that "practice" is the most basic and important starting point of epistemology. Thus, "practice" is the only criterion for testing the truth of theory, as well as being *the* source of theory. This is why the "revolutionary mentors" insist that "practice" is *the* "dialectical materialist standpoint." The article ends with a call for a "freer" country, for to "practice" is to recognize that one is living in an ever-changing world. No doctrine is guaranteed to be true at all times.[15]

Deng on "Seeking Truth from Facts"

Following the publication of the article, in a talk given at the All-Army Conference on Political Work, Deng Xiaoping discussed at length the theme of "seeking truth from facts" (*shishi qiushi*). While Deng refrained from the phrase "practice as the sole criterion for testing truth," it was clear that Deng endorsed the

Guangming ribao article. In the speech, Deng pointed out that to "seek truth from facts" is the most fundamental principle of Marxism-Leninism- Mao Zedong Thought. To grasp this is to be able to "analyze and study actual conditions and solve practical problems." Deng maintained that the "concrete analysis of concrete conditions" is the "living soul of Marxism." Unless the principle of "seeking truth from facts" is adhered to firmly, the Party will fall into the traps of "idealism" and "metaphysics." As such, to "seek truth from facts" is the most effective way to counteract the "pernicious influence" of Lin Biao and the Gang of Four.[16]

At the Third Plenary Session held later that year (1978), Deng stated that "the current debate about whether practice is the sole criterion for testing truth is also a debate about whether people's minds need to be emancipated." The "emancipation of the mind" is a doctrine that encourages people to "think, explore new ways and generate new ideas."[17] Deng also made it very clear that the debate was *not* simply over epistemological issues. Rather, "the debate about the criterion for testing truth is really a debate about ideological line, about politics."[18] The "practice" doctrine was from then on identified as the "ideological line" of Deng and his supporters, who were anxious to distinguish themselves from what Lin Biao and the Gang of Four stood for ideologically.

There is of course nothing new in Deng's characterization of his struggle against the Gang of Four as a struggle over the "correct" ideological line. However, what is distinctive about Deng's statement is that after asserting the importance of *how* Marxism-Leninism-Mao Zedong Thought should be interpreted, he did not extend the analysis beyond the ideological level. To put this in Marxist terms, there is no attempt to trace a problem that exists at the superstructural level to the base. This makes Deng's analysis quite different from Mao's analysis of revisionism in a socialist state, which establishes a causal link between revisionism and the rise of a "privileged stratum" in socialist society.[19] The contrast was a signal to the Chinese people that while the struggle between Deng and the Gang of Four was an ideological struggle, it was not a class struggle.[20] Although this reflects Deng's longstanding view that ideological differences among Party members should be treated only as an internal Party matter, such an analysis still retains the stake involved in what constitutes a correct understanding of the theoretical nature of Marxism-Leninism-Mao Zedong Thought.

In the speech, Deng also noted that "democracy" is an essential condition for emancipating the mind. Here, Deng claimed that a "revolutionary party" should not be afraid of the "voice of the people." But he also added that in the end it is the Party which can tell the "correct" opinions from the "incorrect."[21] Indeed, soon after the Third Plenum, Deng stipulated another "criterion for judging what is right and what is wrong about a political line to supplement that of practice."[22] This other criterion is the "four cardinal principles," which are the socialist system, the dictatorship of the proletariat, Party leadership, and Marxism-Leninism-Mao Zedong Thought. In 1980, when economic reforms had already been well underway, the doctrine of "emancipation of the mind" was further elaborated by Deng as follows:

> Guided by Marxism, we should break the fetters of habit, subjectivism and prejudice, and study new situations and solve new problems. In emancipating our minds, we should never deviate from the four cardinal principles or impair the political situation marked by stability, unity and liveliness.[23]

Two important points are established in this passage. One is that the constructive role of theory, in the age of reforms, is to "study" concrete problems raised by the task of modernization. The second point is that in studying these problems, one should not "deviate from the four cardinal principles." In fact, Deng went so far as to say that emancipation of the mind means "making our thinking conform to reality—making the subjective conform to the objective—and that means seeking truth from facts."[24] This definition obviously raises "objectivity" to a superior position, which is another way of saying that "practice" is the sole criterion for judgment. The trouble is, of course, that "practice" happens to be the Party's current ideological line. And, according to the "four cardinal principles," the line of "practice" is not something to be questioned.

Yu Guangyuan on the Nature of "Scientific" Marxist Analysis

We now turn to the writings of Yu Guangyuan, who is an important figure of the Chinese Academy of Social Sciences and served as the first director of the Institute of Marxism-Leninism-Mao Zedong Thought. In June 1978, at a conference, Yu expressed his view on the practice debate by way of a commentary on a new book—*Shehuizhuyi gongyouzhi yu an lao fenpei* (Public ownership and distribution according to work in socialism). As Yu pointed out, the very subject matter of the book itself challenges a major political view of the Gang of Four, which is that the principle of "distribution accoring to work" is by definition a bourgeois right and therefore antisocialist. Yu maintained that the Gang's claim is basically "theoretically unsound." This is due not so much to its misinterpretation of Marxist theory on the subject per se, but rather to the fact that the theory lacked empirical research. It is in this sense that the Gang's view on "distribution according to work" fails to take "practice" into account and hence, is incorrect and un-Marxist.[25]

In the following year, at the Nationwide Conference on the Scope of Research on Marxism-Leninism-Mao Zedong Thought, Yu noted that the most pressing task facing theoretical workers is to study the major "theoretical" and "concrete" problems by proceeding from reality, and to provide "scientific" responses to these questions. To do so, one must grasp the principle that in science there are no "forbidden zones." Equipped with a "scientific attitude," Marxist theorists must stand in the front-line of the "emancipation of the mind." "Emancipation of the mind" and promotion of democracy are what move Marxism forward; whereas dogmatism and ossified thought are what stifle Marxism.[26]

In 1983, on the Marx Centenury, Yu claimed that the most distinctive characteristic of Marxism is that it is never a "closed system." The agenda for theoretical work on Marxism, in Yu's view, is to "develop Marxism as the science of building socialism." "Marxism as the science of building socialism" is juxtaposed to "Marxism as the science of socialist revolution." The essential distinction between the two is that "Marxism as the science of socialist revolution" is marked by the negative characteristic of destruction, whereas "Marxism as the science of socialist construction" is marked by positive work. This distinction implies, for Yu, that the latter requires more "general scientific knowledge," which may not necessarily belong to the "domain of Marxism." But this by no means lessens the importance of Marxism in socialist construction.[27]

Yu proceeded to lay out in very general terms the subject matter of the project as well as its methodology. Accordingly, the subject matter should include the discovery of the "objective laws" that govern historical development and the exploration of ways to build socialism. The method for developing "Marxism as the science of building socialism" is by studying "concrete practical experiences" within a "scientific" Marxist framework rather than to engage in "empty talks."[28]

To sum up, the task of theory, in the age of reforms, is to apprehend, rather than to criticize "practice." As stated so succinctly by Yu himself, the task of developing "Marxism as the science of building socialism" requires one to "stand higher and examine historical experiences that are of a longer range and a more extensive scope, make further scientific abstraction of them and then systematize and express the conclusions in a strictly logical sequence."[29] Given what Deng had said about the role of theory, Yu's delineation of its nature was one that Deng would endorse. However, Yu did, on a number of occasions, point out that the "emancipation of the mind" and democracy must go together. Perhaps most interesting of all was Yu's claim that to be a "genuine Marxist" is to be able to "emancipate one's mind," "use one's head," and "seek truth from facts." There is therefore nothing mysterious in becoming a Marxist and a Marxist standpoint can be readily acquired by a "large number of people."[30] This can be read as a defense for democracy in that to "democratize" Marxism is obviously to challenge the Party's monopoly on truth. Yet Yu in the end failed to provide a case for a truly "critical" role for theory, one that will call into question the legitimacy of a political party that refuses to share power with its people.

Su Shaozhi and the Development of Marxism in a Reforming China

In 1982, Su Shaozhi was elected by the members of the Institute to become its second director, after Yu's retirement.[31] By then, Su had already established himself as one of the most innovative

Marxist theorists in China, known for his controversial theory of "undeveloped socialism."[32] It is thus important to compare Su's view on the nature of Marxism-Leninism-Mao Zedong Thought with that of Deng and Yu.

In response to the epistemology debate, Su published an article in 1978. He began by providing a definition of "seeking truth from practice."[33] The act of "seeking truth" (*qiushi*) must be preceded by "practice" (*shishi*), which means that one must be able to deal with reality "as it is," including one's achievements as well as weaknesses. It is important to cultivate such an attitude because socialist construction is by definition an experimental endeavor and errors are inevitable. The argument is clearly formulated to criticize the inability of the Gang of Four to deal with any kind of criticism, since they characteristically labelled all criticisms as "rightist opportunistic," "antiparty" and "antisocialist" activities.[34]

Positively, "seeking truth from practice" means developing democracy and following the "mass line." The masses should be able to speak out because they are in constant contact with "reality" and should also be given access to information about their own country. For it is only with the involvement of the masses that the modernization process can proceed.[35] Hence, people should be encouraged to explore the "forbidden zones" in the realm of ideas formerly stipulated by the Gang of Four. By directly linking the "emancipation of the mind" with more power to the people, Su had definitely gone further than Deng and even Yu in drawing a direct connection between openmindedness and democratic practice. However, this plea for democracy was somewhat limited because it was again premised on the Party's agenda for modernization—an agenda that is officially defined by "practice" and guided by the "four cardinal principles."

In an important article published in 1983, Su dealt with the issue of how Marxism could be made relevant to the contemporary world on a global scale. But Su also addressed specifically the way Chinese Marxists could deal with the problem. He pointed out that the Party's program of "building socialism with Chinese characteristics" represents "a creative development of Mao Zedong Thought." This program points to the fact that there is neither a *"standardized"* nor an *"immutable"* model for building socialism in individual countries. Consequently, the task for the Chinese theoretical workers is to find the best way to combine the "basic system of socialism" (that is, its "general features" and "principles") with "specific conditions" (that is, the "particular features" of China and its "given reality"). Su noted that because of the various "creative undertakings" by the Party, especially the responsibility system in agriculture, there is much for the theoretical workers to work on. In fact, Su went so far as to say that China's theoretical work is *lagging behind* the "vigorous development of practical life" in a "fairly large measure." He warned that if theorists remain solely concerned with "abstract" issues divorced from reality, then Marxism will once again provide a "sanctuary and hotbed" for leftist ideology and "offer an ideological ground" for it to censure current reforms.[36]

Su's view points to the significance of having a "correct" theoretical grasp of Marxism, as this was interpreted the most effective way to counter a relapse into the leftist era. More importantly, while the role of Marxism here is a "critical" one (that is, to provide a counterforce to leftism), Su did not intend to use this conception of the role of theory to justify reforms. Indeed, at the concluding section of the article, Su maintained that "*the necessity of reform*" is "*determined by the very character of socialism,*" since socialist construction is essentially an experimental endeavor.[37] Hence, for Su, the source for reform is not so much a "critical" consideration as a "practical" one, that is, the demand of "practice." On this, Su's view echoes Deng's.[38]

II

The "Sovereign Definer" Reconsidered

The basic agreement among Deng, Yu and Su on the nature of "metatheory" in this early phase of the post-Mao era indicated a general agreement on the importance of understanding the nature of theory as the only effective way to combat leftism. It is important to note why the Party under Deng would want to emphasize the point that the "mistakes" of the Gang of Four were a result of their "idealism." Clearly, it was to the advantage of the reformists to contain leftism within "epistemology." For this gave the reformists an opportunity to come up with a "correct" Marxist epistemological standpoint without necessarily threatening the society with another class struggle, which the Chinese could ill afford at the time.

However, what needs to be emphasized is that it was not simply a matter of political expediency for Hu Yaobang and his "ghost writers" to decide to start a debate on epistemology in 1978. The Chinese Communist Party is very conscious of the importance of retaining its role as the "sovereign definer." As Hu noted in 1982, one of the most distinguishing achievements of the Party was its outstanding record in "ideological work." On this ground, Hu urged his fellow Party members that the great tradition had to be maintained by ensuring that the masses grasp the principle of "practice" as the only valid perspective and standpoint.[39] Hu's statement was significant for gauging the outermost perimeter of diversity that the Party would tolerate. For Hu was generally considered to be the most sympathetic among the key Party leaders to democratic reforms in the 1980s and it was in commemoration of his sudden death that the demonstration at Tiananmen Square in 1989 first started.

As for the theorists, one should not simply dismiss them as the mouthpieces of the Party for the same reason that one ought not disregard ideology in post-Mao China as mere propaganda. Moreover, Su, for example, is undoubtedly a committed Marxist who believes that socialism is a worthwhile political goal and that it can be achieved through democratic means.[40] On the basis of the preceding analysis, it should be clear that the reform-minded Marxists took seriously the issue of epistemological standpoint. To them, idealism inevitably leads to extremism in politics and as such, leftism is a misappropriation of Marxism. The dialectical materialist standpoint that these Marxists espoused during the period examined was one that valorized experience by way of a contextualist approach to truth. One can argue with these Marxists whether their understanding of dialectical materialism is correct. But the fact remains that there was an assumed connection between contextualism and democratic practices.

This brief analysis of the ideological developments in China in the period immediately following the leftist era demonstrates that a certain conception of truth can be politically construed in order to achieve the seemingly contradictory goals of maintaining political stability while implementing fundamental structural changes. Such an analysis shows that there is nothing intrinsically democratic in a political practice that recognizes that truth ought to be rooted in the reality of experience. Certainly, Deng's definition of the "emancipation of the mind" has nothing to do with democracy.[41] The Tiananmen Incident of 1989 is a clear indication of how determined that regime is in holding on to its power. The fate of reform-minded Marxist intellectuals in China further indicates that a responsive theory to "practice" is certainly no way to fight the Party. Like many reform-minded intellectuals and activists, Su Shaozhi has been living in exile in the United States since the Tiananmen Incident of 1989. It is significant that Su, in 1993, acknowledged that intellectuals like himself had made mistakes. What was lacking, in Su's words, was "the *requisite independence of thought* to challenge wrong decisions by the Party leadership."[42]

Hence, I see the Chinese case as at once an affirmation of Arendt's insightfulness about the nature of totalitarianism and a revelation of the precariousness of the idea that a concept of truth that is validated on the basis of experience can act as a restraint to power. This precariousness, rather than undercutting the insightfulness of Arendt, shows that she is right in insisting on the distinctiveness of the totalitarian phenomenon and the fundamental role of the state in the inducement of a "fictional discourse," especially at the critical juncture of foundational political act.[43]

CHAPTER EIGHT

Politics, Truth, and Democratic Practice

THIS BOOK POINTS TO THE CENTRALITY of truth in twentieth-century politics. While we are now living in the post-Cold War era, truth and its relation to politics remains a continuing preoccupation for those who want to come up with a nonliberal, non-Marxist political alternative. Of the thinkers considered in this work, it is understandable why Foucault in particular is of interest to the politically committed postmodernists. After all, Foucault helped define what postmodernism is through his intellectual enagagement. As we have seen, Foucault's contribution is not just in providing postmodernism with its critical niche, but also in enriching our understanding of the self as a historical self through his meticulous genealogical works.

What is more perplexing is that there is a certain trend in recent scholarship to interpret Arendt as an early proponent of postmodernist politics, most notably in the works of Bonnie Honig.[1] Honig takes Arendt's theory of political action as providing the basis of agonistic politics. On this reading, the performative aspect of political action is emphasized at the expense of the deliberative aspect. Individuation is formed in each speech act rather than prior to it. In Honig's words,

> Her [Arendt's] connection of political action to the performative production of identities rather than to their constative representation opens up possibilities of political proliferation, reclaiming the practice of politics from representative, *state-centered, and state-centering* institutions

and treating that reclamation . . . as part of a practice of political authority that calls for the perpetual augmentation and amendment of the constitution and practice of politics.[2]

The first obvious reason for Arendt's tremendous appeal to political theorists in the 1990s is that she defies standard ideological labels. As Arendt once put it, "I am neither a liberal nor a positivist nor a pragmatist."[3] In this sense it is rather logical that Arendt becomes the rallying point for those looking for a political alternative in the post–Cold War era.[4] But what is contestable is whether her insight into the antipolitical nature of philosophical truth and her view that we need to think "without a bannister"[5] make her sufficiently postmodernist, at least for the purposes of those who read Arendt as such.

To answer the question, let us reconsider what is at stake for the postmodernist political platform. One conclusion to emerge from my examination of Plato and Hobbes is that an idea of truth lies at the heart of the antidemocratic stance of both thinkers. Whether it be Plato's essentialism or Hobbes's nominalism, truth is by definition beyond the reach of politics and so should be when political power is properly construed. In this regard, Lyotard notes appropriately that since Plato, "the question of the legitimacy of science has been indissociably linked to that of the legitimation of the legislator."[6] It is therefore by no means accidental that the latest attempt at reconceptualizing politics—radical postmodernism—begins as a revolt in philosophy. Ironically, in championing an antifoundationalist notion of truth as the basis for a new politics, postmodernists have not dissolved the intimate link between truth and politics, a link that is at least as old as Plato. If anything, there seems to be a sense that philosophical truth, when properly construed, is now more relevant than ever to politics. Thus, in reassuring us of the feasibility of "agonistic democracy," Connolly notes that "the experience of democracy and the experience of contingency in identity can sustain each other, *especially when the first is supported by an intellectual culture of genealogy.*"[7] Here, Connolly, following Nietzsche and Foucault, sees genealogy as the quintessential philosophical project in dismantling the Western metaphysical baggage.

I surmise that Arendt would have been very skeptical of postmodernist antifoundationalism as the basis for democracy in late modernity. For such a move is not based on the claim that truth is irrelevant to politics. Rather, postmodernism still betrays a basic assumption that underlies the tradition of Western political thought, which is that philosophical truth is the proper guide to politics. In sum, the radical nature of the postmodernist political platform can be assessed by way of two questions: 1) Is a contextualist notion of truth necessarily more conducive to the practice of democracy than a foundationalist notion of truth? (By democratic practice, I mean one that emphasizes the role of individuals as participants as opposed to that of institutions which follow democratic procedures.) 2) What is the ontological assumption behind the postmodernist conviction that displacing the state as the centerpiece in politics is the key to revitalizing democratic practices in the late twentieth century?

On the basis of the preceding discussion in this book, it is clear that a contextualist notion of truth is not necessarily more conducive to democratic practice, especially if such a notion serves as a legitimation discourse. The rationale behind the postmodernist linkage between antifoundationalism and democratic practice strikes me as precisely one such instance. The claim of antifoundationalism is that as an epistemological paradigm, it is in fact more "truthful," if not "truer," than foundationalism because antifoundationalism is free from the illusory metaphysical trappings of traditional philosophy. This new-found philosophical freedom restores human agency in individuals and thereby heightens the efficacy of individuals as political actors. Thus understood, one has to wonder if postmodernism is but a logical sequence to the modern notion of truth, which undoubtedly enhances the role of human agency in the validation of knowledge. In Allen's words, "placing emphasis on the subjective or transcendental constitution of truth encourages the assumption that it is not Nature but subjectivity or the will which makes truth true."[8] As argued earlier, once the modern notion of truth is in place, the way is open for Nietzsche's critique of Truth. And one outcome of Nietzsche's nihilistic defiance is indeed a form of radical individualism in which the self is answerable only to itself.[9] We see versions of this individualism in both Weber and Foucault. In the case of Weber, I describe his position as one of engaged individualism. As for Foucault, much is conveyed by the fact that he increasingly saw philosophy as "an exercise of oneself in the activity of thought."

No one knows how an "agonistic democracy" as the theorists conceive it will play out. But we do have some sense of the kind of politics conducted in the spirit of antifoundationalism and nonessentialism. What I have in mind is identity politics, which, as Elshtain sees it, is a symptom of our "faltering democracy." What is most disturbing is the fact that identity politics has dominated the politics of marginalized groups in multiethnic and multicultural countries like Canada and the United States. Identity politics, as defined by Judy Rebick, a prominent Canadian feminist political activist, is not about "identifying with a group that faces discrimination" because "it is a reality of life." Rather, "identity politics is born when that identity becomes the basis for political thinking, sometimes the *sole basis for politics*."[10] Identity politics therefore tends to be devoted to a single cause that is supported by a monocausal account of one's marginalization.[11]

The inevitable lopsided approach of identity politics is uncompromising and this is why it is divisive. Identity politics means that more and more individuals are asked to take sides on political issues on the basis of which one of a person's many identities is at stake. Thus, political issues are often treated as if they are not only mutually exclusive but fundamentally incompatible. Recently I sat on the Human Rights Art Commissioning Committee at my institution. Its mandate is to see to the production of an art work, preferably a mural, on human rights, which will be on permanent public display on campus. A black male, who served as a student representative, lobbied for an antiracism mural as opposed to a human rights mural. The argument put forth by this activist proceeded as though the two issues could be separated and a positive portrayal of human rights would only have undercut the didactic purpose an antiracism mural is supposed to convey.[12]

But presumably not everything is at stake in taking sides because no one identity should exhaust a person. As Seyla Benhabib notes, "the Clarence Thomas and Anita Hill confrontation was a paradigmatic episode which hightlighted the fungibility of identity categories: which are you—a black professional feminist or a black sister?"[13] The idea that an individual is the potential site of multiple identities brings us to the epistemological premise underlying identity politics—the "standpoint" perspective.

The standpoint perspective originated as a feminist epistemology. This epistemological stance is antifoundationalist in that it challenges the principle of universality as necessarily exclusionary (that is, gender blind) and therefore contradictory. From the standpoint perspective, foundationalism valorizes abstract reasoning rather than concrete experience. Moreover, abstract reasoning privileges the intellectuals, which in the Western world means white males. Nancy Hartsock, who pioneered the adoption of standpoint epistemology in North American feminism, recently restated standpoint epistemology as follows:

> We need a theory of power that recognizes our practical daily activity contains an understanding of the world. . . . Here I am reaffirming Gramsci's argument that everyone is an intellectual and that each of us has an epistemology.[14]

In order to counter the inevitable bias of foundationalism, one must turn to experience as basis for evidence. In Joan Scott's words, "what could be truer, after all, than a subject's own account of what he or she has lived through?"[15] However, as Scott also notes, there is nothing inherently "transparent" about experience. Instead of being "the origin of our explanation," experience should rather be "that which we seek to explain, that about which knowledge is produced."[16] Certainly, Arendt, Foucault, and Weber would agree that much is at stake in how our experiences are recounted and interpreted.

One can of course argue that standpoint epistemology fails to be consistently antifoundationalist because it falls into the trap of making experience the basis of an essentialist self, as if there is a stable subject that underlies all experiences. This is precisely where Hartsock and Foucault part company for she believes that there is such an entity as the oppressed subject.[17] In contrast, "agonistic democracy" will take to heart Foucault's claim that "nothing in man—not even his body—is sufficiently stable to serve as the basis for self-recognition or for understanding other men."[18] To take an antifoundationalist stance is to embrace contingency unreservedly. But, as Paul Veyne notes, "Foucault's originality among the great thinkers of our century lay in his refusal to convert our finitude into the basis for new certainties."[19] One wonders if "agonistic democracy" is not settling for contingency as *the* basis of our "post-Nietzschean identity" when Connolly claims in his more recent work that "the risky, disruptive politics of enactment is . . . *indispensable* to identification."[20]

Does truth justify power? The extremities of all the wars and political conflicts fought in the name of truth should serve as a reminder that truth certainly does imply power but power may not be the best way to serve truth. Plato was the first in the Western philosophical tradition to make the claim that politics ought to serve truth. This truth is by definition abstract. Individuals are subject to the rule of reason via the philosopher because the rule of reason is superior to that of the spirit or of the appetite. Hobbes, motivated more by fear than by some transcendent truth, ironically elevates politics to an even higher level of abstraction. For Hobbes's nominalism points to the need for merging the sovereign with the "sovereign definer" so that politics can validate itself by way of a self-contained train of thought.

Through the study of Weber, Foucault, and Arendt, we see a reverse of this trend, in the return of subjectivity in politics. Weber wants to secure a place for the spirit in the iron cage. Foucault challenges institutional power by locating the human body as the actual repository of otherwise impersonal forces. Arendt reminds us that the world is constituted of people *living*, rather than contemplating, together. It is for these different reasons that politics for each of the three thinkers is, in some fundamental sense, beyond the scope of philosophy. However, as I have argued, none of them, not even Foucault, can therefore be construed as endorsing a kind of politics that would turn politics into a self-indulgent and perhaps even mindless activity. It is on this basis that all three argue that politics and truth must know their respective places vis-à-vis each other. But among Weber, Foucault, and Arendt, Arendt is the only thinker who can give us some principled grounds to ensure that the sovereign and the "sovereign definer" cannot be identical. Arendt pleads for the sake of the human condition of plurality; this to me is fundamentally an essentialist postulation.

Notes

Chapter One

1. Hans J. Morgenthau, *Politics Among Nations: The Struggle for Power and Peace*, 5th ed. rev. (New York: Alfred A. Knopf, 1978), 246; emphasis added.

2. Jean-François Lyotard, *The Postmodern Condition: A Report on Knowledge*, trans. Geoff Bennington and Brian Massumi (Minneapolis: University of Minnesota Press, 1984), xxiii–xxiv.

3. Carl von Clausewitz, *On War*, ed. and trans. Michael Howard and Peter Paret (Princeton: Princeton University Press, 1976), 87.

4. For example, Fang Lizhi, a well-known Chinese astrophysicist and dissident currently living in exile, had written extensively during those years on the subject of intellectual freedom. For a sample of Fang's writing, see "A Hat, A Forbidden Zone, A Question," in *Bringing Down the Great Wall: Writings on Science, Culture, and Democracy in China* (New York: W. W. Norton, 1992), 56–59.

5. In Václav Havel, *Living in Truth*, ed. Jan Vladislav (London: Faber and Faber, 1987), 39.

6. Havel, *Living in Truth*, 55 and 65; emphasis in original.

7. While it is true that it was the collapse of the socialist camp that brought an end to the Cold War, it is also reasonable for us to entertain the alternative. This means that even if the socialist camp had managed to hold out longer, it was unclear that the liberal democracy of the West could have sustained the ideological self-rightousness essential to the

continued confrontation. This scenario would of course have meant a less dramatic end to the Cold War. See Jean Bethke Elshtain, *Democracy On Trial*, 1993 Massey Lectures (Concord, Ontario: Anansi Press, 1993), for a succinct analysis of the "faltering" democracy of the West. The politicization of knowledge as discussed in the text above can certainly be considered as a symptom of this "faltering" democracy.

8. Among those who were instrumental in propagating this view during the highly volatile years of the late 1980s and early 1990s was Francis Fukuyama. See Fukuyama, "The End of History?" *The National Interest* 16 (summer 1989): 3–18; followed by a book-length study, *The End of History and the Last Man* (New York: Free Press, 1992). For a powerful critique of the work, see Alan Ryan, "Professor Hegel Goes to Washington," *The New York Review of Books* 39 (26 March 1992): 7–13. As Ryan notes, "Fukuyama doesn't just argue that liberal democracy is the only political option now open; he argues that liberal democracy is the meaning of history" (8).

9. This is precisely how Fukuyama presents his project. See *The End of History*, xxiii.

10. Richard Rorty, *Philosophy and the Mirror of Nature* (Princeton: Princeton University Press, 1979), 3.

11. Rorty, *Philosophy and the Mirror of Nature*, 389; emphasis in original.

12. Rorty, *Consequences of Pragmatism (Essays: 1972–1980)* (Minneapolis: University of Minnesota Press, 1982), xxxix–xl.

13. Rorty, *Consequences of Pragmatism*, xxxviii.

14. Rorty, "Introduction," in *Objectivity, Relativism, and Truth*, vol.1 of *Philosophical Papers* (New York: Cambridge University Press, 1991), 13.

15. Rorty, "Solidarity or Objectivity," in *Objectivity, Relativism, and Truth*, 22–23.

16. John Patrick Diggins, *The Promise of Pragmatism: Modernism and the Crisis of Knowledge and Authority* (Chicago: University of Chicago Press, 1994), 452.

17. Rorty, "Postmodernist Bourgeois Liberalism," in *Objectivity, Relativism, and Truth*, 198.

18. For a good summary of these critiques, see Diggins, *Promise of Pragmatism*, 451–452.

19. Rorty, "Introduction," in *Objectivity, Relativism, and Truth*, 2.

20. Rorty, "Cosmopolitanism without Emancipation," in *Objectivity, Relativism, and Truth*, 221–222.

21. See, for example, Bonnie Honig, *Political Theory and the Displacement of Politics* (Ithaca: Cornell University Press, 1993). In this work, Honig contrasts a "virtue" theory of politics with a "*virtù*" theory, in which the former identifies "politics with administration" while the latter sees "politics as a disruptive practice" (2).

22. William E. Connolly, *Identity\Difference: Democratic Negotiations of Political Paradox* (Ithaca: Cornell University Press, 1991), 211; emphasis in original.

23. Connolly, *Identity\Difference*, x.

24. Connolly, *Identity\Difference*, 24–25.

25. Connolly, "Democracy and Contingency," in *Democracy and Possessive Individualism: The Intellectual Legacy of C. B. Macpherson*, ed. Joseph H. Carens (Albany: State University of New York Press, 1993), 215.

26. Connolly, *Identity\Difference*, 218; emphasis in original.

27. Sheldon Wolin, *Politics and Vision: Continuity and Innovation in Western Political Thought* (Boston: Little, Brown and Company, 1960), 19.

28. Lyotard, *The Postmodern Explained: Correspondence 1982–1985*, ed. Julian Pefanis and Morgan Thomas, trans. Don Barry et al. (Minneapolis: University of Minnesota Press, 1993), 19.

29. Barry Allen, *Truth in Philosophy* (Cambridge: Harvard University Press, 1993), 31; emphasis in original.

30. Allen, *Truth in Philosophy*, 31–32.

31. Allen, *Truth in Philosophy*, 18.

Chapter Two

1. Plato, *Republic*, trans. G. M. A. Grube (Indianapolis: Hackett, 1974), 473d. Hereafter cited as *Rep*.

2. Karl Popper, *The Spell of Plato*, vol.1 of *The Open Society and Its Enemies*, 5th ed. (Princeton: Princeton University Press, 1966), 90–91.

3. Popper, *Spell of Plato*, 86–119.

4. Popper, *Spell of Plato*, 31–32, 161.

5. See Leo Strauss, "On Plato's Republic," in *The City and Man* (Chicago: University of Chicago Press, 1964), 50–138. Also see Allan Bloom, "Interpretative Essay," in *The Republic of Plato*, trans. Allan Bloom (New York: Basic Books, 1968), 307–436.

6. Strauss, "On Plato's Republic," 127.

7. As Sheldon Wolin notes, while Popper criticizes Plato's political philosophy for being doubly wrong—epistemologically and politically—Popper does not question the basic assumption that truth-claims justify power. See "Hobbes and the Culture of Despotism," in *Thomas Hobbes and Political Theory*, ed. Mary G. Dietz (Lawrence: University Press of Kansas, 1990), 9.

8. For a classical collection of essays on Popper's reading of Plato, see *Plato, Popper and Politics: Some Contributions to a Modern Controversy*, ed. R. Bambrough (Cambridge: Heffer, 1967). For a sample of lively debates on Strauss's position, see M. F. Burnyeat, "Sphinx Without a Secret," *The New York Review of Books* 32 (30 May 1985): 30–36. For responses to the review by Straussian scholars, including Joseph Cropsey, Harry V. Jaffa, Allan Bloom, Ernest J. Weinrib, Thomas L. Pangle, Clifford Orwin, and Robert Gorgis, together with Burnyeat's reply, see "The Studies of Leo Strauss: An Exchange," *The New York Review of Books* (10 October 1985): 41–44. The book under review is Leo Strauss, *Studies in*

Platonic Political Philosophy (Chicago: University of Chicago Press, 1983).

9. Hans-Georg Gadamer, *Truth and Method* ed. Garrett Barden and John Cumming (New York: Cross Road, 1985), xxv–xxvi.

10. While Gadamer's philosophical hermeneutics per se is not political theory, critics are interested in exploring the political implications of such a philosophical project. For example, see Catherine H. Zuckert, "Gadamer's Way: From Heidegger to Plato," (paper presented at the annual meeting of the American Political Science Association, Washington, D.C., September 1993). For a reading of young Gadamer as a "budding political theorist" and the centrality of Plato in the development of Gadamer's thought, see Robert Sullivan, *Political Hermeneutics: The Early Thinking of Hans-Georg Gadamer* (University Park: Pennsylvania State University Press, 1989).

11. Plato, "Letter VII," 341d, trans. L. A. Post, in *The Collected Dialogues of Plato, including the Letters*, ed. Edith Hamilton and Huntington Cairns (Princeton: Princeton University Press, 1961).

12. Gadamer, "Dialectic and Sophism in Plato's *Seventh Letter*," in *Dialogue and Dialectic: Eight Hermeneutical Studies on Plato*, trans. P. Christopher Smith (New Haven: Yale University Press, 1980), 98, 122, 123.

13. Gadamer, *Truth and Method*, 330.

14. Gadamer, *Truth and Method*, 326, 338.

15. Gadamer, *Truth and Method*, 326–327.

16. Gadamer, *Truth and Method*, 330.

17. Ibid.

18. Gadamer, *Truth and Method*, 331–332.

19. For a helpful discussion of Gadamer's hermeneutics in the context of contemporary political theory, see Richard J. Bernstein, *Beyond Objectivism and Relativism: Science, Hermeneutics and Praxis* (Philadelphia: University of Pennsylvania Press, 1983), 109–169.

20. This is in fact one of Bernstein's criticisms, see *Beyond Objectivism and Relativism*, 157–159.

21. For a cogent argument for why Gadamer did not end up following the path of his mentor, Heidegger, in being a supporter of the Nazi Party, see Sullivan, *Political Hermeneutics*, 176–181.

22. Gadamer, *The Idea of the Good in Platonic-Aristotelian Philosophy*, trans. P. Christopher Smith (New Haven: Yale University Press, 1986), 70; emphasis in original.

23. For an interesting account of the relationship between Strauss and Gadamer, see "Gadamer on Strauss: An Interview," *Interpretation* 12 (January 1984): 1–13. Strauss had once remarked, "we have marched from that common ground in opposite directions." See "Correspondence concerning *Wahrheit und Methode*," *The Independent Journal of Philosophy* 2 (1978): 5.

24. Gadamer, *The Idea of the Good*, 70. Also see Strauss, "On Plato's Republic," 124–128 and 138, and Bloom, "Interpretative Essay," 409–412. For a discussion of the difference between Gadamer and Bloom, see Zdravko Planinc, *Plato's Political Philosophy: Prudence in The Republic and The Laws* (Columbia: University of Missouri Press, 1991), 43–47.

25. Gadamer, *The Idea of the Good*, 71.

26. Gadamer, *The Idea of the Good*, 72.

27. Gadamer, "Plato's Educational State," in *Dialogue and Dialectic*, 73–92. For the discussion that follows, see 92.

28. Gadamer, *Plato's Dialectic Ethics: Phenomenological Interpretations Relating to the Philebus*, trans. Robert M. Wallace (New Haven: Yale University Press, 1991), 3.

29. *Rep* 475e.

30. *Rep* 514a–518e.

31. *Rep* 518d; emphasis added.

32. Plato, *Meno* 81d, 84d, 86a, trans. W. K. C. Guthrie, in *Collected Dialogues*.

33. Plato, *Meno* 86b.

34. Plato, *Meno* 86a, 98a.

35. This discussion of the theory of the "Forms" is based on *Rep* 507a–511c.

36. Gregory Vlastos, "Degrees of Reality in Plato," in *Platonic Studies* (Princeton: Princeton University Press, 1981), 58–59, 63.

37. Plato, *Phaedo* 99d–e, trans. Hugh Tredennick, in *Collected Dialogues*.

38. Plato, *Phaedo* 90c.

39. Vlastos, "Degrees of Reality," 69.

40. Allen, *Truth in Philosophy*, 16.

41. *Rep* 414a–417b.

42. *Rep* 474c.

43. *Rep* 428e–429a.

44. For the dating of Plato's dialogues, see George Klosko, *The Development of Plato's Political Theory* (New York: Methuen, 1986), 14–17.

45. Plato, *Statesman* 297c, trans. J. B. Skemp, in *Collected Dialogues*.

46. For a discussion of the education of the philosopher king, see *Rep* 514a–541b.

47. Plato, *Statesman* 292e.

48. Plato, *Meno* 98a.

49. *Rep* 517c.

50. Allen, *Truth in Philosophy*, 18. C. D. C. Reeve interprets "the good as simply being *the* rational order;" without which "there would not be an intelligible realm." See "Platonic Politics and the Good," *Political Theory* 23 (August 1995): 417, 419; emphasis added.

51. *Rep* 430e–431b.

52. *Rep* 441e–442b.

53. *Rep* 443d–444a.

54. *Rep* 544e.

55. *Rep* 546a–547a. I am grateful to Kenneth Dorter for pointing out this stage.

56. This discussion on the various forms of government is based on *Rep* 543a–569c, passim.

57. *Rep* 433b.

58. *Rep* 332d–335e.

59. *Rep* 509e.

60. *Rep* 473a. After having consulted with Brian Calvert and Alkis Kontos on the original Greek text, I decided to use Paul Shorey's translation in the Loeb edition rather than Grube's for this particular passage. Shorey's choice of action/deed versus word/speech is preferred over Grube's choice of theory versus practice because the latter is suggestive of a rather more loaded contrast. The corresponding Greek words involved are *prachthenai, praxis, ergon* on the one hand, and *legetai, lexis and logos* on the other.

61. *Rep* 592a–b.

62. In the *Statesman*, Plato states that a regime constituted by law is "second best" to the "ideal," defined as one ruled by an individual "who understands the art of kingship and has kingly ability." See 294a and 297e.

63. Plato, *Statesman* 294b.

64. Plato, *Phaedrus* 275a–276a, trans. R. Hackforth, in *Collected Dialogues*.

65. Plato, *Statesman* 277c.

66. Plato, *Cratylus* 388c, trans. Benjamin Jowett, in *Collected Dialogues*. Gadamer discusses the importance of this dialogue with regard to the relationship between language and *logos*, see *Truth and Method*, 366–378.

67. Plato, *Cratylus* 439b.

68. Plato, *Cratylus* 391b, 388c, 401b.

69. Plato, *The Laws*, trans. Trevor J. Saunders (Harmondsworth: Penguin Books, 1970), 715c–d.

70. *Laws* 960b.

71. Trevor J. Saunders, "Plato's Later Political Thought," in *The Cambridge Companion to Plato*, ed. Richard Kraut (Cambridge: Cambridge University Press, 1992), 475. On this page and the next, Saunders gives a very succinct summary of how the election is to be conducted to favor those with "intellectual attainments" and "moral character." These characterizations are Plato's own words, see *Laws* 968d.

72. Saunders, in his introduction to the section of the *Laws* that deals with the role of the Nocturnal Council, 516.

73. Plato, *Crito* 50b, in *Collected Dialogues*.

74. Plato, *Crito* 52e. I am thankful to Kenneth Dorter for reminding me of the contrast between *Crito* and the *Apology*, where Socrates defends the right to civil disobedience. In thinking about the problem, I find a recent interpretation by J. Peter Euben helpful. Euben says, "his [Socrates'] argument suggests that radical critics of democracy have special obligations to the city they criticize; that his deference here (he literally calls himself a slave to the laws) has everything to do with his refusal (in the *Apology*) to accept silencing even when enjoined by laws." See "Taking It To the Street: Radical Democracy and Radicalizing Theory," in *Radical Democracy: Identity, Citizenship, and the State*, ed. David Trend (New York: Routledge, 1996), 76, note 24.

75. Saunders, "Plato's Later Political Thought," 465.

76. Saunders, "Plato's Later Political Thought," 483.

77. Popper treats the *Laws* as advocating the same political program as the *Republic;* see *Spell of Plato*, passim.

78. Plato, *Laws* 718a.

79. See, for example, Plato, *Phaedrus* 276a, in which Socrates defends "living speech" over "written discourse."

80. *Rep* 377b.

81. *Rep* 597e.

82. Gadamer, "Plato and the Poets," in *Dialogue and Dialectic*, 64–65; Gadamer's own emphasis.

83. *Rep* 607b.

84. As Sullivan notes, for Gadamer to point out that imitation leads to "self-forgetting," he is in fact "employing that key theme of German nineteenth-century thought: The purpose of education is to construct an authentic human being, and this has to be done in terms of an image of the *self*." See *Political Hermeneutics*, 144; emphasis in original.

85. Plato, *Laws* 801d; see also 719b–e.

86. Elizabeth Asmis, "Plato On Poetic Creativity," in *Cambridge Companion to Plato*, 356.

87. Plato, *Laws* 656d–657b.

88. Plato, *Laws* 700e–701b; my emphasis.

89. Plato, *Laws* 657b–c.

90. In explaining why Plato thinks that the philosopher should be "the city's founder and lawgiver," Popper says the following: "If the state is to be stable, then it must be a true copy of the divine Form or Idea of the State. But only a philosopher who is fully proficient in the highest of sciences, in dialectics, is able to see, and to copy, the heavenly Original." See Popper, *Spell of Plato*, 145.

91. Gadamer, "Plato and the Poets," 67.

92. Wolin, "Hobbes and Despotism," 15.

93. *Rep* 546a. Wolin, *Politics and Vision*, 67–68.

94. Hannah Arendt, *The Human Condition* (Chicago: University of Chicago Press, 1958), 223, 225.

Chapter Three

1. Thomas Hobbes, *Leviathan*, ed. C. B. Macpherson (Harmondsworth: Penguin Books, 1968), chap.13, 186. Hereafter cited as *Lev*.

2. Job 41:33–34 New Oxford Annotated Bible.

3. Tom Sorell, "The Science in Hobbes's Politics," in *Perspectives on Hobbes*, ed. G. A. J. Rogers and Alan Ryan (Oxford: Clarendon Press, 1988), 69.

4. C. B. Macpherson, introduction, to *Lev*, 25–39; *The Political Theory of Possessive Individualism* (Oxford: Oxford University Press, 1962), 19–46.

5. For thoughtful reviews on the contemporary state of scholarship on Hobbes, see M. M. Goldsmith, "The Hobbes Industry," *Political Studies* 39 (March 1991): 135–147; Perez Zagorin, "Hobbes on Our Mind," *Journal of the History of Ideas* 51 (April/June 1990): 317–335.

6. See, for example, Alan Ryan, "Hobbes and Individualism," in *Perspectives on Hobbes*, 85–86; Sorell, "The Science in Hobbes's Politics," 71.

7. Sorell, "The Science in Hobbes's Politics," 70.

8. Thomas Hobbes, *Elements of Philosophy Concerning Body*, in *The English Works of Thomas Hobbes*, ed. Sir William Molesworth, vol.1 (London: John Bohn, 1839–1845), chap. 1, section 6, at 7. One is reminded here of Francis Bacon's formulation: "human knowledge and human power meet in one." See Bacon, *The New Organon*, in *The New Organon and Related Writings*, ed. Fulton H. Anderson (New York: Liberal Arts Press, 1960), bk.1, aphorism 3 at 39. For Bacon's influence on Hobbes, see Richard Peters, *Hobbes* (Westport: Greenwood Press, 1979), chap.1.

9. *Lev*, chap.17, 227.

10. For a detailed account of the debate, see Steven Shapin and Simon Schaffer, *Leviathan and the Air Pump: Hobbes, Boyle, and the Experimental Life* (Princeton: Princeton University Press, 1985).

11. Shapin and Schaffer, *Leviathan and the Air Pump*, 22–79, passim.

12. *Lev*, chap.9, 147.

13. *Lev*, chap.46, 682; also see chap.5, 117.

14. *Lev*, chap. 9, 147; chap.7, 131; emphasis in original.

15. *Lev*, chap.5, 115.

16. *Lev*, chap.5, 111; emphasis in original.

17. *Lev*, chap.46, 683.

18. *Lev*, chap.4, 100–101.

19. *Lev*, chap.4, 101; emphasis in original.

20. *Lev*, chap.4, 100.

21. *Lev*, chap.4, 102.

22. *Lev*, chap.4, 105. For Hobbes's view on truth, see Dorothea Krook, "Thomas Hobbes's Doctrine of Meaning and Truth," *Philosophy* 31 (January 1956): 3–22. Chapters 2 and 5 in Peters, *Hobbes*, and T.A. Heinrichs, "Language and Mind in Hobbes," *Yale French Studies* 49 (1973): 56–70, are helpful as well.

23. *Lev*, chap.4, 106.

24. *Lev*, chap.4, 105; emphasis in original.

25. *Lev*, chap.5, 115.

26. *Lev*, chap.9, 147.

27. *Lev*, chap.46, 682.

28. Ibid; emphasis in original.

29. Hobbes's general distrust of the senses was influenced by Descartes. But more specifically, Hobbes's view on the fallibility of the senses was also shaped by the anti-Aristotelian view of modern skeptics like Pierre Charron in France. See Richard Tuck, "Optics and sceptics: the philosophical foundations of Hobbes's political thought," in *Thomas Hobbes*, ed. Vere Chappell, vol.5 of *Essays On Early Modern Philosophers* (New York: Garland Publishing, 1992), 239.

30. Hobbes, *Six Lessons to the Savilian Professors of the Mathematics*, in *English Works*, vol.7, 183–184. This paragraph is noted in Sorell, "The Science in Hobbes's Politics," 71.

31. Hobbes, *Seven Philosophical Problems and Two Propositions of Geometry*, in *English Works*, vol.7, 3. Again, the importance of this paragraph is pointed out by Sorell, "The Science in Hobbes's Politics," 71.

32. Donald W. Hanson, "The Meaning of 'Demonstration' in Hobbes's Science," *History of Political Thought* 11 (winter 1990): 625.

33. Lyotard, *The Postmodern Condition*, 15.

34. *Lev*, "A Review and Conclusion," 727; emphasis in original.

35. Hobbes, *Six Lessons*, 184. This phrase is taken from the same paragraph that has just been cited at length, see note 30 above. Civil philosophy and geometry are juxtaposed in the original text.

36. *Lev*, chap.17, 227.

37. *Lev*, "The Introduction," 81; emphasis in original.

38. Hobbes, *Behemoth or the Long Parliament*, ed. Ferdinand Tönnies (1889; reprint, Chicago: University of Chicago Press, 1990), 2–4.

39. *Lev*, chap.41, 514; emphasis in original.

40. *Lev*, chap.44, 629.

41. *Lev*, chap.44, 627–628. For a helpful analysis of the relationship between Hobbes's politics and religion, see Arrigo Pacchi, "Hobbes and the Problem of God," in *Perspectives on Hobbes*, 171–187; James Farr, "Atomes of Scripture: Hobbes and the Politics of Biblical Interpretation," in *Thomas Hobbes and Political Theory*, 172–196.

42. *Lev*, chap.4, 100.

43. *Lev*, chap.14, 189–190; emphasis in original.

44. *Lev*, chap.5, 116–117; emphasis in original.

45. Hobbes, "The Autobiography of Thomas Hobbes," trans. Benjamin Farrington, *The Rationalist Annual* (1958), 25.

46. Hobbes, *English Works*, vol.8, vii.

47. W. Robert Connor, *Thucydides* (Princeton: Princeton University Press, 1984), 99.

48. See Connor, *Thucydides*, 96–105, for a discussion of this theme in the Corcyrean episode.

49. Hobbes, *English Works*, vol.8, 348.

50. Connor, *Thucydides*, 99.

51. *Lev*, chap.13, 188; emphasis in original.

52. Ibid; emphasis added.

53. Wolin, *Politics and Vision*, 265.

54. *Lev*, chap.14, 189–190.

55. Peters, *Hobbes*, 125.

56. Hobbes, *De Cive*, ed. Howard Warrender (Oxford: Clarendon Press, 1983), chap.18, 253; first emphasis in original; second emphasis added. The importance of this passage is pointed out by Peters, *Hobbes*, 125.

57. *Lev*, chap.31, 395; emphasis added.

58. Hobbes, *Elements of Philosophy*, chap.3, section 7 at 35; emphasis in original.

59. Martin Heidegger, *The Basic Problems of Phenomenology*, trans. Albert Hofstadter (Bloomington: Indiana University Press, 1982), 187; emphasis in original.

60. Heidegger, *The Basic Problems of Phenomenology*, 189; emphasis in original.

61. Heidegger, *The Basic Problems of Phenomenology*, 192.

62. *Lev*, chap.18, 233.

63. Nietzsche, "On Truth and Lies in a Nonmoral Sense," in *Philosophy and Truth: Selections from Nietzsche's Notebooks of the Early 1870s*, ed. and trans. Daniel Breazeale (Atlantic Highlands, N.J.: Humanities Press, 1979), 81; emphasis in original.

64. *Lev*, chap.30, 376.

65. Hobbes, *De Cive*, chap.13, 158.

66. *Lev*, chap.30, 387. On the issue of providing for the poor, Hobbes appears to be an early supporter of welfare state. See Ryan, "Hobbes's political philosophy," in *The Cambridge Companion to Hobbes*, ed. Tom Sorell (Cambridge: Cambridge University Press, 1996), 235. However, Hobbes's proposal strikes me as closer to "workfare," which is the latest conservative backlash against welfare provisions.

67. Kathleen B. Jones, *Compassionate Authority: Democracy and the Representation of Women* (New York: Routledge, 1993), 87.

68. Hobbes, *De Cive*, chap.13, 160.

69. Hobbes, *Behemoth*, 16.

70. *Lev*, "A Review and Conclusion," 720.

71. Hobbes, *De Cive*, chap.1, 44; emphasis in original.

72. *Lev*, chap.30, 379.

73. *Lev*, chap.23, 291.

74. Hobbes, *Behemoth*, 40; emphasis in original.

75. Hobbes, *Behemoth*, 58.

76. Hobbes, *De Cive*, chap.13, 161. For a comparable statement, see *Lev*, chap.30, 384.

77. Hobbes, *Behemoth*, 58.

78. Ryan, "Hobbes and Individualism," 84 and 100. Perez Zagorin notes that Hobbes was the first thinker "to see that there can be no divine or transcendent source or guarantor of moral values, and that men must create their normativity themselves out of their own reason and human nature." See "Hobbes on Our Mind," 335.

79. *Lev*, chap.21, 380–383.

80. Sheldon Wolin, *Hobbes and the Epic Tradition of Political Theory* (Los Angeles: William Andrews Clark Memorial Library, University of California, Los Angeles, 1970). David Johnston, *The Rhetoric of Leviathan: Thomas Hobbes and the Politics of Cultural Transformation* (Princeton: Princeton University Press, 1986).

81. Sorell, "The Science in Hobbes's Politics," 78.

82. Ryan, "Hobbes's Political Philosophy," 225.

83. See Ryan, "Hobbes, Toleration, and the Inner life," *The Nature of Political Theory*, ed. David Miller and Larry Siedentop (Oxford: Clarendon Press, 1983), 197–218; "A More Tolerant Hobbes?" in *Justifying Toleration: Conceptual and Historical Perspectives*, ed. Susan Mendus (Cambridge: Cambridge University Press, 1988), 37–58.

84. *Lev*, chap.21, 271.

85. Jones, "On Authority: Or, Why Women Are Not Entitled to Speak?" in *Feminism and Foucault*, ed. Irene Diamond and Lee Quinby (Boston: Northeastern University Press, 1988), 122.

86. *Lev*, chap.31, 407. Hobbes also notes that Thucydides had taught him "how stupid democracy is and by how much one man is wiser than an assembly." See "The Autobiography of Hobbes," 25.

87. *Lev*, "Dedication," 75.

88. Johnston, *The Rhetoric of Leviathan*, 14.

89. *Lev*, chap.31, 407.

90. Johnston, *The Rhetoric of Leviathan*, 91.

91. *Lev*, chap.31, 408.

92. Johnston, *The Rhetoric of Leviathan*, 91. See also Wolin, *Hobbes and the Epic Tradition of Political Theory*, where Wolin notes that "Leviathan itself is a metaphor, while the whole argument supporting it is but an extended metaphor" (38).

93. Hobbes, "The Answer of Mr. Hobbes to Sir Will. D'Avenant's Preface before Gondibert," in *Sir William D'Avenant's Gondibert*, ed. David F. Gladish (Oxford: Clarendon Press, 1971), 49–50, quoted in Johnston, *The Rhetoric of Leviathan*, 90.

94. Amos Funkenstein, *Theology and the Scientific Imagination from the Middle Ages to the Seventeenth Centuries* (Princeton: Princeton University Press, 1986), 327.

95. For a good analysis of Hobbes's view on the complexity of human motivations, which are by no means always rational, see Stephen Holmes, introduction to *Behemoth*, vii–l.

Prologue

1. John Locke, *An Essay Concerning Human Understanding*, ed. Peter H. Nidditch (Oxford: Clarendon Press, 1975), bk.2, chap.1, §2, 104; emphasis in original.

2. Norman Hampson, *The Enlightenment* (Harmondsworth: Penguin Books, 1968), chap.6, "The Inner Voice," 186–217.

3. Hampson, *The Enlightenment*, 186.

4. Hampson, *The Enlightenment*, 196. Also see Peter Gay, *The Rise of Modern Paganism*, vol.1 of *The Enlightenment: An Interpretation* (New York: Norton, 1977), 3–27.

5. Immanuel Kant, *Critique of Pure Reason*, trans. Norman Kemp Smith (New York: St Martin's Press, 1965), 152–3 (B131–B132).

6. Kant, *Critique of Pure Reason*, 336–337 (A354); emphasis in original.

Notes to Prologue

7. Schacht, *Hegel and After: Studies in Continental Philosophy Between Kant and Sartre* (Pittsburgh: University of Pittsburgh Press, 1975), 24.

8. Allen, *Truth In Philosophy*, 32.

9. Alexander Nehamas, *Nietzsche: Life as Literature* (Cambridge: Harvard University Press, 1985), 45.

10. Nietzsche, *The Will To Power*, ed. Walter Kaufmann, trans. Walter Kaufmann and R. J. Hollingdale (New York: Vintage Books, 1968), 267.

11. José Ortega y Gasset, "On Point of View in the Arts," trans. Paul Snodgress and Joseph Frank, in *The Dehumanization of Art and Other Essays on Art, Culture, and Literature* (Princeton: Princeton University Press, 1968), 127. I first became aware of this observation when reading Jason Edward Kaufman, "Picasso and Braque: Mano a Mano," *The World & I* 4 (October 1989): 278–283. This is a review article on the exhibition "Picasso and Braque: Pioneering Cubism" at the Museum of Modern Art in New York in the fall of 1989. In the article, Kaufman notes, "what distinguished Cubism from all art that had preceded it, as Spanish philosopher José Ortega y Gasset ingeniously discerned, was its focus on the world as idea" (278).

12. Ortega y Gasset, "On Point of View in the Arts," 127.

13. Cited in Kaufman, "Picasso and Braque," 278; emphasis added.

14. Nehamas, *Nietzsche*, 59; emphasis added.

15. Carl Schorske, *Fin-de-Siècle Vienna: Politics and Culture* (New York: Alfred A. Knopf, 1980), xix.

16. Schorske, *Fin-de-Siècle Vienna*, 4.

17. Lawrence Scaff, *Fleeing the Iron Cage: Culture, Politics, and Modernity in the Thought of Max Weber* (Berkeley: University of California Press, 1989), 79–80.

18. Nietzsche, "On Truth and Lies in a Nonmoral Sense;" emphasis added.

19. Nehamas, *Nietzsche*, 73.

Chapter Four

1. Wilheim Hennis, *Max Weber: Essays in Reconstruction*, trans. Keith Tribe (London: Allen & Unwin, 1988), 44–46; emphasis in original.

2. Scaff, *Fleeing the Iron Cage*, 150.

3. Strauss, *Natural Right and History* (Chicago: University of Chicago Press, 1950), 41–42.

4. Mommsen, "The Antinomical Structure of Max Weber's Political Thought," in *The Political and Social Theory of Max Weber: Collected Essays* (Chicago: University of Chicago Press, 1989), 43. The "moral obligation to rationality" is presumably Weber's liberal premise. Other works by Mommsen on the subject of Weber's politics are *The Age of Bureaucracy: Perspectives on the Political Sociology of Max Weber* (Oxford: Basil Blackwell, 1974); *Max Weber and German Politics, 1890–1920*, trans. Michael S. Steinberg (Chicago: University of Chicago Press, 1984).

5. Christian Lenhardt, "Max Weber and the Legacy of Critical Idealism," in *The Barbarism of Reason: Max Weber and the Twilight of Enlightenment*, ed. Asher Horowitz and Terry Maley (Toronto: University of Toronto Press, 1994), 22.

6. Weber, "'Objectivity' in Social Science and Social Policy," in *The Methodology of Social Sciences*, ed. Edward A. Shils and Henry A. Finch (New York: Free Press, 1949), 106. Hereafter the essay will be cited as "Objectivity." On Weber's interpretation of Kant, see Martin Barker, "Kant as a problem for Weber," *British Journal of Sociology* 31 (June 1980): 224–245; M. A. Brand, "Causality, Objectivity and Freedom: Weber, Kant and The Neo-Kantians," *Australian and New Zealand Journal of Sociology* 15 (March 1979): 6–12.

7. Max Weber, "Science as a Vocation," in *From Max Weber: Essays in Sociology*, ed. and trans. H. H. Gerth and C. Wright Mills (New York: Oxford University Press, 1946), 154. Hereafter the article will be cited as "SV" and the book as *FMW*.

8. "Objectivity," 72.

9. "Objectivity," 81; emphasis in original.

10. "Objectivity," 67, 72, 81.

11. "Objectivity," 90, 93; emphasis in original. For an interpretation of Weber's "ideal-type" in a Kantian context, see Tracy Strong, "Weber and Freud: vocation and self-acknowledgement," *Canadian Journal of Sociology* 10 (fall 1985): 397.

12. "Objectivity," 97–99.

13. W. G. Runciman, in *A Critique of Max Weber's Philosophy of Social Science* (Cambridge: Cambridge University Press, 1972), faults Weber for confusing theoretical presuppositions with value judgments. It seems to me, however, that Runciman's criticism is an indication of his narrow reading of the term "value" in Weber. "Value," especially when contrasted with "facts," belongs to the domain of meaning and consequently, "value" is a question of decision and choice rather than "what ought to be."

14. "Objectivity," 111; emphasis added.

15. "Objectivity," 110; emphasis in original.

16. Weber, *Roscher and Knies: The Logical Problems of Historical Economics*, trans. Guy Oakes (New York: Free Press, 1975), 63–66 and 179–181. Also see Oakes, "Introductory Essay," 25–32; H. Stuart Hughes, *Consciousness and Society: The Reorientation of European Social Thought 1890–1930*, rev. ed. (New York: Vintage Books, 1977), 278–335.

17. As Tracy Strong notes, "the Weber of Talcott Parsons and Edward Shils" is "no longer with us." Here in North America, one can say that "the Europeanness of Weber" is finally restored by the works of a different generation of scholars like Robert Eden, Fredric Jameson, and Lawrence Scaff. This Weber is the "Nietzschean Weber." See "'What have we to do with morals?' Nietzsche and Weber on history and ethics," *History of the Human Sciences* 5 (August 1992): 9, 16. Personally I find Hennis's essay "The Traces of Nietzsche in the Work of Max Weber," in *Max Weber*, 146–162, most helpful.

18. I am referring to Weber's famous remark, which he made to his students: "Our intellectual world has to a great extent been shaped by Marx and Nietzsche" and that "whoever does not admit that he could not perform the most important parts of his work without the work that those two have done swindles himself and others." Eduard Baumgarten, *Max*

Weber: Werk und Person (Tübingen, 1964), 554–555, cited in Arthur Mitzman, *The Iron Cage: An Historical Interpretation of Max Weber* (New York: Grosset & Dunlap, 1969), 182. The same remark is also cited in Hennis, *Max Weber*, 146.

19. Hennis, *Max Weber*, 158.

20. "SV," 139.

21. Weber, "The Social Psychology of the World Religions," in *FMW*, 283.

22. "SV," 139. See also Weber, "Magic and Religion," in *Economy and Society*, vol.1, ed. Guenther Roth and Claus Wittich, trans. Guenther Roth, Claus Wittich et al. (Berkeley: University of California Press, 1978), 422–439.

23. "SV," 147–149.

24. Fredric Jameson, "The Vanishing Mediator: Narrative Structure in Max Weber," *New German Critique* 1 (winter 1974): 61. Jameson's citation can be found in "SV," 148.

25. Weber, "Religious Rejections of the World and Their Directions," in *FMW*, 356; emphasis in original. For Weber's view on the act of choosing and the authentication of being, see "Politics as a Vocation," in *FMW*, 126–128; hereafter cited as "PV."

26. Weber, "The Social Psychology of the World Religions," 282.

27. "SV," 139; emphasis in original.

28. "SV," 147.

29. As Wolin notes, the book *The Protestant Ethic and The Spirit of Capitalism* "marks the first sustained discussion of a theme that was to preoccupy Weber for the remainder of his life, the meaninglessness of human existence." See "Max Weber: Legitimation, Method, and the Politics of Theory," *Political Theory* 9 (August 1981): 412. The article is reprinted in *The Barbarism of Reason*, 287–309. All subsequent citations refer to the original article.

30. "SV," 147.

31. This discussion on religion is based on Weber, "The Social Psychology of the World Religions," 267–301, passim. It should be noted that the sorcerer emerges as the first kind of "spiritual advisor" with regard to human suffering.

32. Weber, *The Protestant Ethic and The Spirit of Capitalism*, trans. Talcott Parsons (New York: Charles Scribner's Sons, 1976). Hereafter cited as *PE*.

33. *PE*, 126. Also see Weber, "Anticritical Last Word on *The Spirit of Capitalism*," trans. Wallace M. Davis, *American Journal of Sociology* 83 (1978): 1129.

34. *PE*, 102–117, passim.

35. *PE*, 104.

36. *PE*, 117; emphasis added.

37. *PE*, 115; emphasis added.

38. The discussion that follows, unless otherwise stated, is based on *PE*, 117–122, passim.

39. Jameson, "The Vanishing Narrator," 74.

40. *PE*, 154.

41. The discussion in this section on the relationship between Protestant asceticism and the spirit of capitalism is based on *PE*, 155–183, passim; especially 174, 181. Also see, Weber, "The Social Psychology of the World Religions," and "Religious Rejections of the World and Their Directions," in *FMW*, 267–359.

42. Wolin, "Max Weber," 416.

43. "SV," 138. This important point will be discussed further in the following section.

44. "SV," 140.

45. *PE*, 28, 180.

46. "SV," 139.

47. "SV," 139; emphasis in original.

48. Weber, "Bureaucracy," in *Economy and Society*, vol.2, 973.

49. Weber, "Bureaucracy," 975.

50. Weber, "Bureaucracy," 975.

51. "SV," 140; Hennis, *Max Weber*, 44.

52. *PE*, 181. See also Wolin, "Max Weber," 415.

53. Kontos, "The World Disenchanted, and the Return of Gods and Demons," in *The Barbarism of Reason*, 237.

54. Weber, "The Meaning of 'Ethical Neutrality,'" in *The Methodology of Social Sciences*, 18. Hereafter cited as "EN."

55. Reading the two essays as "companion-pieces, united by common themes" is an interpretation suggested by Wolin. See "Max Weber," 406.

56. This comparison can be found in "SV," 134–138.

57. "Objectivity," 105.

58. Ibid.

59. It is interesting to note how Rorty echoes Weber on this point. Rorty says, "since he [the post-Philosophy philosopher] has no extra-historical Archimedean point . . . *he is doomed to become outdated*." See Rorty, *Consequences of Pragmatism*, xl; emphasis added.

60. "SV," 143.

61. Ibid.

62. "Objectivity," 111.

63. Wolin, "Max Weber," 409.

64. "EN," 17; "SV," 147.

65. Hennis, *Max Weber*, 158–159.

66. "SV," 147–148, 152.

67. "PV," 128.

68. "Parliament and Government in a Reconstructed Germany (A Contribution to the Political Critique of Officialdom and Party Politics)," in *Economy and Society*, vol.2, 1393; emphasis added. Hereafter the article will be cited as "PG."

69. "PG," 1393.

70. "Domination and Legitimacy," in *Economy and Society*, vol.2, 946; emphasis in original.

71. Weber, "Domination and Legitimation," 954.

72. Weber, "Bureaucracy," 972–973.

73. Weber, "Bureaucracy," 983; emphasis in original.

74. Weber, "Religious Rejections of the World and Their Directions," 333–334.

75. Wolin, "Democracy and the Welfare State: The Political and Theoretical Connection Between *Staatsräson* and *Wohlfahrtsstaatsräson*," in *The Presence of the Past: Essays on the State and the Constitution* (Baltimore: Johns Hopkins University Press, 1989), 178; emphasis added.

76. Fred Dallmayr, "Max Weber and the Modern State," in *Barbarism of Reason*, 57.

77. Weber, "Bureaucracy," 991.

78. Weber, "Bureaucracy," 994.

79. Weber, "Bureaucracy," 999.

80. Weber, "Bureaucracy," 1001–1002; emphasis in original.

81. "PG," 1403–1404; emphasis in original.

82. "PG," 1417.

83. "PG," 1395.

84. "PG," 1451–1452.

85. "The Types of Legitimate Domination," in *Economy and Society*, vol.1, 266–267; emphasis in original.

86. "PG," 1459–1460.

87. As David Beetham notes, Weber's ambivalence to democracy is similar to Mill's. See Beetham, "Max Weber and the Liberal Political Tradition," in *The Barbarism of Reason*, 107. Like Mill, Weber sees the need of educating the ordinary people to become better informed citizens. Also see Scaff, "Max Weber's Politics and Political Education," in *Weber: Critical Assessments 2*, ed. Peter Hamilton, vol.1 (London: Routledge, 1991), 162–182.

88. "PV," 118–128; "SV," 151–152.

89. Martin Luther cited by Weber in "PV," 127. See "Luther at the Diet of Worms, 1521" in *Career of the Reformer II* vol.32 of *Luther's Works,* ed. George W. Forell, trans. Roger A. Hornsby (Philadelphia: Muhlenberg Press, 1958), 113.

90. Wolin notes that there are interesting connections between science and charisma; see "Max Weber," 417.

91. Strong, "Weber and Freud: Vocation and Self-acknowledgement," *Canadian Journal of Sociology* 10 (fall 1985):397.

92. The theme that only "facts" should be taught in classroom is central to the two essays, "EN" and "SV."

93. Weber, "The Academic Freedom of the Universities," in *Max Weber On Universities: The Power of the State and the Dignity of the Academic Calling in Imperial Germany*, ed. and trans. Edward Shils (Chicago: University of Chicago Press, 1973), 20.

94. "EN," 18; emphasis in original.

95. "EN," 19.

96. The division of labor between the politician and the social scientist is noted in Mommsen, "Antinomical Structure," 43.

97. *PE*, 182; "EN," 47; "PV," 128. The theme that the political role of the social scientist comes from the "inherent limitations of science" is one that Wolin develops in "Max Weber," see 419 especially.

98. On the theme of individualism, see Karl Löwith, *Max Weber and Karl Marx*, ed. Tom Bottomore and William Outhwaite, trans. Hans Fantel (London: George Allen & Unwin, 1982), 52–60. As Beetham notes, the crisis of liberalism for Weber was first and foremost "a crisis of individualism"; see "Weber and the Liberal Political Tradition," 108.

99. Scaff, *Fleeing the Iron Cage*, 157.

100. That Weber's politics is ontological is an interpretation that both Kontos and Wolin develop in their respective essays cited in this chapter.

Chapter Five

1. For example, the authors of a recent volume of collected essays on this theme, when citing Foucault, refer exclusively to *Power/Knowledge*, with only one exception. The volume is *Beyond Political Correctness: Toward the Inclusive University*, ed. Stephen Richer and Lorna Weir (Toronto: University of Toronto Press, 1995).

2. Here I am borrowing from Habermas's concept of "legitimation crisis." In *Legitimation Crisis*, Habermas analyzes the question of legitimation in advanced capitalism as a series of crises in economic, political, and sociocultural spheres, which are all profoundly interrelated. See *Legitimation Crisis*, trans. Thomas McCarthy (Boston: Beacon Press, 1975), 33–94, passim. Elshtain regards identity politics as a form of "politics of displacement," whereby "private identity takes precedence over public ends or purposes." As such, identity politics is a symptom of a "faltering democracy." See Elshtain, *Democracy on Trial*, 52.

3. Taylor, "Foucault on Freedom and Truth," *Political Theory* 12 (May 1984): 152–183; Connolly, "Taylor, Foucault, and Otherness," *Political Theory* 13 (August 1985): 365–375. This article marks the beginning of Connolly's major engagement with Foucault.

4. Taylor, "Foucault on Freedom and Truth," 152, 175.

5. Foucault's most deterministic formulation can be found in "What is an Author?" in *Language, Counter-Memory, Practice: Selected Essays and Interviews*, ed. Donald F. Bouchard, trans. Donald F. Bouchard and Sherry Simon (Ithaca: Cornell University Press, 1977). Foucault says, "the subject (and its substitutes) must be stripped of its creative role and analysed as a complex and variable function of discourse" (138). For "global" versus "local" knowledge, see Foucault, "Two Lectures," in *Power/Knowledge: Selected Interviews and Other Writings 1972–1977*, ed. Colin Gordon, trans. Colin Gordon et al. (New York: Pantheon Books, 1980), 80–82.

6. "Power and Sex: An Interview with Michel Foucault," *Telos* 32 (summer 1977): 159; emphasis added.

7. Foucault, "The Subject and Power," in *Michel Foucault: Beyond Structuralism and Hermeneutics*, 2d ed. (Chicago: University of Chicago Press, 1983), 208, 222–223.

8. Thomas McCarthy, "The Critique of Impure Reason: Foucault and the Frankfurt School," *Political Theory* 18 (August 1990): 446.

9. Foucault, "Kant on Enlightenment and Revolution," trans. Colin Gordon, *Economy and Society* 15 (February 1986): 96.

10. Foucault, "What is Enlightenment?" in *The Foucault Reader*, ed. Paul Rabinow (New York: Pantheon Books, 1984), 39.

11. Foucault, "Kant on Enlightenment and Revolution," 89.

12. Ibid.

13. Foucault, "What is Enlightenment?" 42, 45–46.

14. Foucault, "What is Enlightenment?" 50.

15. Colin Gordon, "Question, Ethos, Event," *Economy and Society* 15 (February 1986): 74. For a comparable observation, see Geoffrey Galt Harpham, "So . . . What *Is* Enlightenment? An Inquisition into Modernity," *Critical Inquiry* 20 (spring 1994): 533. Harpham notes, "For both Kant and his disciple Foucault, Enlightenment awakens a compulsion to contradiction, to self-division, to paradox."

16. Maurice Florence notes, "if Foucault is indeed perfectly at home in the philosophical tradition, it is within the *critical* tradition of Kant, and his undertaking could be called *A Critical History of Thought*." See "Foucault, Michel, 1926–," in *The Cambridge Companion to Foucault*, ed. Gary Gutting (Cambridge: Cambridge University Press, 1994), 314; emphasis in original. This piece is a translation of an entry on Michel Foucault, originally published in *Dictionaire des philosophes*, ed. Denis Huisman (Paris: Presses Universitaires de France, 1984). Gutting notes that there is "good reason" to think that "Maurice Florence" is in fact Michel Foucault. See "Preface," vii.

17. The entire work was submitted to the Université de Paris in 1960 as *thèse complémentaire* for Foucault's doctoral degree. The translation is published as *Emmanuel Kant, Anthropologie du point de vue pragmatique* (Paris: Vrin, 1964). The interpretive essay remains unpublished. A copy is available at Centre Michel Foucault, Bibliothèque du Saulchoir, Paris.

18. Foucault, "*Introduction à l'anthropologie de Kant*," 122. The original text reads: "... *cette obstination est liée à la structure meme du problème kantien: comment penser, analyser, justifier et fonder la finitude, dans une réflexion qui ne passe pas par une ontologie de l'infini, et ne s'excuse pas sur une philosophie de l'absolu?*"

19. Foucault, "Kant on Enlightenment and Revolution," 96.

20. Foucault, "Nietzsche, Genealogy, History," in *Language, Counter-Memory, Practice*, 153–154.

21. Foucault, "Nietzsche, Genealogy, History," 151–152.

22. Foucault, "The Discourse on Language," appendix to *The Archaeology of Knowledge*, trans. A.M. Sheridan Smith (New York: Pantheon Books, 1972), 216–220.

23. See, for example, Foucault's discussion on power, "Two Lectures," 92–108.

24. Foucault, *An Introduction*, vol.1 of *The History of Sexuality*, trans. Robert Hurley (New York: Vintage Books, 1980), 85.

25. Foucault, "Two Lectures," 88–89; *Discipline and Punish: The Birth of the Prison*, trans. Alan Sheridan (New York: Vintage Books, 1979), 26–27.

26. Foucault, "Truth and Power," in *Power/Knowledge*, 121.

27. Foucault, "Two Lectures," 97–98; emphasis in original.

28. Foucault, "Subject and Power," 217.

29. Foucault, "Subject and Power," 209.

30. Foucault, *History of Sexuality*, vol.1, 86.

31. It is worth noting that Foucault's account of the concept of power is in the chapter entitled "Method" in Part Four—"The Deployment of Sexuality"—of Volume One of *The History of Sexuality*.

32. For example, see Foucault, "Subject and Power," 209.

33. As Arnold I. Davidson puts it, "genealogy . . . has a wider scope than archaeology." See "Archaeology, Genealogy, Ethics," in *Foucault: A Critical Reader*, ed. David C. Hoy (Oxford: Basil Blackwell, 1986), 224.

34. Foucault, "Nietzsche, Genealogy, History," 140.

35. Foucault, "Subjectivity and Truth," lecture delivered at Dartmouth College, November 17, 1980, *Political Theory* 21 (May 1993): 203–204. Also see Pasquale Pasquino, "Michel Foucault (1926–84): The will to knowledge," *Economy and Society* 15 (February 1986): 104.

36. Foucault, "Subject and Power," 212.

37. "Questions of Method: An Interview with Michel Foucault," trans. Colin Gordon, *Ideology and Consciousness* 8 (spring 1981): 8–9; emphasis added.

38. Foucault, "Technologies of the Self," in *Technologies of the Self: A Seminar with Michel Foucault*, ed. Luther H. Martin, Huck Gutman, Patrick H. Hutton (Amherst: University of Massachusetts Press, 1988), 17.

39. Foucault, "The Confession of the Flesh," in *Power/Knowledge*, 194.

40. Foucault, *History of Sexuality*, vol.1, 145.

41. Foucualt, "Subjectivity and Truth," 203.

42. Foucault, *History of Sexuality*, vol.1, 94–95.

43. Davidson, "Ethics as ascetics," in *Cambridge Companion to Foucault*, 118.

44. Foucault, *The Use of Pleasure*, vol.2 of *The History of Sexuality*, trans. Robert Hurley (New York: Vintage Books, 1986), 6. Also see Davidson, "Archaeology, Genealogy, Ethics" and "Ethics as ascetics."

45. Foucault, "Truth and Power," 122.

46. Foucault, "Truth and Power," 122; "Questions on Geography," in *Power/Knowledge*, 72–73. For a similar formulation, see "Body/Power," in *Power/Knowledge*, 60.

47. Foucault, "Questions on Geography," 73.

48. Foucault, "Subject and Power," 209.

49. Foucault, "Confinement, Psychiatry, Prison," in *Politics, Philosophy, Culture: Interviews and Other Writings 1977–1984*, ed. Lawrence D. Kritzman, trans. Alan Sheridan et al. (New York: Routledge, 1988), 180; emphasis in original.

50. Foucault, "Confinement, Psychiatry, Prison," 181.

51. For a summary of these lectures, see Foucault, *Résumé des cours 1970–1982* (Paris: Julliard, 1989), 99–119.

52. Foucault, "Omnes et Singulatim: Towards a Criticism of 'Political Reason,'" in *The Tanner Lectures on Human Values*, ed. Sterling McMurrin (Salt Lake City: University of Utah Press, 1981), 223–254.

53. Foucault, "Governmentality," lecture given at the Collège de France, February 1978, trans. Rosi Braidotti, *Ideology and Consciouness* 6 (autumn 1979): 20.

54. Foucault, "Space, Knowledge, and Power," in *The Foucault Reader*, 242; emphasis in original.

55. Foucault, *History of Sexuality*, vol.1, 141–143.

56. Foucault, "Governmentality," 21. For a good account of this concept, see Colin Gordon, "Governmental Rationality: An Introduction," in

The Foucault Effect: Studies in Governmentality, ed. Graham Burchell, Colin Gordon, and Peter Miller (Chicago: University of Chicago Press, 1991), 1–51. The volume also contains Foucault's "Governmentality" and "Questions of Method," both with minor revisions by Colin Gordon.

57. Foucault, "Omnes et Singulatim," 227–230.

58. Foucault, "Omnes et Singulatim," 227.

59. Foucault, "Omnes et Singulatim," 235.

60. Foucault, "Omnes et Singulatim," 239. James Tully argues that the philosopher who made a major contribution to what Foucault sees as the "demonic game" was none other than Locke. Locke was caught in a tension—"the tension between his juristic political theory, which limits the degree and manner of control government can exercise over citizens, and some of his methods of reform, which treat the human subject as a malleable resource." See Tully, *An Approach to Political Philosophy: Locke in Contexts* (Cambridge: Cambridge University Press, 1993), 68.

61. Foucault, "Omnes et Singulatim," 235.

62. Foucault, *History of Sexuality*, vol.1, 138–144; emphasis in original.

63. Foucault, *History of Sexuality*, vol.1, 145–147.

64. Foucault, "Foucault at the Collège de France ii: A Course Summary," trans. James Bernauer, *Philosophy and Social Criticism* 8 (fall 1981): 354–355.

65. "Foucault at the Collège de France ii," 354, 356.

66. On Foucault's place in enriching our understanding of liberalism, see Tully, "The Possessive Individualism Thesis: A Reconsideration In Light Of Recent Scholarship," in *Democracy and Possessive Individualism*, 31–34, 37–39.

67. Foucault, "Omnes et Singulatim," 225.

68. Nancy Fraser, "Foucault on Modern Power: Empirical Insights and Normative Confusions," *Praxis International* 1 (fall 1981): 281–286; Nancy Hartsock, "Foucault on Power: A Theory for Women?" *Feminism/Postmodernism*, ed. Linda J. Nicholson (New York: Routledge,

1990), 164. For a comparable line of questioning, see Michael Walzer, "The Politics of Michel Foucault," *Dissent* (fall 1983): 481–490. Richard Rorty, in noting that Foucault is "an ironist who is unwilling to be a liberal," also claims that Foucault shows signs of fundamental contradiction. By this, Rorty means that Foucault is not willing to settle for liberal democracy as the most optimal political condition for what Rorty refers to as the private project of "self-creation." This refusal on Foucault's part is thus indicative of his ultimate "'longing for total revolution'". See "The Contingency of Community," in *Contingency, Irony, and Solidarity* (New York: Cambridge University Press, 1989), 61–65.

69. The exceptions are: Hubert L. Dreyfus and Paul Rabinow, "What is Maturity? Habermas and Foucault on 'What is Enlightenment?'" in *Foucault: A Critical Reader*, 109–121; Ian Hacking, "Self Improvement," in *Foucault: A Critical Reader*, 235–240. More recent works include: James Miller, *The Passion of Michel Foucault* (New York: Simon & Schuster, 1993), 137–142, 332–334, especially; Christopher Norris, "Foucault on Kant," in *The Truth About Postmodernism* (Oxford: Blackwell, 1993), 29–99, and "'What is Enlightenment?': Kant according to Foucault," in *Cambridge Companion to Foucault*, 159–196; David Owen, *Maturity and Modernity: Nietzsche, Weber, Foucault and the Ambivalence of Reason* (London: Routledge, 1994).

70. Norris, "Foucault on Kant," 43. It is interesting to note that Norris's position on this has changed considerably. See *Uncritical Theory: Postmodernism, Intellectuals and the Gulf War* (London: Lawrence & Wishart, 1992), 100–119.

71. For a penetrating critique of Norris's reading of Foucault and Kant, see Harpham, "So . . . What *Is* Enlightenment?" 535–539.

72. Foucault, "What is Enlightenment?" 36–37.

73. Foucault, "What is Enlightenment?" 37.

74. Kant, "What is Enlightenment?" in *On History*, ed. Lewis White Beck, trans. Lewis White Beck et al. (New York: Macmillan, 1963), 5.

75. Arendt, *Lectures on Kant's Political Philosophy*, ed. Ronald Beiner (Chicago: University of Chicago Press, 1982), 50.

76. Foucault, *Remarks on Marx: Conversations with Duccio Trombadori*, trans. R. James Goldstein and James Cascaito (New York: Semiotexte(e), 1991), 27, 33, 38–39; emphasis added.

77. Foucault, "Intellectuals and Power," in *Language, Counter-Memory, Practice*, 209. As Gilles Deleuze puts it, "a theorizing intellectual, for us, is no longer a subject, a representing or representative consciousness. Those who act and struggle are no longer represented. . . . Who speaks and acts? It is always a multiplicity . . . " See "Intellectuals and Power," 206. Foucault's concept of decentralizing discourse through a multiplicity of voices echoes M. M. Bakhtin's notion of "dialogization." See Bakhtin, *The Dialogic Imagination*, ed. Michael Holquist, trans. Caryl Emerson and Michael Holquist, (Austin: University of Texas Press, 1981), 262–263.

78. Foucault, "Discourse on Language," 231.

79. Ibid.

80. Foucault, "Politics and the Study of Discourse," trans. Colin Gordon, in *The Foucault Effect*, 60.

81. Foucault, *Remarks on Marx*, 29.

82. Foucault, "Confinement, Psychiatry, Prison," 197.

83. Taylor, "Foucault on Freedom and Truth," 175. More recently, Ronald Beiner, borrowing from Weber's famous line in *The Protestant Ethic and the Spirit of Capitalism*, describes Foucault as simultaneously a "spiritless specialist" and a "heartless sensualist." See Beiner, "Foucault's Hyper-Liberalism," *Critical Review* 9 (summer 1995): 367.

84. Foucault, "Two Lectures," in *Power/Knowedge*, 80–81; emphasis in original.

85. Foucault, "Truth and Power," 128; "Intellectuals and Power," 207–208.

86. J. Robert Oppenheimer, *Atom and Void: Essays on Science and Community* (Princeton: Princeton University Press, 1989), 64. Foucault, "Truth and Power," 127.

87. Oppenheimer, *Atom and Void*, 69.

88. Foucault, "Truth and Power," 128.

89. Clearly, Foucault was aware of the exclusive nature of modern science. As he puts it, by "subjugated knowledge(s)," he means those

"naive knowledges, located low down on the hierarchy, beneath the required level of cognition or scientificity." See "Two Lectures," 82.

90. Foucault, "Intellectuals and Power," 208.

91. Oppenheimer to the Association of Los Alamos Scientists, speech, November 1945, in *Robert Oppenheimer: Letters and Recollections*, ed. A. K. Smith and C. Weiner (Cambridge: Harvard University Press, 1980), quoted in Richard Rhodes, *The Making of the Atomic Bomb* (New York: Simon & Schuster, 1986), 761.

92. Foucault, "Is it really important to think?" *Philosophy and Social Criticism* 9 (spring 1982): 34.

93. Ibid.

94. Foucault, "Polemics, Politics, and Problemizations: An Interview," in *The Foucault Reader*, 388. The importance of this passage is noted by Norris, "Foucault on Kant," 52. For a very similar though not as eloquent comment by Foucault on the nature of thought, see "Is it really important to think?" 33.

95. Foucault, *The Use of Pleasure*, vol.2 of *The History of Sexuality*, trans. Robert Hurley (New York: Vintage, 1986), 9.

96. I do not agree with Rorty's claim that Foucault has conflated his own moral identity as a "useful citizen in a democratic country" and the ethical identity that Foucault has to himself, which is being a philosopher engaged in the private project of self-invention. Foucault might have devoted his private life to self-invention. But this is indeed Foucault's private life, as opposed to his public life as an intellectual and as a citizen. See Rorty, "Moral Identity and Private Autonomy," in *Essays on Heidegger and Others*, vol.2 of *Philosophical Papers* (New York: Cambridge University Press, 1991), 196.

97. Foucault, "Face aux gouvernements, les droits de l'homme," *Liberation*, July 1, 1984, reprinted in *Actes*, 54 (1986): 22.

98. Tom Keenan, "The 'Paradox' of Knowledge and Power: Reading Foucault on a Bias," *Political Theory* 15 (February 1987): 21.

99. Keenan, "The 'Paradox' of Knowledge and Power," 28. Foucault, "Two Lectures," 108.

100. In Keenan's view, Foucault employs the moribund language of right in order to "destabilize" it. But to me Keenan's very elaborate deconstructionist analysis really amounts to the same observation. See Keenan, "The 'Paradox' of Knowledge and Power," 21–28.

101. Foucault once said, to "counter all forms of fascism" is to "not become enamored of power," preface to *Anti-Oedipus: Capitalism and Schizophrenia*, by Gilles Deleuze and Felix Guattari, trans. Robert Hurley et al. (Minneapolis: University of Minnesota Press, 1983), xiii–xiv. It is a statement worth noting even though Foucault had come a long way since he wrote the preface. Miller points out that Foucault had a change of heart by 1979 when he, along with "much of the French left," began to embrace "a kind of liberal (and chastened) vision of what politics might achieve." See Miller, *The Passion of Michel Foucault*, 314. For a rebuttal, see Connolly, "Beyond Good and Evil: The Ethical Sensibility of Michel Foucault," *Political Theory* 21 (August 1993): 365–389.

102. Rux Martin, "An Interview with Michel Foucault, October 25, 1982," in *Technologies of the Self: A Seminar with Michel Foucault*, ed. Luther H. Martin, Huck Gutman, Patrick H. Hutton (Amherst: The University of Massachusetts Press, 1988), 13.

103. Ibid.

104. Gilles Deleuze, *Foucault*, ed. and trans. Seán Hand (Minneapolis: University of Minnesota Press, 1988), 116.

105. Foucault, *The Use of Pleasure*, 9. Foucault's understanding of philosophy as "spiritual exercise" is profoundly shaped by Pierre Hadot. See Davidson, "Spiritual Exercises and Ancient Philosophy: An Introduction to Pierre Hadot," *Critical Inquiry* 16 (spring 1990): 475–482.

106. Deleuze characterizes Foucault's project as "a sort of neo-Kantianism unique to Foucault," see *Foucault*, 60.

107. Foucault, "Discourse and Truth: The Problematization of *Parrhesia*" (Notes to the Seminar Given by Foucault at the University of California at Berkeley, 1983), 114. I consulted the copy at Centre Michel Foucault.

108. Foucault, "Discourse and Truth," 113.

109. Foucault, *History of Sexuality*, vol.1, 137.

110. While Foucault obviously has provided us with important insights into the rationale behind genocide in modern states, he has been criticized in particular for being silent on Nazism and the Holocaust—an experience that he had actually lived through. A recent article by Alan Milchman and Alan Rosenberg vindicates Foucault against this charge. See "Michel Foucault, Auschwitz and modernity," *Philosophy and Social Criticism* 22 (January, 1996): 101–113. The purpose of the paper is "to weave together these strands of a genealogy of Nazism which Foucault did not live to write, but which we believe cannot be written without him" (110). The construction of this genealogy by Milchman and Rosenberg is convincing and true to the spirit of Foucault's genealogy. However, I find the article, like Foucault's view on the matter, lacking in accounting for why the Holocaust occurred in Germany and other European enclaves under the Nazi Party and not anywhere else.

111. Foucault, "Two Lectures," 81.

112. "Questions of Method," 10. See also *Discipline and Punish*, 200–208.

113. For Foucault's comment on the relationship between "truth" and "fiction," see "The History of Sexuality," in *Power/Knowledge*, 193.

Chapter Six

1. Hannah Arendt, *The Origins of Totalitarianism*, rev. ed. (New York: Harcourt Brace Jovanovich, 1973), viii–ix. Hereafter cited as *OT*. All subsequent citations are from this edition unless otherwise stated.

2. Arendt, "Understanding and Politics," in *Essays in Understanding 1930–1954*, ed. Jerome Kohn (New York: Harcourt Brace & Company, 1994), 324. This essay was originally published in *Partisan Review* 20 (July–August 1953): 377–392. Kohn includes portions of the manuscript that did not appear in the 1953 article. The words cited here are one such instance. An earlier comparable formulation can be found in the first edition of *The Origins of Totalitarianism*. Arendt said, "the fact is that the true problem of our time cannot be understood, let alone solved, without the acknowledgment that totalitarianism became this century's curse only because it so terrifyingly took care of its problems." See "Concluding Remarks," in *The Origins of Totalitarianism*, 1st ed. (New York: Harcourt, Brace and Company), 430.

3. Canovan, *Hannah Arendt: A Reinterpretation of Her Political Thought* (Cambridge: Cambridge University Press, 1992), 7.

4. Canovan, *Hannah Arendt*, vii; emphasis in original. Canovan's earlier work is *The Political Thought of Hannah Arendt* (London: J. M. Dent, 1974).

5. However, at the end of the book, Canovan appears to retract her position when she says that Arendt's "thinking about Nazism and Stalinism may be something of an embarrassment: a brilliant, ambitious and highly questionable interpretation of totalitarianism and modernity." See Canovan, *Hannah Arendt*, 279. As Seyla Benhabib points out, what Canovan has trouble with is Arendt's "interconnected accounts of totalitarianism, modernity and 'society.'" Benhabib disagrees with Canovan's reading insofar as it suggests that Arendt sees totalitarianism as "an inevitable growth of western modernity." See Benhabib, review of *Hannah Arendt: A Reinterpretation of Her Political Thought*, by Margaret Canovan, and *Arendt, Camus, and Modern Rebellion*, by Jeffrey C. Isaac, *Journal of Modern History* 67 (September 1995): 689.

6. *OT*, 468–474.

7. Arendt, "Truth and Politics," in *Between Past and Future*, enl. ed. (New York: Penguin Books, 1977), 241.

8. Arendt, "What is Authority?" in *Between Past and Future*, 137.

9. *The Origins of Totalitarianism*, 2d ed. (New York: Meridian Books, 1958), xi; emphasis added. "Ideology and Terror" first appeared in *The Review of Politics* 15 (July 1953): 303–327.

10. *OT*, 1st ed., 433 and 439. For an excellent account of the development of Arendt's thought between the publication of the first edition of *The Origins of Totalitarianism* and that of *The Human Condition*, see Canovan, *Arendt*, 17–154. On pages 60 to 62, Canovan gives an overview of how "Arendt's mature political thought flows directly" from the preoccupations addressed in the first edition.

11. *OT*, xv.

12. *OT*, 460–461.

13. *OT*, 468–474, passim.

14. *OT*, 353

15. *OT*, 474.

16. *OT*, 323.

17. *OT*, 311–315.

18. *OT*, 352.

19. *OT*, 352–353, 323.

20. Arendt, "Truth and Politics," 249–254.

21. Arendt, "Truth and Politics," 253–254.

22. Arendt, "Truth and Politics," 227n. The book is *Eichmann in Jerusalem: A Report on the Banality of Evil*, rev. and enl. (Harmondsworth: Penguin Books, 1965). Hereafter cited as *Eichmann*. The book is based on a series of reports that Arendt wrote for the *New Yorker* on the trial of Adolf Eichmann. He was a former Gestapo officer in the Head Office for Reich Security under Himmler. For a detailed account of Arendt's experience of the trial, see Elisabeth Young-Bruehl, *Hannah Arendt: For Love of the World* (New Haven: Yale University Press, 1982), 328–378.

23. Arendt, "Truth and Politics," 264.

24. Arendt, "Truth and Politics," 231.

25. Ibid.

26. Arendt, "Truth and Politics," 246.

27. Arendt, "Truth and Politics," 231.

28. Arendt, "Truth and Politics," 238.

29. Arendt, "Thinking, " pt.1 *of The Life of the Mind*, ed. Mary McCarthy, one-volume ed. (New York: Harcourt Brace Jovanovich, 1978). Arendt says, "there exists a sharp dividing line between what is authentically Socratic and the philosophy taught by Plato" (168). Hereafter the book will be cited as *LM*.

30. Arendt, "Philosophy and Politics," *Social Research* 57 (spring 1990): 73. Hereafter cited as "PP." As stated in the introduction by the editor, this article is the third and final part of a series of lectures that Arendt delivered at Notre Dame University in 1954. The original title of the whole series is "The Problem of Action and Thought after the French Revolution." See also Canovan, "Philosophy and Politics," in *Hannah Arendt*, 253–274.

31. "PP," 73–74.

32. "PP," 80.

33. "PP," 74–75. Whether or not one can characterize Plato's conclusion as truly "anti-Socratic" will of course depend on how one understands the historical Socrates, which is a much-debated subject among scholars. However, as readers can tell from my interpretation of Plato in chapter 2, Arendt's reading is one that I support.

34. "PP," 78–80, 90.

35. "PP," 93.

36. "PP," 95–96.

37. Arendt, "On the Nature of Totalitarianism," in *Essays in Understanding*, 359–360.

38. For an excellent and thorough exposition of Arendt's theory of political action, see Dana R. Villa, *Arendt and Heidegger: The Fate of the Political* (Princeton: Princeton University Press, 1996), 15–109. Also see George Kateb, *Hannah Arendt: Politics, Conscience, Evil* (Totowa, N.J.: Rowman & Allanheld, 1983), 1–51.

39. Arendt, *The Human Condition*, 7; emphasis added.

40. Arendt, *The Human Condition*, 3. On pages 178–179, Arendt points out that action and speech are so closely related that it would not be possible to separate them, The importance of this passage is pointed out by Bernstein, in *Beyond Objectivity and Relativism*, 208.

41. Villa, *Arendt and Heidegger*, 31.

42. Villa, *Arendt and Heidegger*, 47; emphasis in original.

43. Arendt, "Truth and Politics," 241–242.

44. Lisa Disch, *Hannah Arendt and the Limits of Philosophy* (Ithaca: Cornell University Press, 1994), 162.

45. Like Foucault, Arendt's reading of Kant is by no means standard, as critics have noted; and indeed, even she herself acknowledges this. See Arendt, *Lectures on Kant's Political Philosophy*, ed. Ronald Beiner (Chicago: University of Chicago Press, 1982), 19 and 61. Arendt's idiosyncratic interpretation revolves around her claim that Kant's political philosophy is yet to be written and it is in the *Critique of Judgment* rather than the *Critique of Practical Reason* and Kant's other political writings that we find his political philosophy. For critiques of Arendt's use of Kant, see Ronald Beiner, "Interpretive Essay: Hannah Arendt on Judging" in *Lectures on Kant's Political Philosophy*, 142–144, and more recently, "Rereading Hannah Arendt's Kant Lectures," *Philosophy and Social Criticism* (January 1997): 21–32; Patrick Riley, "Hannah Arendt on Kant, Truth and Politics," *Political Studies* 35 (September 1987): 379–392.

46. Arendt, "The Crisis in Culture," in *Between Past and Future*, 220–223.

47. Arendt, *Lectures on Kant's Political Philosophy*, 72.

48. Beiner, "Interpretive Essay: Hannah Arendt on Judging," 109. However, Beiner questions whether Kant constitutes the best source for understanding the nature of political judgment. He goes on to suggest that Arendt chooses Kant as her source on the subject primarily because it facilitates her aesthetic notion of politics; see 131–144.

49. Arendt, "Truth and Politics," 231.

50. Arendt, "Truth and Politics," 238.

51. Villa, *Arendt and Heidegger*, 96.

52. Arendt, "Truth and Politics," 257.

53. *OT*, 296. Arendt also notes in "Truth and Politics" that "freedom of opinion is a farce" anyway "unless factual information is guaranteed" (238).

54. *OT*, 477.

55. Arendt, "The Archimedean Point," Hannah Arendt Papers, Library of Congress, Box 61, 031394. This was a lecture delivered at the College of Engineering, University of Michigan, in November 1968. I first became aware of the lecture when reading Disch, *Hannah Arendt and the Limits of Philosophy*. Hereafter the lecture will be cited as "AP." Parts of the lecture were published in the essay "The Conquest of Space and the Stature of Man," in *Between Past and Future*, 265–280.

56. "AP," 031395.

57. Arendt, "The Conquest of Space," 265, 267.

58. Arendt, "AP" 0331395; "The Conquest of Space," 273.

59. "AP," 031399.

60. "AP," 031398.

61. "AP," 031401; emphasis in original.

62. Arendt, "The Conquest of Space," 278.

63. Villa, *Arendt and Heidegger*, 257; emphasis in original. Villa notes that Arendt's observation about totalitarianism as the "plastic art" of politics owes much to Heidegger's later work on the essence of technology.

64. *OT*, 463.

65. Arendt, "Intellectuals and Responsibility," lecture delivered at the University of Chicago, 1967, Hannah Arendt Papers, Library of Congress, Box 71, 2.

66. For example, see Beiner, "Interpretive Essay," 97–101. Also, see Wolin, "Stopping to Think," *The New York Review of Books* 25 (26 October 1978): 16–21.

67. Arendt, "On Hannah Arendt," in *Hannah Arendt: The Recovery of the Public World*, ed. Melvyn A. Hill (New York: St. Martin's Press, 1979), 303; emphasis in original. Hereafter the aricle will be cited as "HA."

68. Ibid.

69. *Eichmann*, 287–288; emphasis in original.

70. "HA," 313–314.

71. *Eichmann*, 289.

72. *Eichmann*, 294–295.

73. *LM*, pt.1, 5.

74. *LM*, pt.1, 167.

75. *LM*, pt.1, 185–186; emphasis in original.

76. "PP," 84–86, 89.

77. "PP," 86, 89.

78. Arendt, "Thinking and Moral Considerations," *Social Research* 38 (autumn 1971): 446.

79. *The Human Condition*, 325.

80. *LM*, pt.1, 179, 186, 187–188, 192–193.

81. *LM*, pt.1, 191.

82. Ibid.; emphasis added.

83. Arendt, "Thinking and Moral Considerations," 422.

84. "HA," 308.

85. "HA," 303.

86. Arendt, "Truth and Politics," 261–262.

87. *LM*, pt.1, 13–15.

88. Arendt, "Isak Dinesen," in *Men in Dark Times* (New York: Harcourt Brace Jovanovich, 1968), 105.

89. "HA," 308.

90. Arendt, "Truth and Politics," 262. On the theme of Arendt herself as a storyteller, see Seyla Benhabib, "Hannah Arendt and the Redemptive Power of Narrative," *Social Research* 57 (spring 1990): 167–196; Elisabeth Young-Bruehl, "Hannah Arendt's Storytelling," in *Mind and the Body Politic* (New York: Routledge, 1988), 1–6.

91. Arendt, "Intellectuals and Responsibility," 2.

92. Riley, "Hannah Arendt on Kant," 392.

93. Arendt, "Truth and Politics," 262–263.

94. "AP," 031394. For a fine comparison between Arendt and Thucydides, see Disch, *Hannah Arendt and the Limits of Philosophy*, 127–131.

95. Beiner, "Interpretive Essay," 92–109.

96. Beiner, "Rereading Hannah Arendt's Kant Lectures," typescript, 13–15.

97. *OT*, xiv.

98. Kant, *Critique of Judgment*, trans. Werner S. Pluhar (Indianapolis: Hackett Publishing, 1987), pt.1, §31, 144.

99. Arendt, "Truth and Politics," 260–261.

100. Arendt, "Truth and Politics," 231.

101. Arendt, "Truth and Politics," 261.

102. Arendt, "A Reply," *The Review of Politics* 15 (January 1953): 80; emphasis in original. The reply is to Eric Voegelin's review of *OT*, which appears in the same volume.

Chapter Seven

1. Foucault, "Truth and Power," 133.

2. Lynn T. White III, *Policies of Chaos: The Organizational Causes of Violence in China's Cultural Revolution* (Princeton: Princeton University Press, 1989).

3. For an analysis of the kind of psychological ordeal that victims of the Cultural Revolution endured, see Anne F. Thurston, *Enemies of the People: The Ordeal of the Intellectuals in China's Great Cultural Revolution* (New York: Knopf, 1987).

4. I think that the case of China does vindicate Arendt against Benhabib's claim when she says, ". . . as explanatory categories, the experiences of isolation and the formation of superfluous masses are limited." See Benhabib, review of *Hannah Arendt*, 690.

5. Lucian W. Pye, "On Chinese Pragmatism in the 1980s," *The China Quarterly* 106 (June 1986): 207.

6. Pye, "On Chinese Pragmatism," 209.

7. Stuart Schram, *Ideology and Policy in China Since the Third Plenum, 1978–84*, Research Notes and Studies no.6 (London: Contemporary China Institute, School of Oriental and African Studies, University of London, 1984), 1.

8. For an in-depth and superb study of post-Mao ideological development, see Yan Sun, *The Chinese Reassessment of Socialism, 1976–1992* (Princeton: Princeton University Press, 1995).

9. I have done a much more detailed study of the debate elsewhere. See "Deng Xiaoping, Yu Guangyuan and Su Shaozhi: The Reformist View on Marxism-Leninism-Mao Zedong Thought as a Guiding Ideology to Building Socialism in China," in *East Asia Insight: Selected Papers from the CASA Annual Conferences 1985–1987*, ed. Larry N. Shyu, Min-sun Chen, Claude-Yves Charron, and Matsuo Soga (Montreal: Canadian Asian Studies Association, 1988), 69–92.

10. Su Shaozhi, "A Decade of Crises at the Institute of Marxism-Leninism-Mao Zedong Thought, 1979–89," *The China Quarterly* 134 (June 1993): 345.

11. Su, "A Decade of Crises," 335, 338.

12. Michael Schoenhals, "The 1978 Truth Criterion Controversy," *The China Quarterly* 126 (June 1991): 256. Hu's piece was titled "Practice is the criterion of all truths."

13. Schoenhals, "The 1978 Truth Criterion Controversy," 260.

14. For an account of how the Chinese Communist Party handled the problem of ultra-leftism, see William A. Joseph, *The Critique of Ultra-Leftism in China, 1958–1981* (Stanford: Stanford University Press, 1984).

15. "Practice is the sole criterion for testing truth," reprint, *Renmin ribao,* May 12, 1978, 2.

16. Deng Xiaoping, "Speech at the All-Army Conference on Political Work," June 2, 1978, in *Selected Works of Deng Xiaoping (1975–1982)*, trans. the Bureau for the Compilation and Translation of Works of Marx, Engels, Lenin and Stalin (Beijing: Foreign Language Press, 1984), 127–128, 132. Hereafter the collection will be cited as *SW*.

17. Deng, "Emancipate the Mind, Seek Truth from Facts and Unite As One in Looking to the Future," December 13, 1978, in *SW*, 154.

18. Ibid.

19. Mao Zedong, "On Khrushchev's Phoney Communism and Its Historical Lessons for the World: Comment on the Open Letter of the Central Committee of the CPSU," in *Sino-Soviet Relations, 1964–1965* by William E. Griffith (Cambridge: MIT Press, 1967), document 14 at 326.

20. As Joseph points out, when the Gang of Four was brought to trial in 1980, all four were charged specifically with "counterrevolutionary crimes" rather than "ultra-leftism." See Joseph, *The Critique of Ultra-Leftism*, 234–235.

21. Deng, "Emancipate the Mind," 156.

22. Schoenhals, "The 1978 Truth Criterion Controversy," 268.

23. Deng, "Adhere to the Party Line and Improve Methods of Work," February 29, 1980, in *SW*, 264.

24. Deng, "Implement the Policy of Readjustment, Ensure Stability and Unity," December 25, 1980, in *SW*, 345.

25. Yu Guangyuan, "Jianyi xie lianxi dangqian shiji de sizhong lilun jiaocai" (Proposal on writing four types of theoretical teaching material that integrates current reality), in *Sikao yu shijian* (Reflection and practice) (Changsha: Hunan renmin chubanshe, 1984), 83–85. The book is a collection of Yu's writings from 1977 to 1983 covering a wide range of subjects. Hereafter the volume will be cited as *SS*.

26. Yu, "Yanjiu Makesizhuyizhe mianlin de zhongda lilun wenti he shiji wenti" (A study on the major theoretical and practical problems confronting Marxists), in *SS*, 202–203.

27. Yu, "Fazhan zuowei shehuizhuyi jianshe de kexue de Makesizhuyi," (Develop Marxism as the science of building socialism), in *SS*, 642–642, 644–647.

28. Yu, "Fazhan," 642–644.

29. Yu, "Fazhan," 649.

30. Yu, "Makesizhuyi yu shehuizhuyi" (Marxism and socialism), in *Makesizhuyi yanjiu* (Research in Marxism) 1 (1983): 38–39.

31. As Su notes, it was due to "a new election procedure in which members of the various institutes of the Academy [of Social Sciences] were allowed to vote and elect their own directors" that he got the position. See Su, "Crises at the Institute of Marxism," 342.

32. For an analysis of Su's theory, see Sun, *The Chinese Reassessment of Socialism*, 183–190.

33. During his visit to Princeton University on April 8, 1985, Su explained why he preferred the translation of *shishi qiushi* into "seeking truth from practice" rather than the official version of "seeking truth from facts." To me, this was an indication that Su realized the ambiguity of the term *shishi* in that the "reality" which the theorists proceed from is not just one consisting of "pure facts." Instead, it is a "reality" that is shaped by "practice"—an ideological line.

34. Su, "Zai shijian zhong zhengque renshi he yunyong jingji guilu" (Correctly understand and apply economic laws through practice), in *Shijian shi jianyan zhenli de weiyi biaozhun wenti taolunji* (Collected essays on the question of practice as the sole criterion for testing truth), ed. the Editorial Department of *Zhexue yanjiu* (Research in Philosophy) vol.2 (Beijing: Zhongguo shehui kexue chubanshe, 1979), 497–500.

35. Ibid. Su has written extensively on the topic of modernization and democratization, see, for example, Su, *Democratization and Reform* (Nottingham: Spokesman, 1988).

36. Su, "Develop Marxism Under Contemporary Conditions—In Commemoration of the Centenary of the Death of Karl Marx," *Selected Writings on Studies of Marxism* 2 (1983): 31–38, see pages 31 to 32 in particular for the discussion on theory lagging behind practice.

37. Su, "Develop Marxism under Contemporary Conditions," 35; emphasis in original.

38. Su was cited as echoing Deng's remark that "socialism needs constant reform" in a speech given at a luncheon gathering with foreign journalists in Beijing. Ann Scott, untitled report, UPI wire service, electronic edition, 11 October 1985.

39. Hu Yaobang, *Guanyu sixiang zhengzhi gongzhuo wenti* (Notes on problems in ideological and political work) (Beijing: Renmin chubanshe, 1983), 2, 4–8.

40. For a more recent essay on these themes, see Su, "Rethinking Marxism in the light of Chinese Reforms," in *Whither Marxism?: Global Crises in International Perspective*, ed. Bernd Magnus and Stephen Cullenberg (New York: Routledge, 1995), 235–250.

41. In *The Chinese Assessment of Socialism*, Sun discusses the differences between the Chinese approach to the reappraisal of socialism and that of the Soviet Union. Sun notes that the Soviets took a more radical approach and the process in general was less orchestrated and monitored by the Party. In Sun's words, "in terms of the content of reassessment, the Soviet appraisal went beyond the major taboo areas of the Chinese case. It uprooted the foundation of the established system, political and economic, by pruning it down to its Stalinist core; it exposed the normative deficiency of this system by establishing the person as the goal of political life and social development; and it delegitimized the political vanguard of that system by recognizing the legitimacy of competing political opinions and interests" (254). For details of the contrasts, see 237–257. It is certainly no accident that the Chinese Communist Party, in contrast to its Russian counterpart, is still in power.

42. Su, review of *Chinese Marxism in the Post-Mao Era*, by Bill Brugger and David Kelly, *The Australian Journal of Chinese Affairs* 29 (January 1993): 169; emphasis added. I first became aware of Su's

statement when I read Sun, *The Chinese Reassessment of Socialism*, 18. For a thoughtful analysis of why Chinese intellectuals tend to be remonstrators rather than dissidents, at least until 1989, see Merle Goldman, *Sowing the Seeds of Democracy in China: Political Reform in the Deng Xiaoping Era* (Cambridge: Harvard University Press, 1994), especially 1–24, 338–360.

43. For Arendt's view on the American founding and how the "discourse" of the founders helps to preserve a "body politic" informed by "common deliberation," see Arendt, *On Revolution* (New York: Penguin Books, 1977), 201–214.

Chapter Eight

1. Honig, *Political Theory and the Displacement of Politics*, 76–125. More recently, "Toward an Agonistic Feminism: Hannah Arendt and the Politics of Identity," in *Feminist Interpretations of Hannah Arendt*, ed. Bonnie Honig (University Park: Pennsylvania State University Press, 1995), 135–166. Another work that interprets Arendt as proposing a "postmodern conception of political action" is Michael G. Gottsegen, *The Political Thought of Hannah Arendt* (Albany: State University of New York Press, 1994), especially 139–234. As to Dana Villa, if one only reads his 1992 essay, "Beyond Good and Evil: Arendt, Nietzsche, and the Aestheticization of Political Theory," *Political Theory* 20 (May 1992): 274–308, then Villa does appear to be a "postmodernist" interpreter of Arendt. But his book, *Arendt and Heidegger*, which I cite in several places in chapter 6, offers a very complex and insightful reading of Arendt—one that I will hestitate to call "postmodernist," at least in the way the term is defined here.

2. Honig, *Political Theory and the Displacement of Politics*, 125; emphasis added.

3. Arendt, "A Reply," 80.

4. For a non-postmodernist reading of Arendt as providing us with a political alternative, see Jeffrey C. Isaac, *Arendt, Camus, and Modern Rebellion* (New Haven: Yale University Press, 1992). I find Isaac's association of Arendt with a vision of "rebellious politics" a lot more convincing than Honig's interpretation.

5. Arendt, "On Hannah Arendt," 336.

6. Lyotard, *The Postmodern Condition*, 8.

7. Connolly, *Identity\Difference*, 200; my emphasis.

8. Allen, *Truth in Philosophy*, 41.

9. Leslie Paul Thiele uses the term "heroic individualism" to describe Nietzsche's individualism. See *Friedrich Nietzsche and the Politics of the Soul: A Study of Heroic Individualism* (Princeton: Princeton University Press, 1990).

10. Judy Rebick, "Bridging Identity: A Creative Response to Identity Politics," in *Clash of Identities: Media, Manipulation, and Politics of the Self*, ed. James Littleton (Toronto: Prentice-Hall, 1996), 31; emphasis added.

11. For a thoughtful piece on the subject, see Sheldon Wolin, "Democracy, Difference, and Re-cognition," *Political Theory* 21 (August 1993): 464–483.

12. Minutes, 2 July 1996, The Human Rights Art Commissioning Committee, University of Guelph.

13. Seyla Benhabib, "From Identity Politics to Social Feminism: A Plea for the Nineties," in *Radical Democracy*, 36.

14. Hartsock, "Foucault on Power: A Theory for Women?" 172. Also see Benhabib, "From Identity Politics to Social Feminism," 30–33.

15. Joan Scott, "The Evidence of Experience," *Critical Inquiry* 17 (summer 1991): 777.

16. Scott, "The Evidence of Experience," 780.

17. Hartsock, "Foucault on Power," 163–164.

18. Foucault, "Nietzsche, Genealogy, History," 153.

19. Paul Veyne, "The Final Foucault and His Ethics," trans. Catherine Porter and Arnold I. Davidson, *Critical Inquiry* 20 (autumn 1990): 5.

20. Connolly, *The Ethos of Pluralization* (Minneapolis: University of Minnesota Press, 1995), xvi; my emphasis. Connolly also says, through the "politics of enactment," "new, positive identities are forged out of old differences, injuries, and energies . . . " (xiv).

Selected Bibliography

Allen, Barry. *Truth in Philosophy.* Cambridge: Harvard University Press, 1993.

Arac, Jonathan, ed. *After Foucault: Humanistic Knowledge, Postmodern Challenges.* New Brunswick, N.J.: Rutgers University Press, 1988.

Arendt, Hannah. *The Origins of Totalitarianism.* 1st ed. New York: Harcourt, Brace and Company, 1951.

———. "A Reply." *The Review of Politics* 15 (January 1953): 76–84.

———. "Ideology and Terror." *The Review of Politics* 15 (July 1953): 303–327.

———. "Understanding and Politics." *Partisan Review* 20 (July–August 1953): 377–392.

———. *The Human Condition.* Chicago: University of Chicago Press, 1958.

———. *The Origins of Totalitarianism.* 2d edition. New York: Meridian Books, 1958.

———. "Intellectuals and Responsibility." Lecture delivered at the University of Chicago, 1967. Hannah Arendt Papers. Library of Congress. Box 71.

---. *Men in Dark Times.* New York: Harcourt Brace Jovanovich, 1968.

---. "The Archimedean Point." Lecture delivered at the College of Engineering, University of Michigan, November 1968. Hannah Arendt Papers. Library of Congress. Box 61

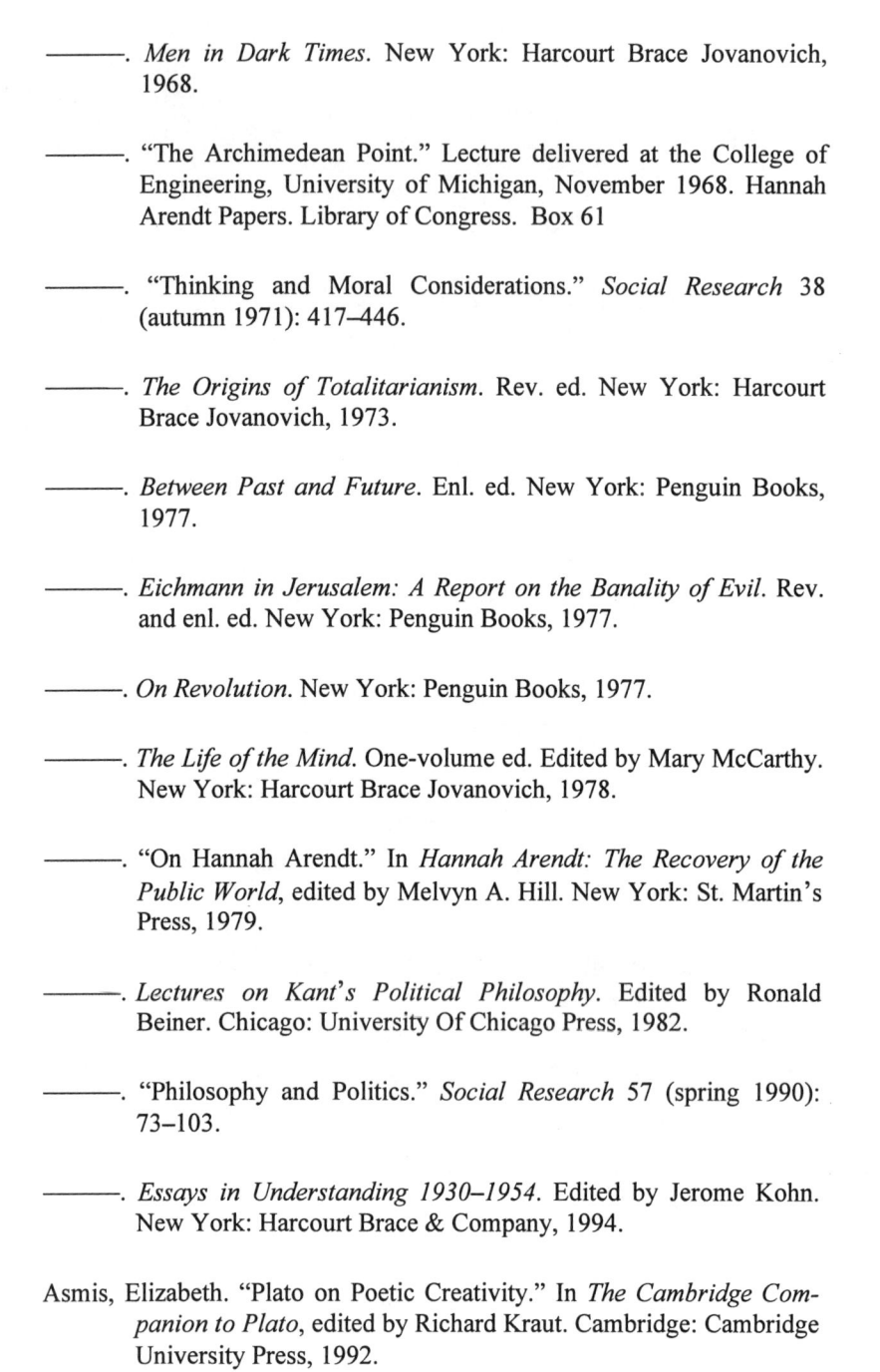

---. "Thinking and Moral Considerations." *Social Research* 38 (autumn 1971): 417–446.

---. *The Origins of Totalitarianism.* Rev. ed. New York: Harcourt Brace Jovanovich, 1973.

---. *Between Past and Future.* Enl. ed. New York: Penguin Books, 1977.

---. *Eichmann in Jerusalem: A Report on the Banality of Evil.* Rev. and enl. ed. New York: Penguin Books, 1977.

---. *On Revolution.* New York: Penguin Books, 1977.

---. *The Life of the Mind.* One-volume ed. Edited by Mary McCarthy. New York: Harcourt Brace Jovanovich, 1978.

---. "On Hannah Arendt." In *Hannah Arendt: The Recovery of the Public World*, edited by Melvyn A. Hill. New York: St. Martin's Press, 1979.

---. *Lectures on Kant's Political Philosophy.* Edited by Ronald Beiner. Chicago: University Of Chicago Press, 1982.

---. "Philosophy and Politics." *Social Research* 57 (spring 1990): 73–103.

---. *Essays in Understanding 1930–1954.* Edited by Jerome Kohn. New York: Harcourt Brace & Company, 1994.

Asmis, Elizabeth. "Plato on Poetic Creativity." In *The Cambridge Companion to Plato*, edited by Richard Kraut. Cambridge: Cambridge University Press, 1992.

Bacon, Francis. *The New Organon and Related Writings*. Edited by Fulton H. Anderson. New York: Liberal Arts Press, 1960.

Bakhtin, M. M. *The Dialogic Imagination*. Edited by Michael Holquist. Translated by Caryl Emerson and Michael Holquist. Austin: University of Texas Press, 1981.

Ball, Terence. "Hobbes' Linguistic Turn." *Polity* 17 (summer 1985): 739–760.

Bambrough, Renford, ed. *Plato, Popper and Politics: Some Contributions to a Modern Controversy*. Cambridge: Heffer, 1967.

Barker, Martin. "Kant as a problem for Weber." *British Journal of Sociology* 31 (June 1980): 224–245.

Beetham, David. "Max Weber and the Liberal Political Tradition." In *Barbarism of Reason: Max Weber and the Twilight of Enlightenment*, edited by Asher Horowitz and Terry Maley. Toronto: University of Toronto Press, 1994.

Beiner, Ronald. "Hannah Arendt on Judging." Interpretive essay in *Lectures on Kant's Political Philosophy*, by Hannah Arendt. Chicago: University of Chicago Press, 1982.

———. "Foucault's Hyper-Liberalism." *Critical Review* 9 (summer 1995): 349–370.

———. "Rereading Hannah Arendt's Kant Lectures." *Philosophy and Social Criticism* (January 1997): 21–32.

Benhabib, Seyla. "Hannah Arendt and the Redemptive Power of Narrative." *Social Research* 57 (spring 1990): 167–196.

———. Review of *Hannah Arendt: A Reinterpretation of Her Political Thought*, by Margaret Canovan and *Arendt, Camus, and Modern Rebellion*, by Jeffrey C. Isaac. *Journal of Modern History* 67 (September 1995): 687–691.

———. "From Identity Politics to Social Feminism: A Plea for the Nineties." In *Radical Democracy: Identity, Citizenship and the State*, edited by David Trend. New York: Routledge, 1996.

Bernauer, James. "On Reading and Mis-reading Hannah Arendt." *Philosophy and Social Criticism* 11 (summer 1985): 1–34.

Bernauer, James, and Thomas Keenan, comps. "The Works of Michel Foucault 1954–1984." In *The Final Foucault,* edited by James Bernauer and David Rasmussen. Cambridge: MIT Press, 1988.

Bernstein, Richard J. *Beyond Objectivity and Relativism: Science, Hermeneutics, and Praxis.* Philadelphia: University of Pennsylvania Press, 1983.

Bloom, Allan. "Interpretive Essay." In *The Republic of Plato,* translated by Allan Bloom. New York: Basic Books, 1968.

Brand, M. A. "Causality, Objectivity and Freedom: Weber, Kant and The Neo-Kantians." *Australian and New Zealand Journal of Sociology* 15 (March 1979): 6–12.

Burnyeat, M. F. "Sphinx Without a Secret." *The New York Review of Books* 32 (30 May 1985): 30–36.

―――. "M. F. Burnyeat replies." In "The Studies of Leo Strauss: An Exchange." *The New York Review of Books* 32 (10 October 1995): 43–44.

Canovan, Margaret. *The Political Thought of Hannah Arendt.* London: J. M. Dent, 1974.

―――. "Socrates or Heidegger? Hannah Arendt's Reflections on Philosophy and Politics." *Social Research* 57 (spring 1990): 135–165.

―――. *Hannah Arendt: A Reinterpretation of Her Political Thought.* Cambridge: Cambridge University Press, 1992.

Connolly, William E. "Taylor, Foucault, and Otherness." *Political Theory* 13 (August 1985): 365–375.

―――. *Identity\Difference: Democratic Negotiations of Political Paradox.* Ithaca: Cornell University Press, 1991.

———. "Beyond Good and Evil: The Ethical Sensibility of Michel Foucault." *Political Theory* 21 (August 1993): 365–389.

———. "Democracy and Contingency." In *Democracy and Possessive Individualism: The Intellectual Legacy of C. B. Macpherson*, edited by Joseph H. Carens. Albany: State University of New York Press, 1993.

———. *The Ethos of Pluralization.* Minneapolis: University of Minnesota Press, 1995.

Connor, W. Robert. *Thucydides*. Princeton: Princeton University Press, 1984.

Cropsey, Joseph et al. "The Studies of Leo Strauss: An Exchange." *The New York Review of Books* 32 (10 October 1985): 41–43.

Dallmayr, Fred. "Max Weber and the Modern State." In *Barbarism of Reason: Max Weber and the Twilight of Enlightenment*, edited by Asher Horowitz and Terry Maley. Toronto: University of Toronto Press, 1994.

Davidson, Arnold I. "Archaeology, Genealogy, Ethics." In *Foucault: A Critical Reader*, edited by David Couzens Hoy. Oxford: Basil Blackwell, 1986.

———. "Spiritual Exercises and Ancient Philosophy: An Introduction to Pierre Hadot." *Critical Inquiry* 16 (spring 1990): 475–482.

Deleuze, Gilles. *Foucault*. Edited and translated by Seán Hand. Minneapolis: University of Minnesota Press, 1988.

Deng, Xiaoping. *Selected Works of Deng Xiaoping (1975–1982)*. Translated by the Bureau for the Compilation and Translation of Works of Marx, Engels, Lenin and Stalin. Beijing: Foreign Language Press, 1984.

Diggins, John Patrick. *The Promise of Pragmatism: Modernism and the Crisis of Knowledge and Authority*. Chicago: University of Chicago Press, 1994.

Disch, Lisa. *Hannah Arendt and the Limits of Philosophy*. Ithaca: Cornell University Press, 1994.

Dreyfus, Hubert L., and Paul Rabinow. *Michel Foucault: Beyond Structuralism and Hermeneutics*. 2d ed. Chicago: University of Chicago Press, 1983.

———. "What is Maturity? Habermas and Foucault on 'What is Enlightenment?'" In *Foucault: A Critical Reader*, edited by David Couzens Hoy. Oxford: Basil Blackwell, 1986.

Elshtain, Jean Bethke. *Democracy On Trial*. 1993 Massey Lectures. Concord, Ontario: Anansi Press, 1993.

Euben, J. Peter. "Taking It To The Street." In *Radical Democracy: Identity, Citizenship, and the State*, edited by David Trend. New York: Routledge, 1996.

Fang, Lizhi. *Bringing Down the Great Wall: Writings on Science, Culture, and Democracy in China*. Edited and translated by James H. Williams. New York: W.W. Norton, 1992.

Farr, James. "Atomes of Scripture: Hobbes and the Politics of Biblical Interpretation." In *Thomas Hobbes and Political Theory*, edited by Mary G. Dietz. Lawrence: University of Kansas Press, 1990.

Florence, Maurice. "Foucault, Michel, 1926–." In *The Cambridge Companion to Foucault*, edited by Gary Gutting. Cambridge: Cambridge University Press, 1994.

Foucault, Michel. "Introduction à l'Anthropologie de Kant." Part of *thèse complémentaire* for doctoral degree, Université de Paris, 1960. From copy in Centre Michel Foucault, Bibliothèque du Saulchoir, Paris.

———. *The Archaeology of Knowledge*. Translated by A. M. Sheridan Smith. New York: Pantheon Books, 1972.

———. "The Discourse on Language." Appendix. Translated by Rupert Swyer. In *The Archaeology of Knowledge*. New York: Pantheon Books, 1972.

———. *Language, Counter-Memory, Practice: Selected Essays and Interviews.* Edited by Donald F. Bouchard. Translated by Donald F. Bouchard and Sherry Simon. Ithaca: Cornell University Press, 1977.

———. "Power and Sex: An Interview with Michel Foucault." *Telos* 32 (summer 1977): 152–161.

———. *Discipline and Punish: The Birth of the Prison.* Translated by Alan Sheridan. New York: Vintage Books, 1979.

———. "Governmentality." *Ideology and Consciousness* 6 (autumn 1979): 5–21.

———. *An Introduction.* Vol.1 of *The History of Sexuality.* Translated by Robert Hurley. New York: Vintage Books, 1980.

———. *Power/Knowledge: Selected Interviews and Other Writings 1972–1977.* Edited by Colin Gordon. Translated by Colin Gordon, Leo Marshall, John Mepham, and Kate Soper. New York: Pantheon Books, 1980.

———. "Foucault at the Collège de France i: A Course Summary." Translated by James Bernauer. *Philosophy and Social Criticism* 8 (summer 1981): 235–242.

———. "Foucault at the Collège de France ii: A Course Summary." Translated by James Bernauer. *Philosophy and Social Criticism* 8 (fall 1981): 351–359.

———. "Omnes et Singulatim: Towards a Criticism of 'Political Reason.'" Lectures delivered at Stanford University on October 10 and 16, 1979. In *The Tanner Lectures on Human Values,* edited by Sterling McMurrin. Salt Lake City: University of Utah Press, 1981.

———. "On Revolution." *Philosophy and Social Criticism* 8 (spring 1981): 5–9.

———. "Questions of Method: An Interview with Michel Foucault." Translated by Colin Gordon. *Ideology and Consciousness* 8 (spring 1981): 3–14.

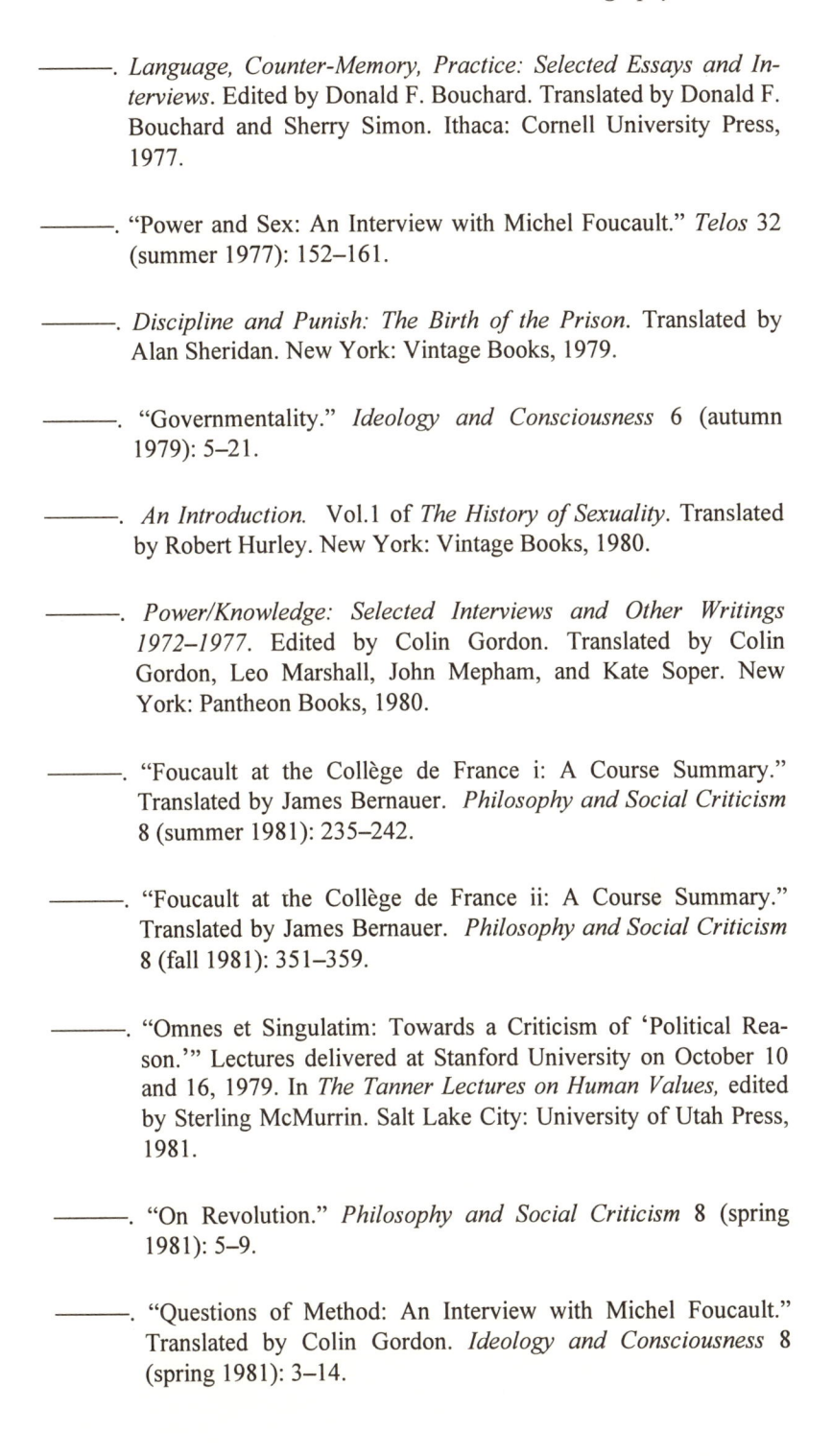

———. "Is It Really Important to Think?" Translated by Thomas Keenan. *Philosophy and Social Criticism* 9 (spring 1982): 31–35.

———. "Discourse and Truth: The Problematization of *Parrhesia*." Note to the Seminar Given by Foucault at the University of California at Berkeley, 1983. Copy at Centre Michel Foucault, Bibliothèque du Saulchoir, Paris.

———. "Preface." In *Anti-Oedipus: Capitalism and Schizophrenia*, by Gilles Deleuze and Felix Guattari. Translated by Robert Hurley, Mark Seem, and Helen R. Lane. Minneapolis: University of Minnesota Press, 1983.

———. "The Subject and Power." In *Michel Foucault: Beyond Structuralism and Hermeneutics*, by Hubert L. Dreyfus and Paul Rabinow. 2d ed. Chicago: University of Chicago Press, 1983.

———. "Face aux gouvernements, les droits de l'homme." *Libération* 1 July 1984. Reprinted in *Actes* 54 (1986): 22.

———. "Polemics, Politics, and Problemizations: An Interview." In *The Foucault Reader*, edited by Paul Rabinow. New York: Pantheon Books, 1984.

———. "Kant on Enlightenment and Revolution." Translated by Colin Gordon. *Economy and Society* 15 (February 1986): 88–96.

———. *The Use of Pleasure*. Vol. 2 of *The History of Sexuality*. Translated by Robert Hurley. New York: Vintage Books: 1986.

———. *The Care of the Self*. Vol. 3 of *The History of Sexuality*. Translated by Robert Hurley. New York: Pantheon Books, 1986.

———. "Confinement, Psychiatry, Prison." In *Politics, Philosophy, Culture: Interviews and other Writings 1977–1984*, edited by Lawrence D. Kritzman and translated by Alan Sheridan et al. New York: Routledge, 1988.

———. *Madness and Civilization: A History of Insanity in the Age of Reason*. Translated by Richard Howard. New York: Vintage Books, 1988.

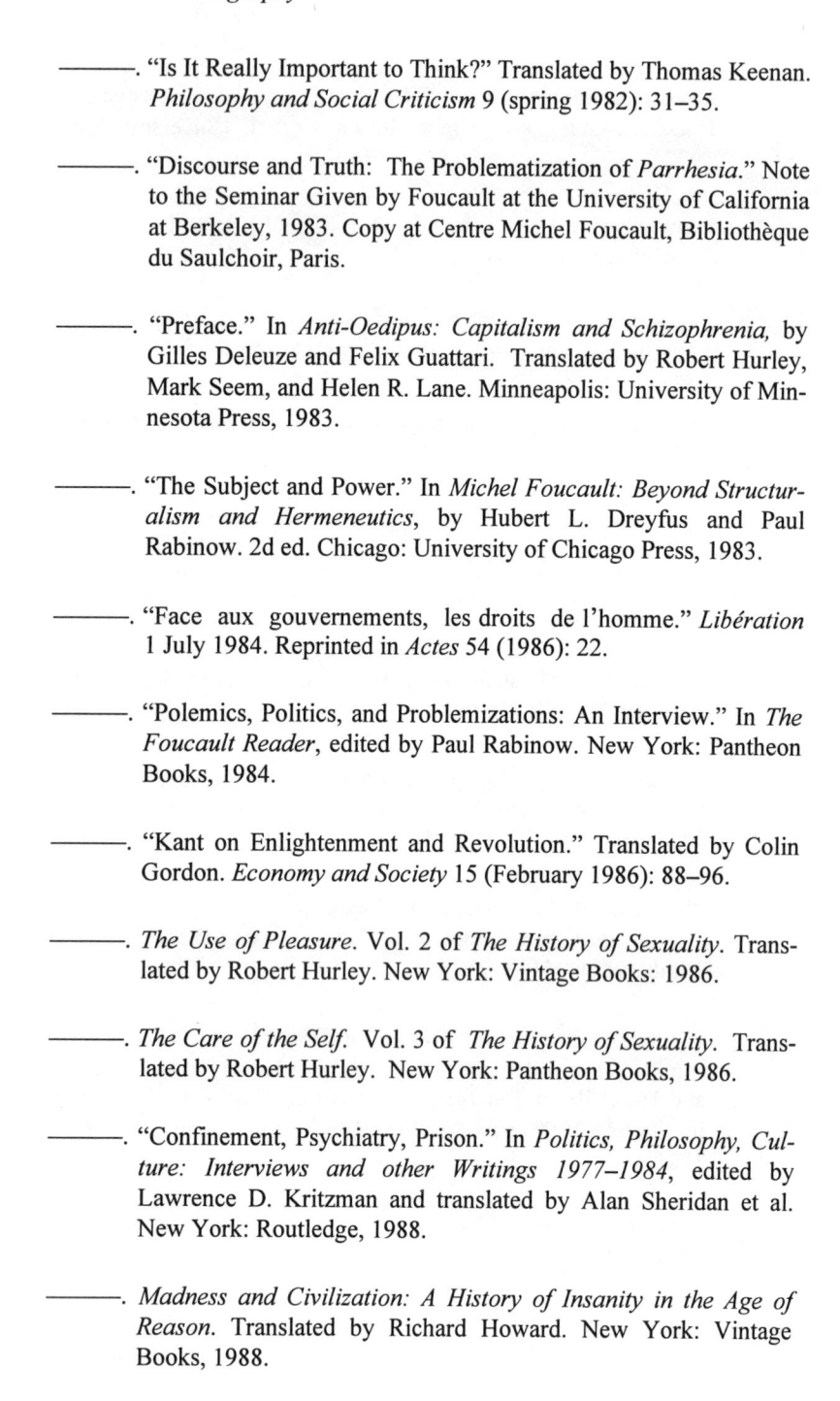

---. "Technologies of the Self." In *Technologies of the Self: A Seminar with Michel Foucault*, edited by Luther H. Martin, Huck Gutman, and Patrick H. Hutton. Amherst: University of Massachusetts Press, 1988.

---. *Résumé des cours 1970–1982*. Paris: Julliard, 1989.

---. "Politics and the Study of Discourse." Translated by Colin Gordon. In *The Foucault Effect: Studies in Governmentality*, edited by Graham Burchell, Colin Gordon, and Peter Miller. Chicago: University of Chicago Press, 1991.

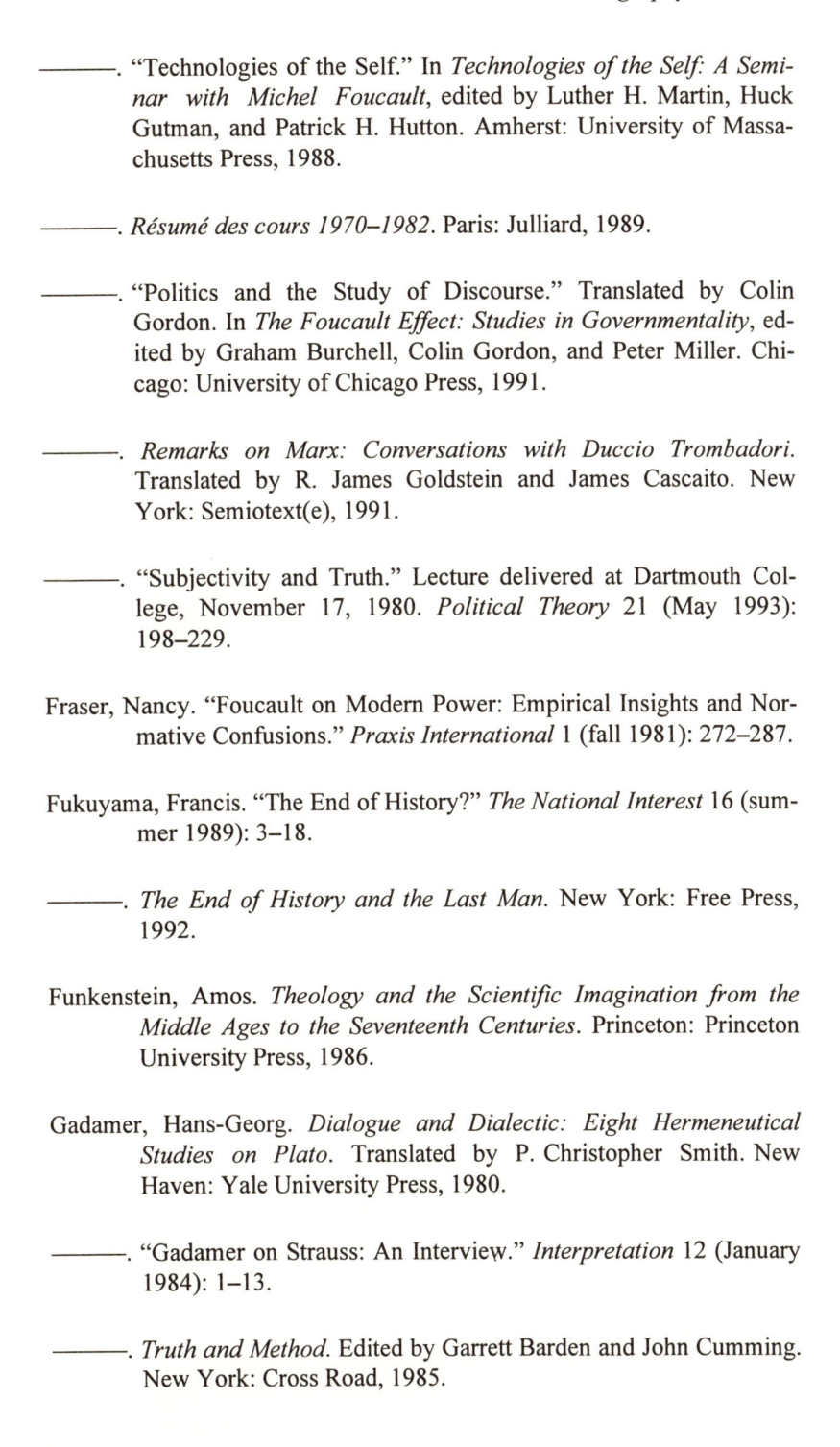

---. *Remarks on Marx: Conversations with Duccio Trombadori*. Translated by R. James Goldstein and James Cascaito. New York: Semiotext(e), 1991.

---. "Subjectivity and Truth." Lecture delivered at Dartmouth College, November 17, 1980. *Political Theory* 21 (May 1993): 198–229.

Fraser, Nancy. "Foucault on Modern Power: Empirical Insights and Normative Confusions." *Praxis International* 1 (fall 1981): 272–287.

Fukuyama, Francis. "The End of History?" *The National Interest* 16 (summer 1989): 3–18.

---. *The End of History and the Last Man*. New York: Free Press, 1992.

Funkenstein, Amos. *Theology and the Scientific Imagination from the Middle Ages to the Seventeenth Centuries*. Princeton: Princeton University Press, 1986.

Gadamer, Hans-Georg. *Dialogue and Dialectic: Eight Hermeneutical Studies on Plato*. Translated by P. Christopher Smith. New Haven: Yale University Press, 1980.

---. "Gadamer on Strauss: An Interview." *Interpretation* 12 (January 1984): 1–13.

---. *Truth and Method*. Edited by Garrett Barden and John Cumming. New York: Cross Road, 1985.

———. *The Idea of the Good in Platonic-Aristotelian Philosophy.* Translated by P. Christopher Smith. New Haven: Yale University Press, 1986.

———. *Plato's Dialectic Ethics: Phenomenological Interpretations Relating to the Philebus.* Translated by Robert M. Wallace. New Haven: Yale University Press, 1991.

Gay, Peter. *The Rise of Modern Paganism.* Vol. 1 of *The Enlightenment: An Interpretation.* New York: W.W. Norton, 1977.

Goldman, Merle. *Sowing the Seeds of Democracy in China: Political Reform in the Deng Xiaoping Era.* Cambridge: Harvard University Press, 1994.

Goldsmith, M. M. "The Hobbes Industry." *Political Studies* 39 (March 1991): 135–147.

Gordon, Colin. "Question, Ethos, Event." *Economy and Society* 15 (Febrary 1986): 71–87.

———. "Governmental Rationality: An Introduction." In *The Foucault Effect: Studies in Governmentality,* edited by Graham Burchell, Colin Gordon, and Peter Miller. Chicago: University of Chicago Press, 1991.

Gottsegen, Michael G. *The Political Thought of Hannah Arendt.* Albany: State University of New York Press, 1994.

Habermas, Jürgen. *Legitimation Crisis.* Translated by Thomas McCarthy. Boston: Beacon Press, 1975.

Hacking, Ian, "Self Improvement." In *Foucault: A Critical Reader,* edited by David Couzens Hoy. Oxford: Basil Blackwell, 1986.

Hampson, Norman. *The Enlightenment.* Harmondsworth: Penguin Books, 1968.

Hanson, Donald W. "The Meaning of 'Demonstration' in Hobbes's Science." *History of Political Thought* 11 (winter 1990): 587–626.

Harpham, Geoffrey Galt. "So . . . What *Is* Enlightenment? An Inquisition into Modernity." *Critical Inquiry* 20 (spring 1994): 524–556.

Hartsock, Nancy. "Foucault on Power: A Theory for Women?" In *Feminism/Postmodernism*, edited by Linda J. Nicholson. New York: Routledge, 1990.

Havel, Václav. *Living in Truth*. Edited by Jan Vladislav. London: Faber and Faber, 1987.

Heidegger, Martin. *The Basic Problems of Phenomenology*. Translated by Albert Hofstadter. Bloomington: Indiana University Press, 1982.

Heinrichs, T.A. "Language and Mind in Hobbes." *Yale French Studies* 49 (1973): 56–70.

Hennis, Wilheim. *Max Weber: Essays in Reconstruction*. Translated by Keith Tribe. London: Allen & Unwin, 1988.

Hill, Melvyn A., ed. *Hannah Arendt: The Recovery of the Public World*. New York: St. Martin's Press, 1979.

Hobbes, Thomas. *The English Works of Thomas Hobbes*. Vols. 1, 7, and 8. Edited by Sir William Molesworth. London: John Bohn, 1839–1845.

———. "The Autobiography of Thomas Hobbes." Translated by Benjamin Farrington. *The Rationalist Annual* (1958): 22–31.

———. *Leviathan*. Edited by C. B. Macpherson. Harmondsworth: Penguin Books, 1968.

———. "The Answer of Mr. Hobbes to Sir Will. D'Avenant's Preface before Gondibert." In *Sir William D'Avenant's Gondibert*, edited by David F. Gladish. Oxford: Clarendon Press, 1971.

———. *De Cive*. Edited by Howard Warrender. Oxford: Clarendon Press, 1983.

———. *Behemoth or The Long Parliament*. Edited by Ferdinand Tönnies. 1889. Reprint, Chicago: University of Chicago Press, 1990.

Holmes, Stephen. Introduction to *Behemoth or The Long Parliament*, edited by Ferdinand Tönnies. 1889. Reprint, Chicago: University of Chicago Press, 1990.

Honig, Bonnie. *Political Theory and the Displacement of Politics*. Ithaca: Cornell University Press, 1993.

———. "The Politics of Agonism: A Critical Response to 'Beyond Good and Evil: Arendt, Nietzsche, and the Aestheticization of Political Action' by Dana R. Villa." *Political Theory* 21 (August 1993): 528–533.

———. "Towards an Agonistic Feminism: Hannah Arendt and the Politics of Identity." In *Feminist Interpretations of Hannah Arendt*, edited by Bonnie Honig. University Park: Pennsylvania State University Press, 1995.

Hoy, David Couzens, ed. *Foucault: A Critical Reader*. Oxford: Basil Blackwell, 1986.

Hu, Yaobang. *Guanyu sixiang zhengzhi gongzhuo wenti* (Notes on problems in ideological and political work). Beijing: Renmin chubanshe, 1983.

Hughes, H. Stuart. *Consciousness and Society: The Reorientation of European Social Thought 1890–1930*. Rev. ed. New York: Vintage Books, 1977.

Isaac, Jeffrey C. "Arendt, Camus, and Postmodern Politics." *Praxis International* 9 (April and July 1989): 48–71.

———. *Arendt, Camus, and Modern Rebellion*. New Haven: Yale University Press, 1992.

———. "Situating Hannah Arendt on Action and Politics." *Political Theory* 21 (August 1993): 534–540.

Jaeger, Werner. *Paideia: The Ideals of Greek Culture*. Vol. 1. 2d ed. Translated by Gilbert Highet. New York: Oxford University Press, 1945.

Jameson, Fredric. "The Vanishing Narrator: Narrative Structure in Max Weber." *New German Critique* 1 (winter 1974): 52–89.

Johnston, David. *The Rhetoric of Leviathan: Thomas Hobbes and the Politics of Cultural Transformation.* Princeton: Princeton University Press, 1986.

Joseph, William A. *The Critique of Ultra-Leftism in China, 1958–1981.* Stanford: Stanford University Press, 1984.

Jones, Kathleen B. "On Authority: Or, Why Women Are Not Entitled to Speak?" In *Feminism and Foucault*, edited by Irene Diamond and Lee Quinby. Boston: Northeastern University Press, 1988.

———. *Compassionate Authority: Democracy and the Representation of Women.* New York: Routledge, 1993.

Kant, Emmanuel. "What is Enlightenment?" Translated by Lewis White Beck. In *On History.* Edited by Lewis White Beck. Translated by Lewis White Beck, Robert E. Anchor, and Emil L. Fackenheim. New York: Macmillan, 1963.

———. *Anthropologie du point de vue pragmatique.* Translated by Michel Foucault. Paris: Vrin, 1964.

———. *Critique of Pure Reason.* Unabridged ed. Translated by Norman Kemp Smith. New York: St Martin's Press, 1965.

———. *Critique of Judgment.* Translated by Werner S. Pluhar. Indianapolis: Hackett, 1987.

Kateb, George. *Hannah Arendt: Politics, Conscience, Evil.* Totowa, N.J.: Rowman & Allanheld, 1983.

Kaufman, Jason Edward. "Picasso and Braque: Mano a Mano." *The World & I* 4 (October 1989): 278–283.

Keenan, Thomas. "Translator's Afterword: Foucault on Government." *Philosophy and Social Criticism* 9 (spring 1982): 35–38.

———. "The 'Paradox' of Knowledge and Power: Reading Foucault on a Bias." *Political Theory* 15 (February 1987): 5–37.

Klosko, George. *The Development of Plato's Political Theory.* New York: Methuen, 1986.

Kontos, Alkis. "The World Disenchanted and the Return of Gods and Demons." In *The Barbarism of Reason: Max Weber and the Twilight of Enlightenment*, edited by Asher Horowitz and Terry Maley. Toronto: University of Toronto Press, 1994.

Krook, Dorothea. "Thomas Hobbes's Doctrine of Meaning and Truth." *Philosophy* 31 (January 1956): 3–22.

Lee, Theresa Man Ling. "Deng Xiaoping, Yu Guangyuan and Su Shaozhi: The Reformist View on Marxism-Leninism-Mao Zedong Thought as a Guiding Ideology to Building Socialism in China." In *East Asia Insight: Selected Papers from the CASA Annual Conferences 1985–1987*, edited by Larry N. Shyu, Min-sun Chen, Claude-Yves Charron, and Matsuo Soga. Montreal: Canadian Asian Studies Association, 1988.

Lenhardt, Christian. "Max Weber and the Legacy of Critical Idealism." In *The Barbarism of Reason: Max Weber and the Twilight of Enlightenment*, edited by Asher Horowitz and Terry Maley. Toronto: University of Toronto Press, 1994.

Locke, John. *An Essay Concerning Human Understanding.* Edited by Peter H. Nidditch. Oxford: Clarendon Press, 1975.

Löwith, Karl. *Max Weber and Karl Marx.* Edited by Tom Bottomore and William Outhwaite. Translated by Hans Fantel. London: Allen & Unwin, 1982.

Lyotard, Jean-François. *The Postmodern Condition: A Report on Knowledge.* Translated by Geoff Bennington and Brian Massumi. Minneapolis: University of Minnesota Press, 1984.

———. *The Postmodern Explained: Correspondence 1982–1985.* Edited by Julian Pefanis and Morgan Thomas. Translated by Don Barry et al. Minneapolis: University of Minnesota Press, 1993.

Macpherson, C. B. *The Political Theory of Possessive Individualism.* Oxford: Oxford University Press, 1962.

———. Introduction to *Leviathan*, by Thomas Hobbes. Edited by C. B. Macpherson. Harmondsworth: Penguin Books, 1968.

Mao, Zedong. "On Khrushchev's Phoney Communism and Its Historical Lessons for the World: Comment on the Open Letter of the Central Committee of the CPSU." In *Sino-Soviet Relations, 1964–1965*, by William E. Griffith. Document 14. Cambridge: MIT Press, 1967.

Martin, Luther H., Huck Gutman, and Patrick H. Hutton, eds. *Technologies of the Self*. Amherst: University of Massachusetts Press, 1988.

Martin, Rux. "An Interview with Michel Foucault, October 25, 1982." In *Technologies of the Self: A Seminar with Michel Foucault*, edited by Luther H. Martin, Huck Gutman, Patrick H. Hutton. Amherst: University of Massachusetts, 1988.

May, Derwent. *Hannah Arendt*. Harmondsworth: Penguin Books, 1986.

McCarthy, Thomas. "The Critique of Impure Reason: Foucault and the Frankfurt School." *Political Theory* 18 (August 1990): 437–469.

Milchman, Alan, and Alan Rosenberg. "Michel Foucault, Auschwitz and Modernity." *Philosophy and Social Criticism* 22 (January 1996): 101–113.

Miller, James. *The Passion of Michel Foucault*. New York: Simon & Schuster, 1993.

Mitzman, Arthur. *The Iron Cage: An Historical Interpretation of Max Weber*. New York: Grosset & Dunlap, 1969.

Mommsen, Wolfgang J. *The Age of Bureaucracy: Perspectives on the Political Sociology of Max Weber*. Oxford: Basil Blackwell, 1974.

———. *Max Weber and German Politics, 1890–1920*. Translated by Michael S. Steinberg. Chicago: University Of Chicago Press, 1984.

———. *The Political and Social Theory of Max Weber: Collected Essays*. Chicago: University of Chicago Press, 1989.

Morgenthau, Hans J. *Politics Among Nations: The Struggle for Power and Peace.* 5th ed. New York: Alfred A. Knopf, 1978.

Nehamas, Alexander. *Nietzsche: Life as Literature.* Cambridge: Harvard University Press, 1985.

Nietzsche, Frederick. *The Will To Power.* Edited by Walter Kaufmann. Translated by Walter Kaufmann and R. J. Hollingdale. New York: Vintage Books, 1968.

———. *Philosophy and Truth: Selections from Nietzsche's Notebooks of the Early 1870s.* Edited and translated by Daniel Breazeale. Atlantic Highlands, N.J.: Humanities Press, 1979.

Norris, Christopher. *Uncritical Theory: Postmodernism, Intellectuals and the Gulf War.* London: Lawrence & Wishart, 1992.

———. "Foucault on Kant." In *The Truth About Postmodernism.* Oxford: Blackwell, 1993.

———. "'What is Enlightenment?': Kant according to Foucault." In *The Cambridge Companion to Foucault*, edited by Gary Gutting. Cambridge: Cambridge University Press, 1994.

Oppenheimer, J. Robert. *Atom and Void: Essays on Science and Community.* Princeton: Princeton University Press, 1989.

Ortega y Gasset, José. *The Dehumanization of Art and Other Essays on Art, Culture, and Literature.* Princeton: Princeton University Press, 1968.

Owen, David. *Maturity and Modernity: Nietzsche, Weber, Foucault and the Ambivalence of Reason.* London: Routledge, 1994.

Pacchi, Arrigo. "Hobbes and the Problem of God." In *Perspectives on Hobbes*, edited by G. A. J. Rogers and Alan Ryan. Oxford: Clarendon Press, 1988.

Pasquino, Pasquale. "Michel Foucault (1926–84): The will to knowledge." Translated by Chloe Chard. *Economy and Society* 15 (February 1986): 97–109.

Peters, Richard. *Hobbes*. Westport: Greenwood Press, 1979.

Planinc, Zdravko. *Plato's Political Philosophy: Prudence in the Republic and the Laws*. Columbia: University of Missouri Press, 1991.

Plato. *Meno*. Translated by W. K. C. Guthrie. In *The Collected Dialogues of Plato, including the Letters*, edited by Edith Hamilton and Huntington Cairns. Princeton: Princeton University Press, 1961.

———. *Phaedo*. Translated by Hugh Tredennick. In *The Collected Dialogues*.

———. *Statesman*. Translated by J. B. Skemp. In *The Collected Dialogues*.

———. *Phaedrus*. Translated by R. Hackforth. In *The Collected Dialogues*.

———. *Cratylus*. Translated by B. Jowett. In *The Collected Dialogues*.

———. *Crito*. Translated by Hugh Tredennick. In *The Collected Dialogues*.

———. "Letter VII." Translated by L. A. Post. In *The Collected Dialogues*.

———. *Laws*. Translated by Trevor J. Saunders. Harmondsworth: Penguin Books, 1970.

———. *Republic*. Translated by G. M. A. Grube. Indianapolis: Hackett, 1974.

Popper, Karl. *The Spell of Plato*. Vol. 1 of *The Open Society and Its Enemies*. 5th ed. Princeton: Princeton University Press, 1966.

Pye, Lucian W. "On Chinese Pragmatism in the 1980's." *The China Quarterly* 106 (June 1986): 207–234.

Rebick, Judy. "Bridging Identity: A Creative Response to Identity Politics." In *Clash of Identities: Media, Manipulation, and Politics of the Self*, edited by James Littleton. Toronto: Prentice-Hall, 1996.

Reeve, C. D. C. "Platonic Politics and the Good." *Political Theory* 23 (August 1995): 411–424.

Richer, Stephen, and Lorna Weir, eds. *Beyond Political Correctness: Toward the Inclusive University*. Toronto: University of Toronto Press, 1995.

Riley, Patrick. "Hannah Arendt on Kant, Truth and Politics." *Political Studies* 35 (September 1987): 379–392.

Rhodes, Richard. *The Making of the Atomic Bomb*. New York: Simon & Schuster, 1986.

Rogow, Arnold A. *Thomas Hobbes: Radical in the Service of Reaction*. New York: W.W. Norton, 1986.

Rorty, Richard. *Philosophy and the Mirror of Nature*. Princeton: Princeton University Press, 1979.

———. *Consequences of Pragmatism (Essays: 1972–1980)*. Minneapolis: University of Minnesota Press, 1982.

———. *Contingency, Irony, and Solidarity*. New York: Cambridge University Press, 1989.

———. *Objectivity, Relativism, and Truth*. Vol. 1 of *Philosophical Papers*. New York: Cambridge University Press, 1991.

———. *Essays on Heidegger and Others*. Vol. 2 of *Philosophical Papers*. New York: Cambridge University Press, 1991.

Runciman, W. G. *A Critique of Max Weber's Philosophy of Social Science*. Cambridge: Cambridge University Press, 1972.

Ryan, Alan. "Hobbes, Toleration, and the Inner Life." In *The Nature of Political Theory*, edited by David Miller and Larry Siedentop. Oxford: Clarendon Press, 1983.

———. "A More Tolerant Hobbes?" In *Justifying Toleration: Conceptual and Historical Perspectives*, edited by Susan Mendus. Cambridge: Cambridge University Press, 1988.

———. "Hobbes and Individualism." In *Perspectives on Hobbes*, edited by G. A. J. Rogers and Alan Ryan. Oxford: Clarendon Press, 1988.

———. "Professor Hegel Goes to Washington." *The New York Review of Books* 39 (26 March 1992): 7–13.

———. "Hobbes's Political Philosophy." In *The Cambridge Companion to Hobbes*, edited by Tom Sorell. Cambridge: Cambridge University Press, 1996.

Said, Edward W. *The World, the Text, and the Critic*. Cambridge: Harvard University Press, 1983.

Saunders, Trevor J. "Plato's Later Political Thought." In *The Cambridge Companion to Plato*, edited by Richard Kraut. Cambridge: Cambridge University Press, 1992.

Scaff, Lawrence. *Fleeing the Iron Cage: Culture, Politics, and Modernity in the Thought of Max Weber*. Berkeley: University of California Press, 1989.

———. "Max Weber's Politics and Political Education." In *Weber: Critical Assessments 2*, edited by Peter Hamilton. Vol. 1. London: Routledge, 1991. First Published in *American Political Science Review* 67 (March 1973): 129–141.

Schacht, Richard. *Hegel and After: Studies in Continental Philosophy Between Kant and Sartre*. Pittsburgh: University of Pittsburgh Press, 1975.

Schoenhals, Michael. "The 1978 Truth Criterion Controversy." *The China Quarterly* 126 (June 1991): 243–268.

Schorske, Carl. *Fin-de-Siècle Vienna: Politics and Culture*. New York: Alfred A. Knopf, 1980.

Schram, Stuart. *Ideology and Policy in China Since the Third Plenum, 1978–1984*. Research Notes and Studies No. 6. London: Contemporary China Institute, School of Oriental and African Studies, University of London, 1984.

Schurmann, Franz. *Ideology and Organization in Communist China.* 2d. enl. ed. Berkeley: University of California Press, 1968.

Scott, Joan. "The Evidence of Experience." *Critical Inquiry* 17 (summer 1991): 773–797.

Shapin, Steven, and Simon Schaffer. *Leviathan and the Air Pump: Hobbes, Boyle, and the Experimental Life.* With a translation of Thomas Hobbes's *Dialogus Physicus De Natura Aeris* by Simon Schaffer. Princeton: Princeton University Press, 1985.

Shapiro, William. "The Nietzschean Roots of Max Weber's Social Science." Ph.D. dissertation, Cornell University, 1978.

Sorell, Tom. "The Science in Hobbes's Politics." In *Perspectives on Hobbes*, edited by G. A. J. Rogers and Alan Ryan. Oxford: Clarendon Press, 1988.

Strauss, Leo. *Natural Right and History.* Chicago: University of Chicago Press, 1950.

———. "On Plato's Republic." In *The City and Man.* Chicago: University of Chicago Press, 1964.

———. "Correspondence Concerning *Wahrheit und Methode.*" *The Independent Journal of Philosophy* 2 (1978): 5–12.

Strong, Tracy. "Weber and Freud: Vocation and Self-Acknowledgement." *Canadian Journal of Sociology* 10 (fall 1985): 391–409.

———. "What Have We to Do With Our Morals? Nietzsche and Weber on History and Ethics." *History of the Human Sciences* 5 (August 1992): 9–16.

Su, Shaozhi. "Zai shijian zhong zhengque renshi he yunyong jingji guilu" (Correctly understand and apply economic laws through practice). In *Shijian shi jianyan zhenli de weiyi biaozhun wenti taolunji* (Collected essays on the question of practice as the sole criterion for testing truth), edited by The Editorial Department of *Zhexue yanjiu* (Research on Philosophy). Vol. 2. Beijing: Zhongguo shehui kexue chubanshe, 1979.

———. "Develop Marxism Under Contemporary Conditions—In Commemoration of the Centenary of the Death of Karl Marx." *Selected Writings on Studies of Marxism* 2 (1983): 1–39.

———. *Democratization and Reform.* Nottingham: Spokesman, 1988.

———. Review of *Chinese Marxism in the Post-Mao Era*, by Bill Brugger and David Kelly. *The Australian Journal of Chinese Affairs* 29 (January 1993): 168–169.

———. "A Decade of Crises at the Institute of Marxism-Leninism-Mao Zedong Thought, 1979–1989." *The China Quarterly* 134 (June 1993): 335–351.

———. "Rethinking Marxism in the light of Chinese Reforms." In *Whither Marxism?: Global Crises in International Perspective*, edited by Bernd Magnus and Stephen Cullenberg. New York: Routledge, 1995.

Sullivan, Robert R. *Political Hermeneutics: The Early Thinking of Hans-Georg Gadamer.* University Park: Pennsylvania State University Press, 1989.

Sun, Yan. *The Chinese Reassessment of Socialism, 1976–1992.* Princeton: Princeton University Press, 1995.

Taylor, Charles. "Foucault on Freedom and Truth." *Political Theory* 12 (May 1984): 152–183.

Thiele, Leslie Paul. *Friedrich Nietzsche and the Politics of the Soul: A Study of Heroic Individualism.* Princeton: Princeton University Press, 1990.

Thucydides. *History of the Peloponnesian War.* Rev. ed. Translated by Rex Warner. Harmondsworth: Penguin Books, 1972.

Thurston, Anne F. *Enemies of the People: The Ordeal of the Intellectuals in China's Great Cultural Revolution.* New York: Knopf, 1987.

Tuck, Richard. "Optics and Sceptics: the Philosophical Foundations of Hobbes's Political Thought." In *Thomas Hobbes.* Volume 5 of

Essays on Early Modern Philosophers, edited by Vere Chappell. New York: Garland Publishing, 1992.

Tully, James. *An Approach to Political Philosophy: Locke in Contexts*. Cambridge: Cambridge University Press, 1993.

———. "The Possessive Individualism Thesis: A Reconsideration In Light of Recent Scholarship." In *Democracy and Possessive Individualism: The Intellectual Legacy of C. B. Macpherson*, edited by Joseph H. Carens. Albany: State University of New York Press, 1993.

Veyne, Paul. "The Final Foucault and His Ethics." Translated by Catherine Porter and Arnold I. Davidson. *Critical Inquiry* 20 (autumn 1993): 1–9.

Villa, Dana R. "Beyond Good and Evil: Arendt, Nietzsche, and the Aestheticization of Political Theory." *Political Theory* 20 (May 1992): 274–308.

———. *Arendt and Heidegger: The Fate of the Political*. Princeton: Princeton University Press, 1996.

Vlastos, Gregory. "Degrees of Reality in Plato." In *Platonic Studies*. Princeton: Princeton University Press, 1981.

Voegelin, Eric. Review of *The Origins of Totalitarianism*, by Hannah Arendt. *Review of Politics* 15 (January 1953): 68–76.

Von Clausewitz, Carl. *On War*. Edited and Translated by Michael Howard and Peter Paret. Princeton: Princeton University Press, 1976.

Walzer, Michael. "The Politics of Michel Foucault." *Dissent* (fall 1983): 481–490.

Weber, Max. *From Max Weber: Essays in Sociology*. Edited and translated by H. H. Gerth and C. Wright Mills. New York: Oxford University Press, 1946.

———. *The Methodology of Social Sciences*. Edited and translated by Edward A. Shils and Henry A. Finch. New York: Free Press, 1949.

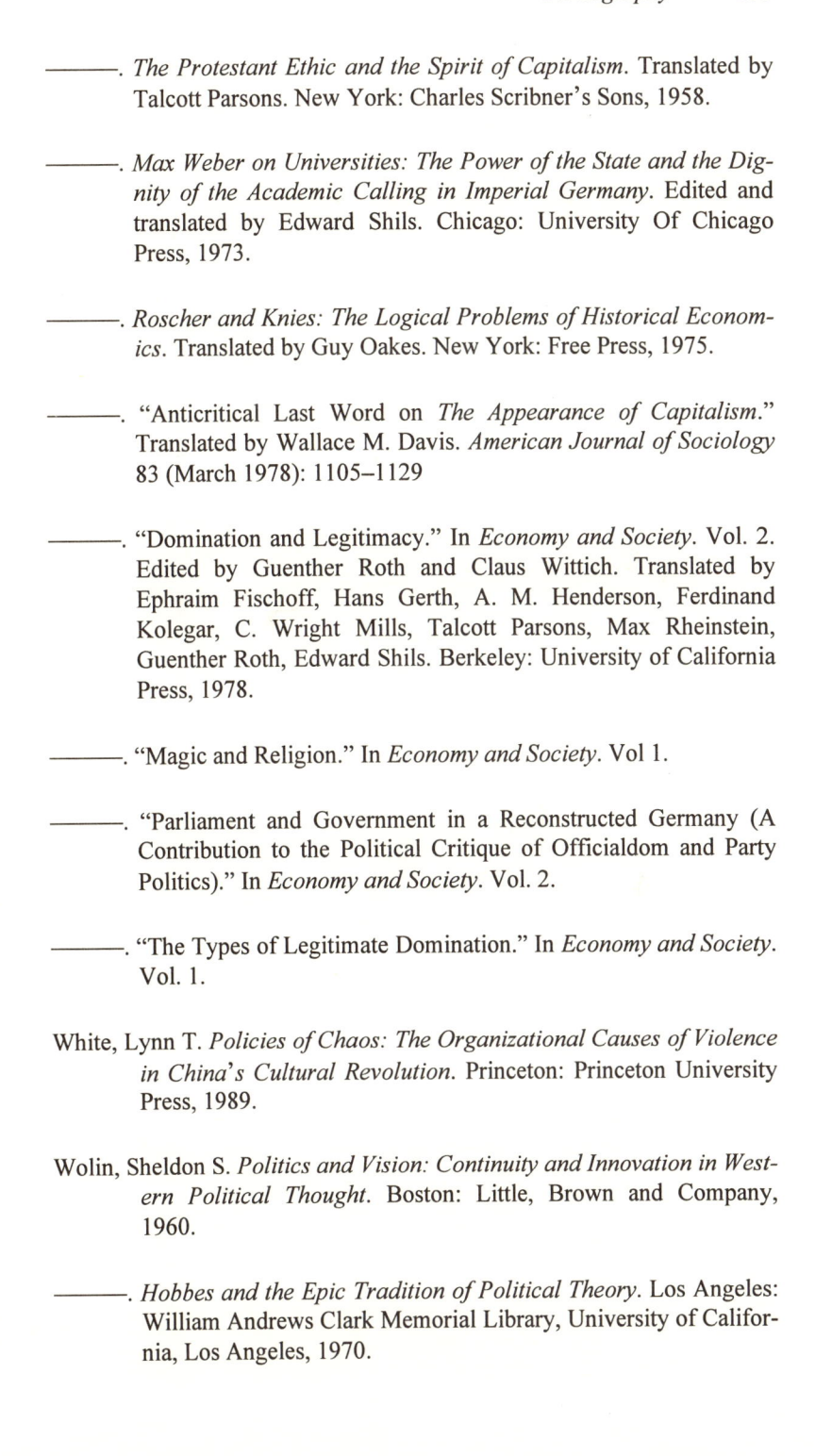

------. *The Protestant Ethic and the Spirit of Capitalism*. Translated by Talcott Parsons. New York: Charles Scribner's Sons, 1958.

------. *Max Weber on Universities: The Power of the State and the Dignity of the Academic Calling in Imperial Germany*. Edited and translated by Edward Shils. Chicago: University Of Chicago Press, 1973.

------. *Roscher and Knies: The Logical Problems of Historical Economics*. Translated by Guy Oakes. New York: Free Press, 1975.

------. "Anticritical Last Word on *The Appearance of Capitalism*." Translated by Wallace M. Davis. *American Journal of Sociology* 83 (March 1978): 1105–1129

------. "Domination and Legitimacy." In *Economy and Society*. Vol. 2. Edited by Guenther Roth and Claus Wittich. Translated by Ephraim Fischoff, Hans Gerth, A. M. Henderson, Ferdinand Kolegar, C. Wright Mills, Talcott Parsons, Max Rheinstein, Guenther Roth, Edward Shils. Berkeley: University of California Press, 1978.

------. "Magic and Religion." In *Economy and Society*. Vol 1.

------. "Parliament and Government in a Reconstructed Germany (A Contribution to the Political Critique of Officialdom and Party Politics)." In *Economy and Society*. Vol. 2.

------. "The Types of Legitimate Domination." In *Economy and Society*. Vol. 1.

White, Lynn T. *Policies of Chaos: The Organizational Causes of Violence in China's Cultural Revolution*. Princeton: Princeton University Press, 1989.

Wolin, Sheldon S. *Politics and Vision: Continuity and Innovation in Western Political Thought*. Boston: Little, Brown and Company, 1960.

------. *Hobbes and the Epic Tradition of Political Theory*. Los Angeles: William Andrews Clark Memorial Library, University of California, Los Angeles, 1970.

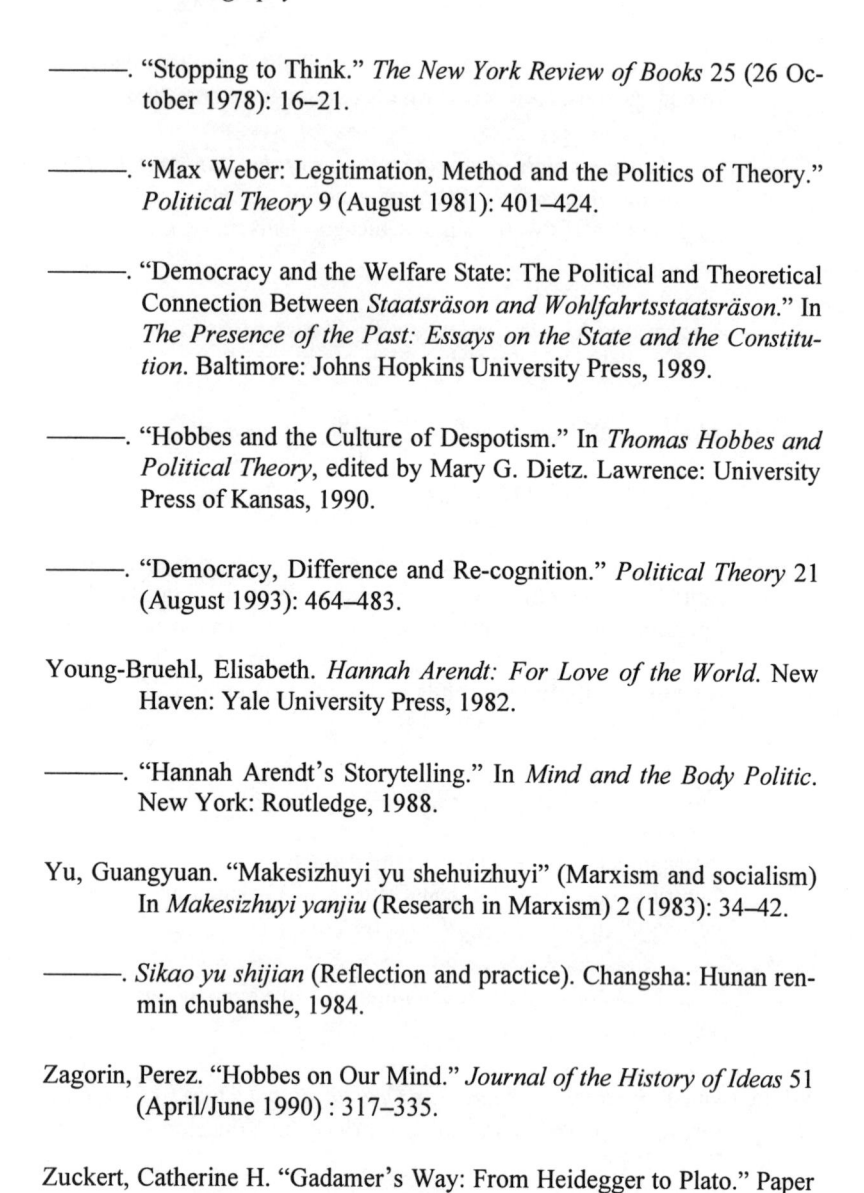

———. "Stopping to Think." *The New York Review of Books* 25 (26 October 1978): 16–21.

———. "Max Weber: Legitimation, Method and the Politics of Theory." *Political Theory* 9 (August 1981): 401–424.

———. "Democracy and the Welfare State: The Political and Theoretical Connection Between *Staatsräson and Wohlfahrtsstaatsräson*." In *The Presence of the Past: Essays on the State and the Constitution*. Baltimore: Johns Hopkins University Press, 1989.

———. "Hobbes and the Culture of Despotism." In *Thomas Hobbes and Political Theory*, edited by Mary G. Dietz. Lawrence: University Press of Kansas, 1990.

———. "Democracy, Difference and Re-cognition." *Political Theory* 21 (August 1993): 464–483.

Young-Bruehl, Elisabeth. *Hannah Arendt: For Love of the World*. New Haven: Yale University Press, 1982.

———. "Hannah Arendt's Storytelling." In *Mind and the Body Politic*. New York: Routledge, 1988.

Yu, Guangyuan. "Makesizhuyi yu shehuizhuyi" (Marxism and socialism) In *Makesizhuyi yanjiu* (Research in Marxism) 2 (1983): 34–42.

———. *Sikao yu shijian* (Reflection and practice). Changsha: Hunan renmin chubanshe, 1984.

Zagorin, Perez. "Hobbes on Our Mind." *Journal of the History of Ideas* 51 (April/June 1990) : 317–335.

Zuckert, Catherine H. "Gadamer's Way: From Heidegger to Plato." Paper presented at the annual meeting of the American Political Science Association, Washington, D.C., September 1993.

Index

abstraction, 9, 11, 38, 58, 60, 75, 91, 94, 125, 127–28, 132, 134, 141, 149, 151, 159, 160. *See also* essentialism, idealism, rationalization
academy, 55, 91, 135, 136, 137. *See also* university and state, relation between
aesthetic, 34, 66, 136
Allen, Barry, 9, 63, 157
American founding, 208n. 43
anarchy, 50
anthropomorphism, 44, 66, 75, 127
antisemitism, 117
anti-statism, 8, 89, 92, 155–57
Apology, 169n. 74
Archimedean point, 127, 128, 129, 135, 183n. 59
Archimedes, 127
Arendt, Hannah, compared with Weber, 131; on speech as action, 122, 125, 132, 199n. 40; on Kant, 106, 125, 133–34, 136, 200nn. 45, 48; on judgment, 125–26, 129, 135–36, 200n. 48; on Plato, 38, 121, 122–24, 129, 130, 198n. 29, 199n. 33; on Socrates, 122–23, 129, 131–32, 198n. 29; on thinking, 129–30, 131–34
aristocracy, 26
asceticism, 74, 76
atomization, 118–19, 142
authoritarianism, 20, 32, 85, 91
authority, 3, 8, 31, 32, 51, 54, 55, 56, 57, 82, 86, 156
autonomy, 56, 68, 106, 109, 112, 136

Bacon, Francis, 83, 91, 171n. 8
Bakhtin, M. M., 193n. 77
Beetham, David, 185n. 87, 186n. 98
Behemoth, 47, 177n. 95
Beiner, Ronald, 126, 136, 193n. 83, 200nn. 45, 48, 201n. 66
being, 34, 72, 96; politics and, 53–4, 88, 94, 124, 181n. 25; thought and, 9, 23, 28, 38, 65, 133, 135
Benhabib, Seyla, 158, 197n. 5, 203n. 90, 204n. 4
Bentham, Jeremy, 112, 113
Bernstein, Richard J., 165n. 19, 166n. 20
biopolitics, 101, 103, 104

235

Bloom, Allan, 164nn. 5, 8, 166n. 24
Boyle, Robert, 41–2, 43, 45
Braque, Georges, 65
bureaucracy, as principle of organization, 74, 78; state and, 81–5, 131

caesarism, 85
Calvinism, 74–6
Canovan, Margaret, 115, 197nn. 5, 10
capitalism, 82, 100, 186n. 2; bureaucracy and, 78, 79; Protestantism and, 74, 76, 79
Cato, 133
censorship, 32–5, 56–7, 58, 59
China, 3, 141–42, 145, 149–51; compared with Soviet Union, 207n. 41; Foucault on, 141; post-Mao, 12, 143–44, 151–53
Chinese Academy of Social Sciences, 144, 148, 206n. 31
Chinese Communist Party, 141, 150, 151, 152, 153, 207n. 41
class, 83, 107, 117, 119, 120, 141
classless society, 131, 141
class struggle, 117, 142, 146, 152
cognition, 23, 133, 134
Cold War, 1–2, 4, 100, 113, 155, 156, 161–62n. 7
communism, 113, 117, 118
Connolly, William E., 5, 7–8, 92, 156, 195n. 101
Connor, W. Robert, 49–50
conscience, 133
consciousness, 108, 142, 193n. 77
consent, 32, 51, 134
contextualism, 8, 12, 152, 157. *See also* foundationalism/ antifoundationalism

contingency, 7, 11, 134, 156, 159
Copernicus, Nicholaus, 128
Corcyrean Civil War, 49
Cratylus, 30, 31, 169n. 66
Crito, 32, 169n. 74
cubism, 65–6, 178n. 11
Cultural Revolution (Chinese), 141–42, 144, 204n. 4
cultural warfare, 92

Dallmayr, Fred, 83
Davidson, Arnold, 189n. 33,
Deleuze, Gilles, 111, 193n. 77, 195n. 106
democracy, agonistic, 7, 92, 155, 156, 157, 159; and liberalism, 4, 162n. 8; and socialism, 147, 149, 150, 152, 207n. 35; Hobbes on, 8, 176n. 86; Plato on, 8, 26–7, 35, 169n. 74; Weber on, 82–3, 84–6, 185n. 87. *See also* Elshtain; identity politics; postmodernism
democratization, 4, 85, 86, 207n. 35
Deng Xiaoping, 143–47, 149–51, 153, 207n. 38
Descartes, René, 173n. 29
despotism, 37, 118, 126
determinism, 39, 64, 109, 187n. 5
Dewey, John, 5
dialectic, 16, 17–20, 21, 29, 33, 36, 57, 123, 132, 170n. 90
dialectical materialism, 145, 152
dictatorship, 118, 145
Dinesen, Isak, 134
Disch, Lisa, 125, 201n. 55, 203n. 94
dissidents, political, 3, 100, 207–8, n. 42
dogma, 18, 19, 30, 36–7, 148

domination, 38, 117; Foucault on, 96, 99, 107; Weber on, 82–6
Dreyfus, Hubert L., 192n. 69

Eddington, Sir Arthur Stanley, 128
Eichmann, Adolf, 129–31, 135, 198n. 22
Eichmann in Jerusalem, 120
Elshtain, Jean Bethke, 158, 161–2n. 7, 186n. 2
emancipation, 7, 118; in post-Mao ideology, 146, 147, 148, 149, 150, 153
empathy, 71, 125
empiricism, 63, 64
English Civil War, 47
Enlightenment, 2, 7, 63–64, 91; Foucault on, 94–5, 104, 105–6, 187n. 15
epistemology, 2, 10, 11, 12, 40, 56, 59, 65, 69, 71, 157; and feminism, 158–9; and post-Mao China, 142, 145, 146, 150, 151–2
equality, 15, 50, 83
essentialism, and Plato, 9, 23, 27–8, 30–1, 34, 60, 170n. 90; and political identity, 6–7, 159, 160
ethnocentrism, 6
ethos, 76, 78, 84, 94, 95, 105, 111
Euben, J. Peter, 169n. 74
evil and politics, relation between, 15, 16, 68, 116, 129–31, 133. *See also* Eichmann
exclusion, 15, 96, 159, 193–94n. 89
experience and knowledge, relation between, 66, 71, 118; Arendt on, 118, 124, 127–28, 131, 133, 134–35, 136;

Foucault on, 104–6; Hobbes on 43, 44; in standpoint epistemology, 159; Kant on, 64

Fang, Lizhi, 161n. 4
Farr, James, 173n. 41
fascism, 100, 195n. 101
feminism, 158–59
fiction, 114, 118, 153, 196n. 113
Florence, Maurice, 188n. 16. *See also* Foucault
Foucault, Michel, on discourse, 95, 96, 98, 99, 106–7, 108, 110, 112, 114; on Hobbes, 97; on Kant, 94, 95–6, 104, 106; on Nietzsche, 96; on Plato, 102–3; on Weber, 98–9; politics of, 107, 110–11, 114, 195n. 101
foundationalism/antifoundationalism, 6, 8, 156–59; and Foucault, 98, 110; and Weber, 67, 68, 89
Fraser, Nancy, 105
freedom of expression/speech, 3, 57, 106, 127, 161n. 4, 200n. 53
Fukuyama, Francis, 162nn. 8, 9
Funkenstein, Amos, 59

Gadamer, Hans-Georg, 16, 30, 31, 33, 36, 37, 170n. 84; as political theorist, 165nn. 10, 19; in contrast with Strauss, 19, 29, 166n. 23; on Plato, 17–21, 34, 169n. 66; politics of, 166nn. 20, 21
Galileo, 39, 128
Gang of Four, 143, 145, 146, 148, 150, 151

genealogy, 94, 96, 97, 98, 99, 105, 106, 107, 141, 156, 189n. 33, 196n. 110
genocide, 112, 196n. 110
globalization, 4, 7–8
God, 43, 46, 47–8, 71, 74–5, 88
Goldman, Merle, 207–8n. 42
Goldsmith, M. M., 171n. 5
Gordon, Colin, 95, 190–91n. 56
Gottsegen, Michael G., 208n. 1
Gramsci, Antonio, 159

Habermas, Jügen, 186n. 1, 192n. 69
Hacking, Ian, 192n. 69
Hadot, Pierre, 195n. 105
Hampson, Norman, 63
Hanson, Donald W., 46
Harpham, Geoffrey Galt, 187n. 15, 192n. 71
Hartsock, Nancy, 105, 159
Havel, Václav, 5–6
Heidegger, Martin, 52–3, 165n. 10, 166n. 21, 201n. 63
Heinrichs, T. A., 172n. 22
Hennis, Wilheim, 67, 180n. 17
hermeneutics, 16, 17, 18
hierarchy, 25, 27, 32, 58, 100, 123, 193–94n. 89
Hill, Anita, 158
History of Sexuality, 93, 94, 99, 101, 112
Hobbes, compared with Plato, 57–8, 60; on civil philosophy, 44–6, 173n. 35; on indoctrination, 54–6; on Plato, 57; on social contract, 40, 51, 54; on state of nature, 39, 50, 51, 53, 54
Holmes, Stephen, 177n. 95
Holocaust, 196n. 110
Honig, Bonnie, 7, 155, 163n. 21, 208n. 1
Hu Fuming, 144, 205n. 12
Hu Yaobang, 144, 152
Human Condition, 115–16, 133, 197n. 10
Huo Guofeng, 143

idealism, 69; and leftism, 145, 146, 151, 152; and totalitarianism, 116, 117, 120, 127–28, 129
identity politics, 12, 91, 158, 186n. 2,
ideology, 1, 2, 82, 113, 143–44, 204n. 8; Arendt on, 117, 118, 119, 127
imperialism, 117
inclusiveness, 91
individualism, 56, 85, 88, 157, 186n. 98, 209n. 9
intellectuals, political role of, 3, 4, 156, 157; Arendt on, 135–36; Foucault on, 93, 107, 108–10, 193n. 77; in China, 144, 152–53, 207–8n. 42
interpretation, 65, 70, 96, 136
intuitionism, 71
"iron cage," 77, 79, 89
Isaac, Jeffrey C., 208n. 4

Jameson, Fredric, 73, 180n. 17
Johnston, David, 56, 58–9
Jones, Kathleen B., 54
Joseph, William A., 205nn. 14, 20

Kant, Emmanuel, 6, 63–5; influence on Foucault, 94–6, 105–6, 111, 187n. 15, 188n. 16, 192n. 69, 195n. 106; influence on Weber, 11, 69, 71, 179n. 6, 180n. 11

Kateb, George, 199n. 38
Keenan, Thomas, 110, 195n. 100
Klosko, George, 167n. 44
Kontos, Alkis, 79, 186n. 100
Krook, Dorothea, 172n. 22

language and politics, relation between, Hobbes on, 43–4, 48–51, 59–60; Plato on, 30–31; Rorty on, 5. *See also* Foucault on discourse
law of nature, 48, 51, 129
Laws, 17, 31, 33, 34, 36, 169nn. 71, 72
leadership, 24, 143, 147, 153; charismatic, 85–6; plebiscitary, 85–6
leftism, 142, 143, 145, 151, 152; ultra-, 145, 152, 205nn. 14, 20
legitimacy, 17, 32, 37, 57, 63, 68, 86, 92, 124, 126, 149, 156, 207n. 41
legitimation, 8, 12, 54, 111, 153, 156, 157; crisis of, 92, 105, 186n. 1; Weber on, 82, 85
Lenhardt, Christian, 69
Leninist-Stalinist state, 1, 2, 3, 100, 141
"Letter VII," 17
Leviathan, as sovereign, 40, 41, 46, 51, 53, 54, 55, 56–8, 59, 97; in Book of Job, 39; truth and, 51–4, 59
Leviathan, 40, 42, 46, 53, 57; rhetoric in, 56, 58–9, 177n. 92
liberal democracy, 1, 2, 4, 5, 8, 33, 100, 112, 161–62n. 7, 162n. 8, 191–92n. 68
liberalism, 4, 58, 66, 186n. 98; Foucault on, 93, 104, 105, 111, 191n. 66; postmodernist critique of, 5–7, 91, 92

Life of the Mind, 129
Locke, John, 63, 191n. 60
Lyotard, Jean-François, 2, 46, 156

Machiavelli, Niccoló, 116
Macpherson, C. B., 39–40
Mao Zedong, 142, 143, 145, 146, 150
marginalization, 4, 158
Marx, Karl, 4, 144, 148, 180n. 18
Marxism, 4, 7, 83, 92; Deng Xiaoping on, 146–47; Su Shaozhi on, 149–51; Yu Guangyuan on, 148–49
Marxism-Leninism, 142,
Marxism-Leninism-Mao Zedong Thought, as ideology, 143, 144, 145, 146, 147, 148, 150; Institute of, 144, 148, 149
McCarthy, Thomas, 94
Meno, 22
metaphysics, 11, 32, 77, 81, 116, 146, 157
Milchman, Alan, 196n. 110
Mill, John Stuart, 185n. 87
Miller, James, 192n. 69, 195n. 101
modernity, 2, 11, 12, 64, 65, 101, 157. *See also* Enlightenment
modernization, 147, 150, 207n. 35
Mommsen, Wolfgang J., 68, 186n. 96
Morgenthau, Hans, 1
movement, political, 2–3, 4, 106, 116, 117, 118, 129, 136, 142
multiculturalism, 158
multiethnicity, 158

Nazism, 117, 118, 196n. 110, 197n. 5
Nehamas, Alexander, 65, 66

Nietzsche, Frederick, 2, 4, 8, 10, 53, 65–6, 137, 156, 157; influence on Foucault, 92, 96, 107, 112; influence on Weber, 11, 68, 71–2, 80, 81, 89, 180nn. 17, 18
nihilism, 68, 157
nominalism, 10, 40, 48, 51–2
normalization, 10, 11, 103, 112
Norris, Christopher, 105, 192nn. 69, 70, 71

objectivity, 2, 3, 5, 93, 135, 147; Boyle's definition of, 42; Weber on, 69–71, 87, 180n. 13, 185n. 92
oligarchy, 26
ontology and truth, relation between, 9, 52–3, 94–6, 109. *See also* being
opinion, Arendt on, 122–23, 125–27, 132, 135; Plato on, 22, 25
Oppenheimer, J. Robert, 108–9
oppression, 118, 142
order, political, 8, 10, 48, 49, 53, 55, 56–7, 59, 82, 100
Origins of Totalitarianism, 115–16, 117, 196n. 2, 197n. 10
Ortega y Gasset, José, 65, 178n. 11

Pacchi, Arrigo, 173n. 41
parrhesia, 112
Peloponnesian War, 49
perspectivism, 65, 66, 71, 88
persuasion, 17, 18–19, 20, 37, 49, 56, 75, 122–23, 126
Peters, Richard, 171n. 8, 172n. 22
Phaedrus, 170n. 79

Picasso, Pablo, 65
Planinc, Zdravko, 166n. 24
Plato, on action and thought, relation between, 28–9, 30, 32, 37–8; on education, 21–2; on justice, 26, 27–8; on poetry, 34; on rule-by-law, 30–3, 168n. 62, 169n. 71; on rule-by-philosopher king, 15, 26–7
pluralism, 111, 144
plurality, condition of, 12, 73, 116, 119, 121, 124, 125, 129, 131, 132–33, 160
politicization, 2–3, 91–2, 93, 101, 113–14, 161–62n. 7
Pol Pot, 112
Popper, Karl, 15–16, 29, 33, 36, 164n. 7, 169n. 77, 170n. 90
positivism, 71, 156
postmodernism, 16, 155; Arendt and, 155–56, 208n. 1; definition of, 2; Foucault and, 92–3, 98, 101, 105, 107, 111–12, 114, 115; Hobbes and, 10, 46; Nietzsche and, 2, 4, 10; politics of, 4, 8, 12, 91–2, 156–57; Weber and, 11, 68, 89. *See also* Connolly; Rorty
power, 3, 8, 114, 129, 135, 136, 137, 149, 150, 153, 160; Foucault on, 11, 93, 107–8, 110, 141, 189n. 31; Hobbes on, 46, 55, 58, 60; knowledge and, 2, 41, 91, 45, 83, 96, 127–28. *See also* domination, feminism, subjection
pragmatism, 156; Deng's definition of, 143, 144; Rorty's definition of, 5–6
progress, 2, 66, 77, 80, 82
propaganda, 1, 117, 119, 152

Protestant Ethic and the Spirit of Capitalism, 74, 77
Protestantism, 73, 74, 76–7; in contrast with Catholicism, 75
Puritanism, 76–7
Pye, Lucian W., 143

Rabinow, Paul, 192n. 69
racism, 117, 131, 158
radicalism, 4, 91, 101, 105, 111, 156, 157
rationalization, as condition of modernity, 11, 67, 68, 73–4, 79; definition of, 72, 73; factors of, 74–9; political impact of, 81–6
reason and knowledge, relation between, 2, 69; Arendt on, 134–35; Hobbes on, 43, 45–6; Plato on, 9, 22–3, 25
reason versus emotion/passion, 59, 63–4, 66; in Weber's politics, 68, 86; Plato on, 25–7, 35, 123, 160
Rebick, Judy, 158
Reeve, C. D. C., 167n. 50
relativism, 92, 105, 107, 112
religion and politics, relation between, 1–2, 47–8, 173n. 41
representation, Arendt on, 125; Kant on, 64; Plato on, 22–3, 30–31, 34, 36; political, 155–56; Rorty on, 5–6
Republic, 15–17, 21, 24, 30, 33; compared with *Laws*, 32–3, 169n. 77; Gadamer on, 19–20, 29
responsibility, 47, 81, 84–5, 86 87, 105, 131. *See also* intellectuals, political role of
revisionism, 146

rights, 97; anti-disciplinarian, 110, 195n. 100; bourgeois, 148; human, 127, 158; natural, 40, 51
Riley, Patrick, 135, 200n. 45
Rorty, Richard, 5–6, 183n. 59; on Foucault, 191–92n. 68, 194n. 96
Rosenberg, Alan, 196n. 110
Rousseau, Jean-Jacques, 63, 64
Runciman, W. G., 180n. 13
Ryan, Alan, 40, 56–7, 162n. 8, 175n. 66

Saunders, Trevor J., 32, 169nn. 71, 72
Scaff, Lawrence, 88, 180n. 17
Schacht, Richard, 64
Schaffer, Simon, 172n. 10
Schoenhals, Michael, 145
Schorske, Carl, 65–6
science, 156; Arendt on, 127–28; Foucault on, 108, 193–94n. 89; Hobbes on, 40, 43, 44–6; Marxism as, 145, 148–149; Oppenheimer on, 108–9; Weber on, 77–8, 80–81, 83, 87, 88. *See also* specialization
Scott, Joan, 159
Shapin, Simon, 172n. 10
skepticism, 9, 111
socialism, 1, 2, 4, 100, 148–9, 150–51, 152, 207nn. 38, 41
Socrates, in *Crito*, 32, 169n. 74; in *Meno*, 22; in *Phaedrus*, 170n. 79; in *Republic*, 15, 16, 21, 24, 27–9; in *Statesman*, 24, 30
Sorell, Tom, 39–40, 56
sovereign, 11, 48, 93, 103, 113, 152, 160. *See also* Leviathan
sovereignty, 8, 15, 46, 47, 97, 103, 110

Soviet Union, 3, 100. *See also* China
specialization, 83–4, 88, 108, 133
Stalinism, 1, 100, 117, 197n. 5, 207n. 41
Statesman, 24, 25, 30, 168n. 62
statesmanship, 25
storytelling, 33–4, 134–36
Strauss, Leo, controversy on, 164n. 8; on Gadamer, 166n. 23; on Plato, 16, 24, 29, 36; on Weber, 67
Strong, Tracy, 87, 180nn. 11, 17
subjection, 94, 98–101; in modern state, 101–4, 112, 113
subjectivity, 64, 65, 71, 88, 157; inter-, 5, 126; intra-, 65, 66
Sullivan, Robert R., 165n. 10, 166n. 21, 170n. 84
Sun Yan, 204n. 8, 207n. 41
Su Shaozhi, 144, 149–53, 206nn. 31, 33, 207nn. 35, 38

Taylor, Charles, 92, 100
technology, 41–2, 128, 201n. 63
Thiele, Leslie Paul, 209n. 9
Thomas, Clarence, 158
Thucydides, 48–50, 136, 174n. 48, 176n. 86, 203n. 94
Thurston, Anne F., 204n. 3
Tiananmen, 152–53
timarchy, 26
totalitarianism, 10, 12; as crisis of modernity, 115, 118–19, 128, 129–31, 197n. 5; as mode of thought, 115–16, 117–18; China and, 141, 142, 153, 204n. 4; in contrast with liberalism, 100, 112, 113, 137; relation to truth, 119–20, 126–27, 128–29
Tower of Babel, 43

truth, Arendt on, 120–21, 124–25, 126–27, 129–30, 132, 136–37; Foucault on truth, 93, 96, 98, 108, 110, 111–12, 113, 114; Hobbes on, 44, 45, 46, 50–51, 52, 53, 55, 58, 60, 172n. 22; Nietzsche on, 53–4, 65–6, 137, 157; Plato on, 23, 25, 30–31, 36–7; Weber on, 69–71
Tuck, Richard, 173n. 29
Tully, James, 191nn. 60, 66
tyranny, 118, 123, 124

universalism, 7, 91; Arendt and, 136; Foucault's critique of, 95, 106, 108, 111; Hobbes on, 44; Plato on, 22–3, 24, 28; science and, 77, 108
universality, principle of, 91, 92, 108, 159
university and state, relation between, Arendt on, 136–37; Hobbes on, 55–6; Weber on, 87
utopia, 16, 19, 113

validation, 1, 8, 10, 40, 41–2, 43, 63, 70–71, 81, 86, 88, 91, 119, 121, 124, 153, 157, 160
Veyne, Paul, 159
Villa, Dana, 125, 126, 199n. 38, 201n. 63, 208n. 1
virtù, 116, 163n. 21
Vlastos, Gregory, 23
Voegelin, Eric, 203n. 102
Von Clausewitz, Carl, 1, 2

Walzer, Michael, 191–92n. 68
Weber, Max; on crisis of modernity, 67, 68, 72–4, 78–9;

Weber, Max; (*Continued*)
    on culture, 69–70, 73; on
    religion and modernity, 72–3,
    74–7, 181n. 29, 182n. 31; on
    vocation, 11, 79, 80–81, 86,
    87–8; politics of, 67–8,
    80–81, 86–9, 179n. 4, 186n.
    100
welfare state, 83, 105, 175n. 66
Whateverists, 143
White, Lynn, 142
Wolin, Sheldon, 37, 164n. 7, 201n.
    66, 209n. 11; on Hobbes, 51,
    80, 177n. 92; on Weber, 181n.
    29, 183n. 55, 185n. 90,
    186nn.97, 100

Young-Bruehl, Elisabeth, 198n. 22, 203n. 90
Yu Guangyuan, 144, 148–49, 150, 151

Zagorin, Perez, 171n. 5, 176n. 78
Zuckert, Catherine H., 165n. 10